MAY 31

INFINITE CRISIS AFTERMATH: THE SPECTRE

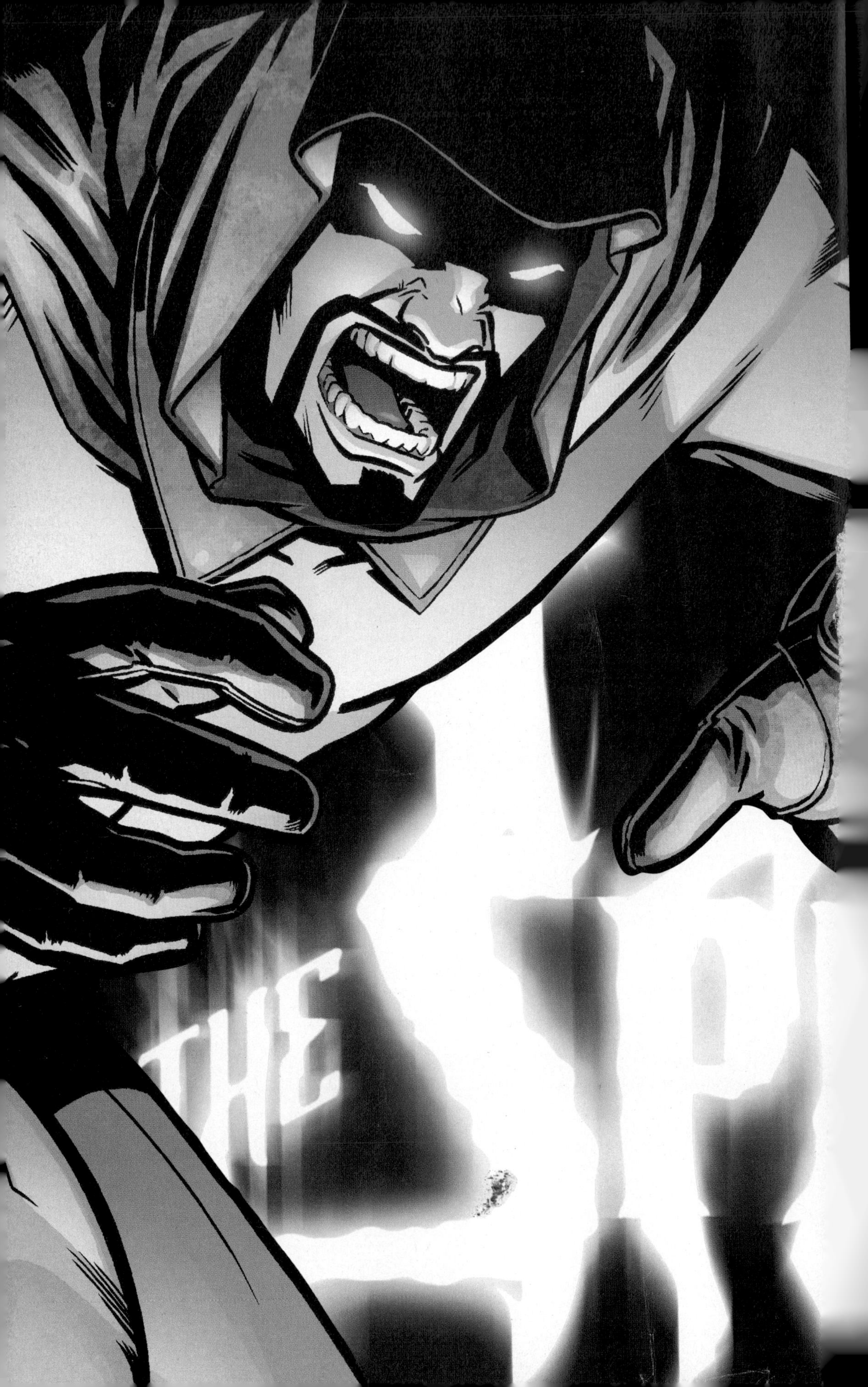
THE

DEAD AGAIN

Will Pfeifer *writer* **Cliff Chiang** *artist and covers*
David Baron *colorist* **Rob Leigh** *letterer*
Based on ideas and characters developed by **Greg Rucka**

THE COLD HAND OF VENGEANCE

David Lapham *writer* **Eric Battle** *penciller* **Prentis Rollins** *inker*
Guy Major *colorist* **Pat Brosseau** *letterer*

Mike Mignola & Dave Stewart **Neal Adams & Moose Baumann**
Michael Wm. Kaluta & David Baron **Matt Wagner & Dave Stewart**
original series covers

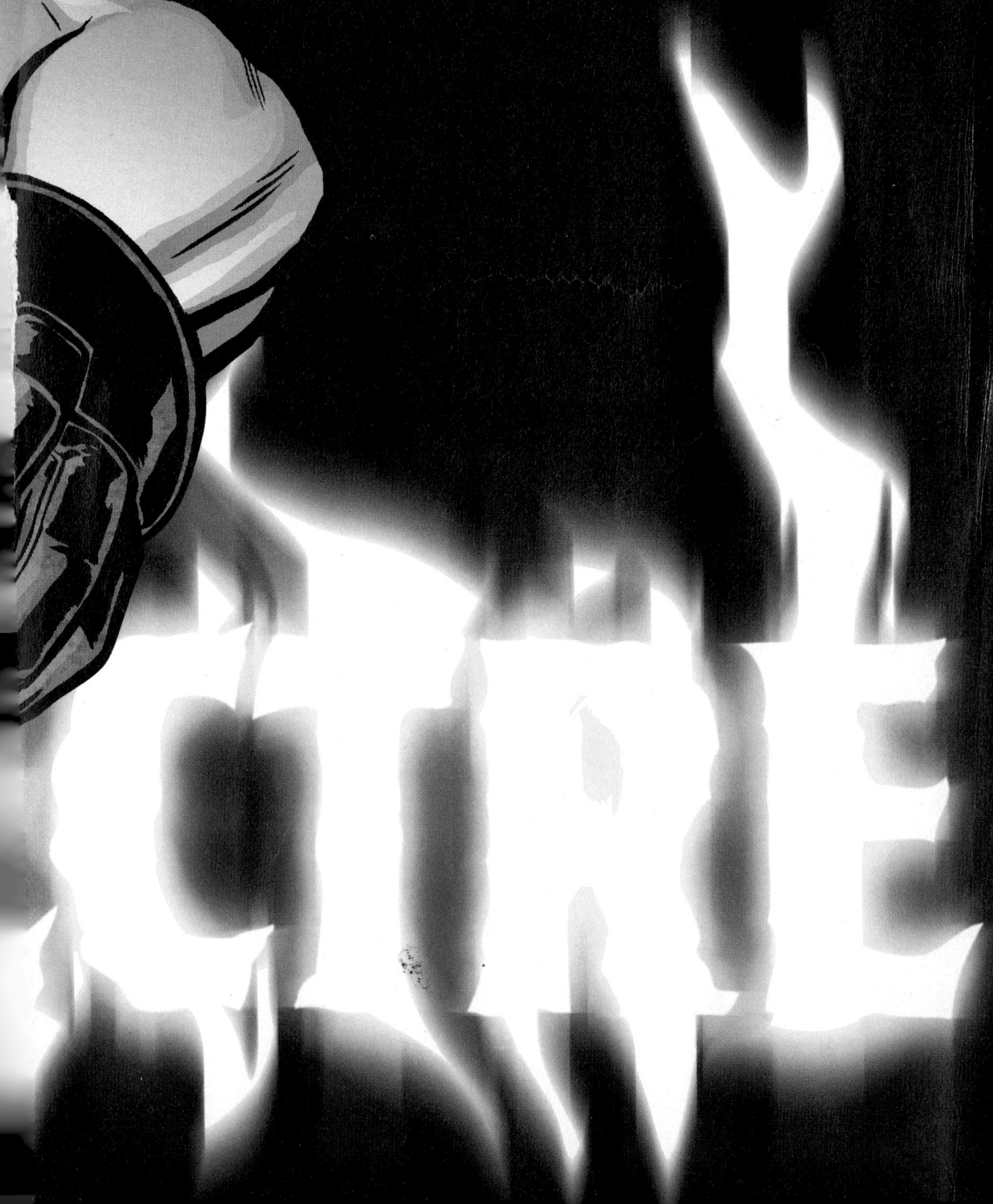

Dan DiDio Senior VP-Executive Editor
Matt Idelson, Bob Schreck Editors-original series
Nachie Castro Associate Editor-original series
Brandon Montclare Assistant Editor-original series
Peter Hamboussi Editor-collected edition
Robbin Brosterman Senior Art Director
Louis Prandi Art Director
Paul Levitz President & Publisher
Georg Brewer VP-Design & DC Direct Creative
Richard Bruning Senior VP-Creative Director
Patrick Caldon Executive VP-Finance & Operations
Chris Caramalis VP-Finance
John Cunningham VP-Marketing
Terri Cunningham VP-Managing Editor
Alison Gill VP-Manufacturing
Hank Kanalz VP-General Manager, WildStorm
Jim Lee Editorial Director-WildStorm
Paula Lowitt Senior VP-Business & Legal Affairs
MaryEllen McLaughlin VP-Advertising & Custom Publishing
John Nee VP-Business Development
Gregory Noveck Senior VP-Creative Affairs
Sue Pohja VP-Book Trade Sales
Cheryl Rubin Senior VP-Brand Management
Jeff Trojan VP-Business Development, DC Direct
Bob Wayne VP-Sales

Cover illustration by **Matt Wagner** & **Dave Stewart**.

Crisis Aftermath: The Spectre
Published by DC Comics. Cover and compilation copyright © 2007 DC Comics. All Rights Reserved.

Originally published in single magazine form in CRISIS AFTERMATH: THE SPECTRE 1-3 and TALES OF THE UNEXPECTED 1-3 © 2006, 2007 DC Comics. All Rights Reserved. All characters, their distinctive likenesses and related elements featured in this publication are trademarks of DC Comics. The stories, characters and incidents featured in this publication are entirely fictional. DC Comics does not read or accept unsolicited submissions of ideas, stories or artwork.

DC Comics, 1700 Broadway,
New York, NY 10019

A Warner Bros. Entertainment Company
Printed in Canada. First Printing.
ISBN 1-4012-1380-4
ISBN 13 978-1-4012-1380-0

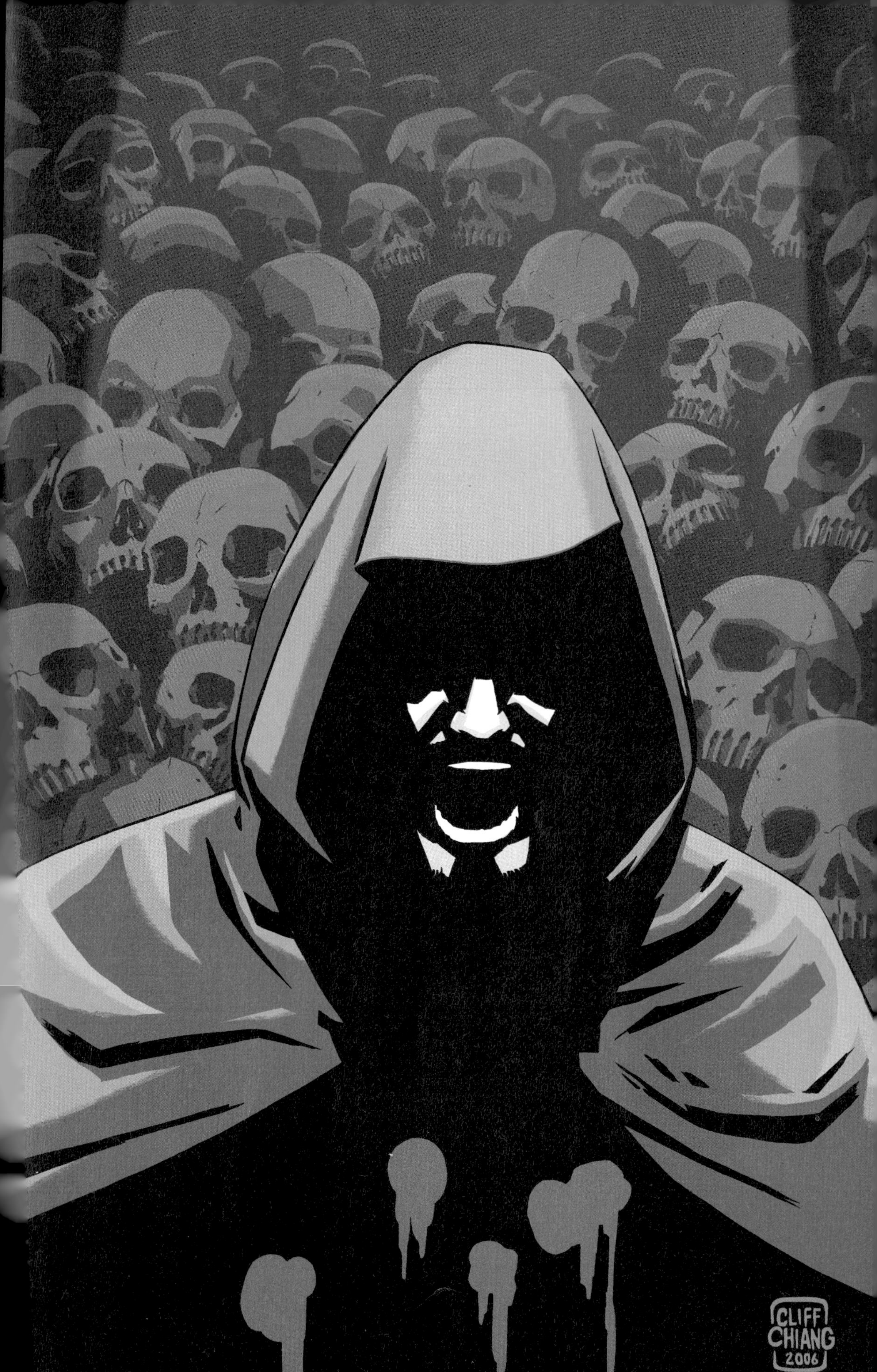
CLIFF
CHIANG
2006

rt by Cliff Chiang

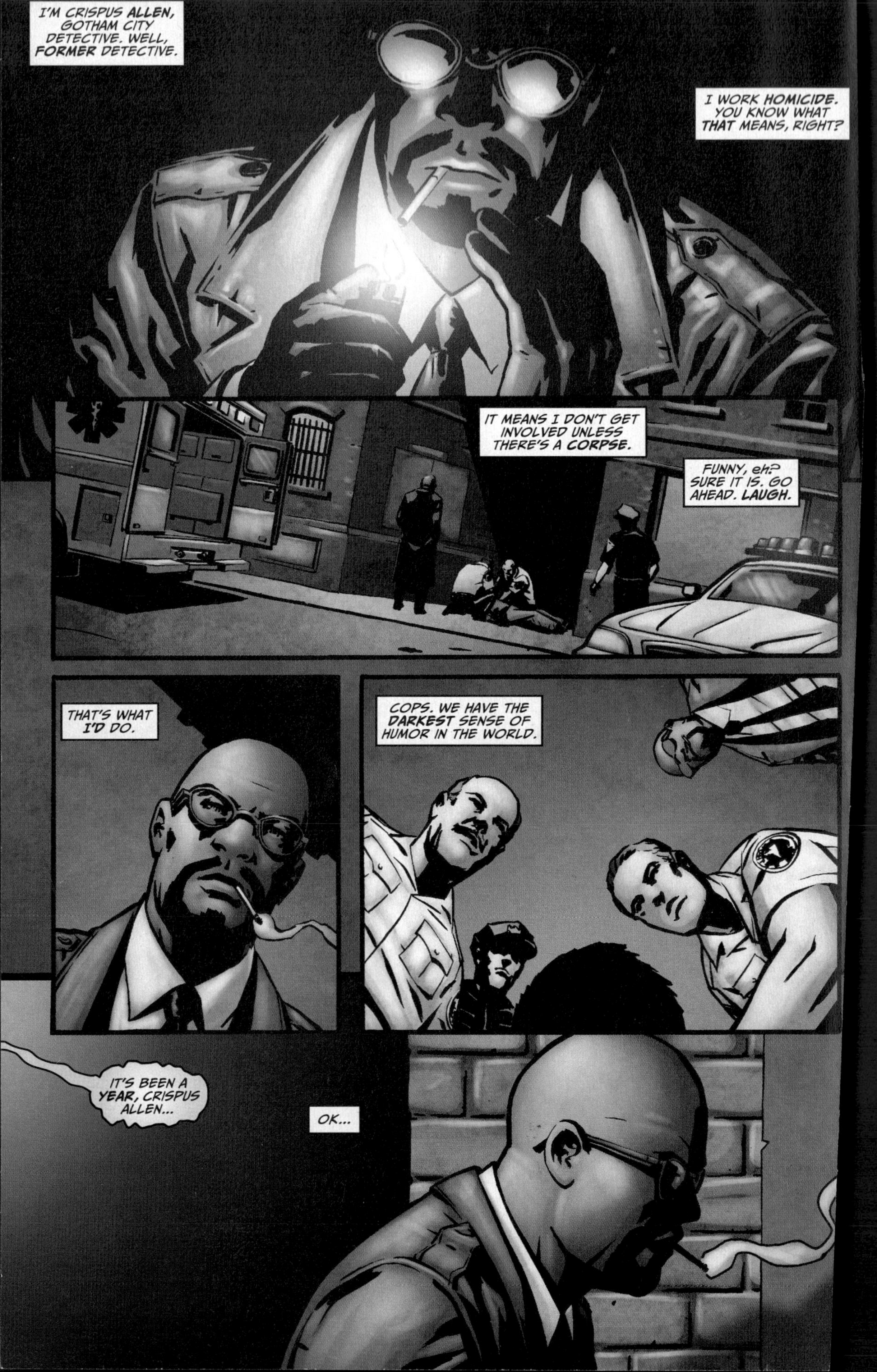
I'M CRISPUS ALLEN, GOTHAM CITY DETECTIVE. WELL, FORMER DETECTIVE.
I WORK HOMICIDE. YOU KNOW WHAT THAT MEANS, RIGHT?
IT MEANS I DON'T GET INVOLVED UNLESS THERE'S A CORPSE.
FUNNY, eh? SURE IT IS. GO AHEAD. LAUGH.
THAT'S WHAT I'D DO.
COPS. WE HAVE THE DARKEST SENSE OF HUMOR IN THE WORLD.
IT'S BEEN A YEAR, CRISPUS ALLEN...
OK...

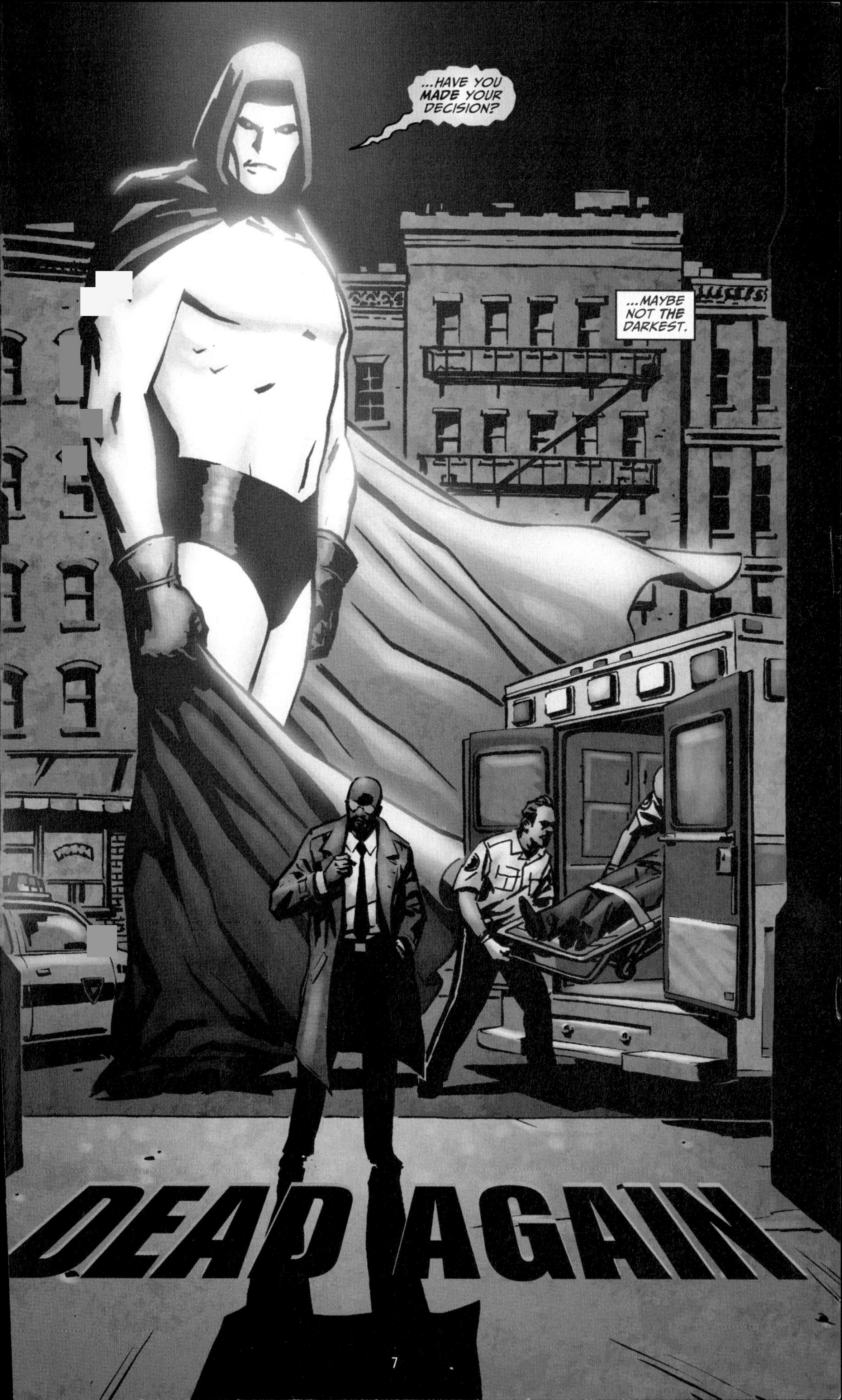
...HAVE YOU MADE YOUR DECISION?
...MAYBE NOT THE DARKEST.
DEAD AGAIN

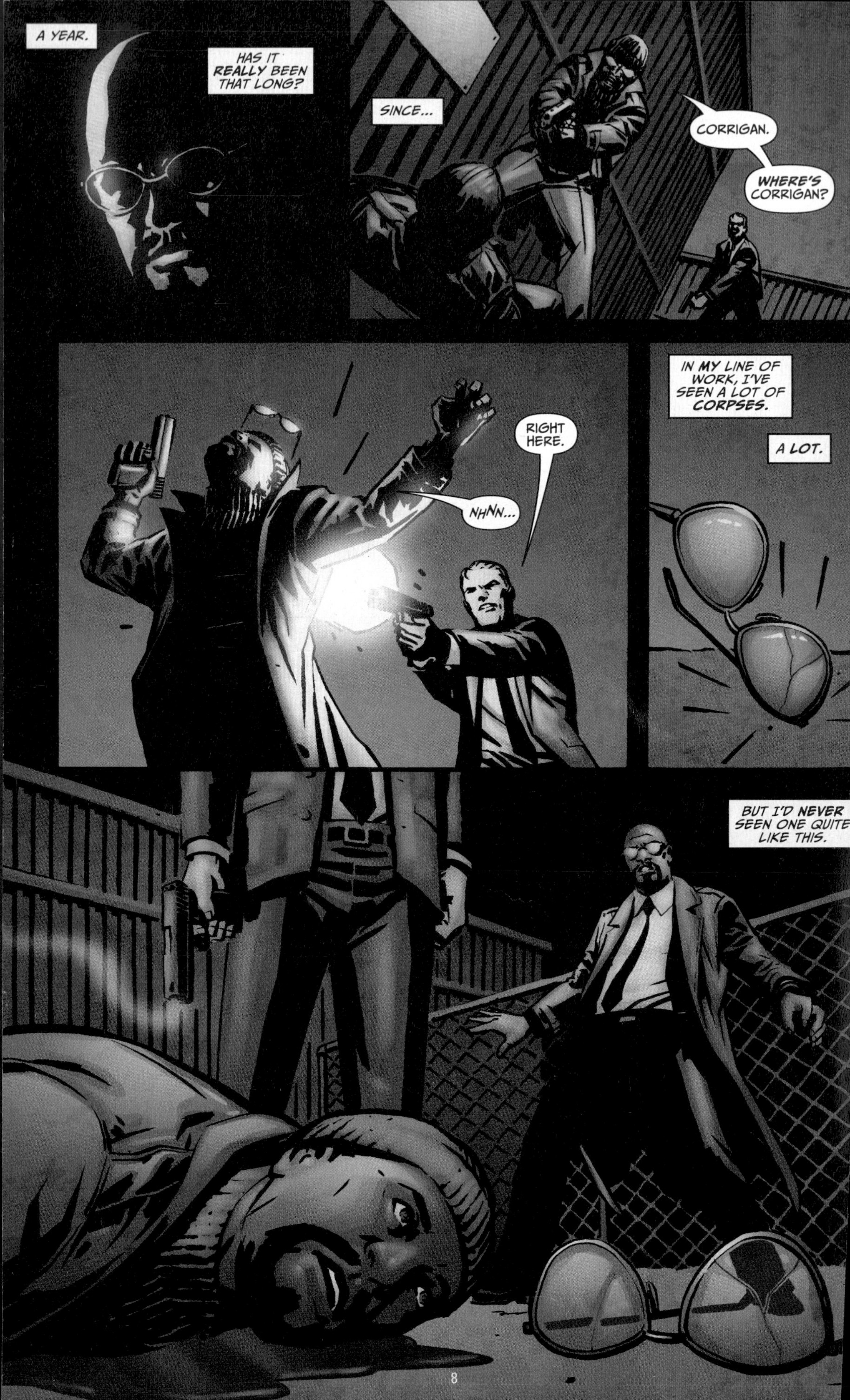
A YEAR.
HAS IT REALLY BEEN THAT LONG?
SINCE...
CORRIGAN.
WHERE'S CORRIGAN?
RIGHT HERE.
NHNN...
IN MY LINE OF WORK, I'VE SEEN A LOT OF CORPSES.
A LOT.
BUT I'D NEVER SEEN ONE QUITE LIKE THIS.

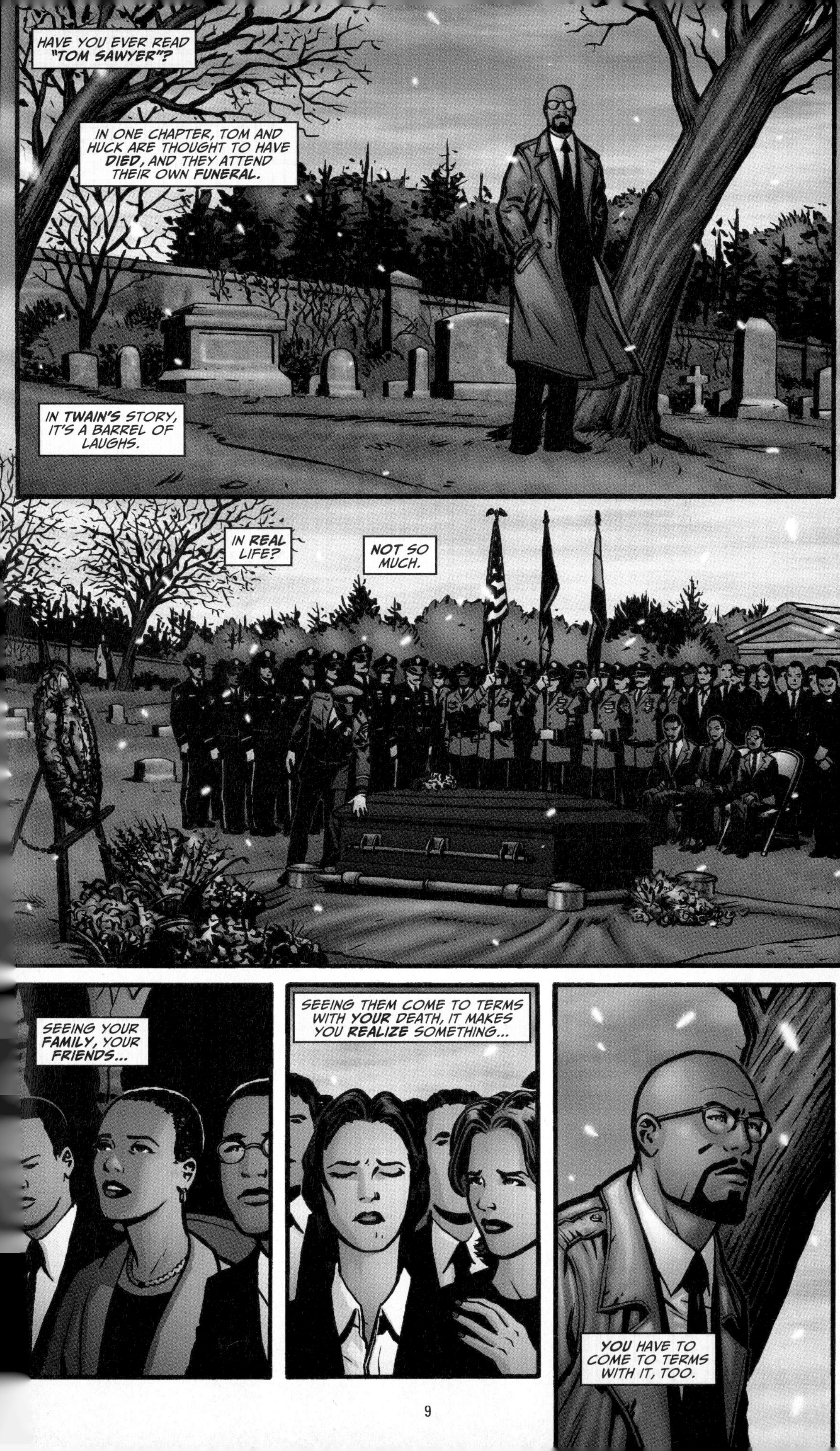

HAVE YOU EVER READ "TOM SAWYER"?
IN ONE CHAPTER, TOM AND HUCK ARE THOUGHT TO HAVE DIED, AND THEY ATTEND THEIR OWN FUNERAL.
IN TWAIN'S STORY, IT'S A BARREL OF LAUGHS.
IN REAL LIFE?
NOT SO MUCH.
SEEING YOUR FAMILY, YOUR FRIENDS...
SEEING THEM COME TO TERMS WITH YOUR DEATH, IT MAKES YOU REALIZE SOMETHING...
YOU HAVE TO COME TO TERMS WITH IT, TOO.

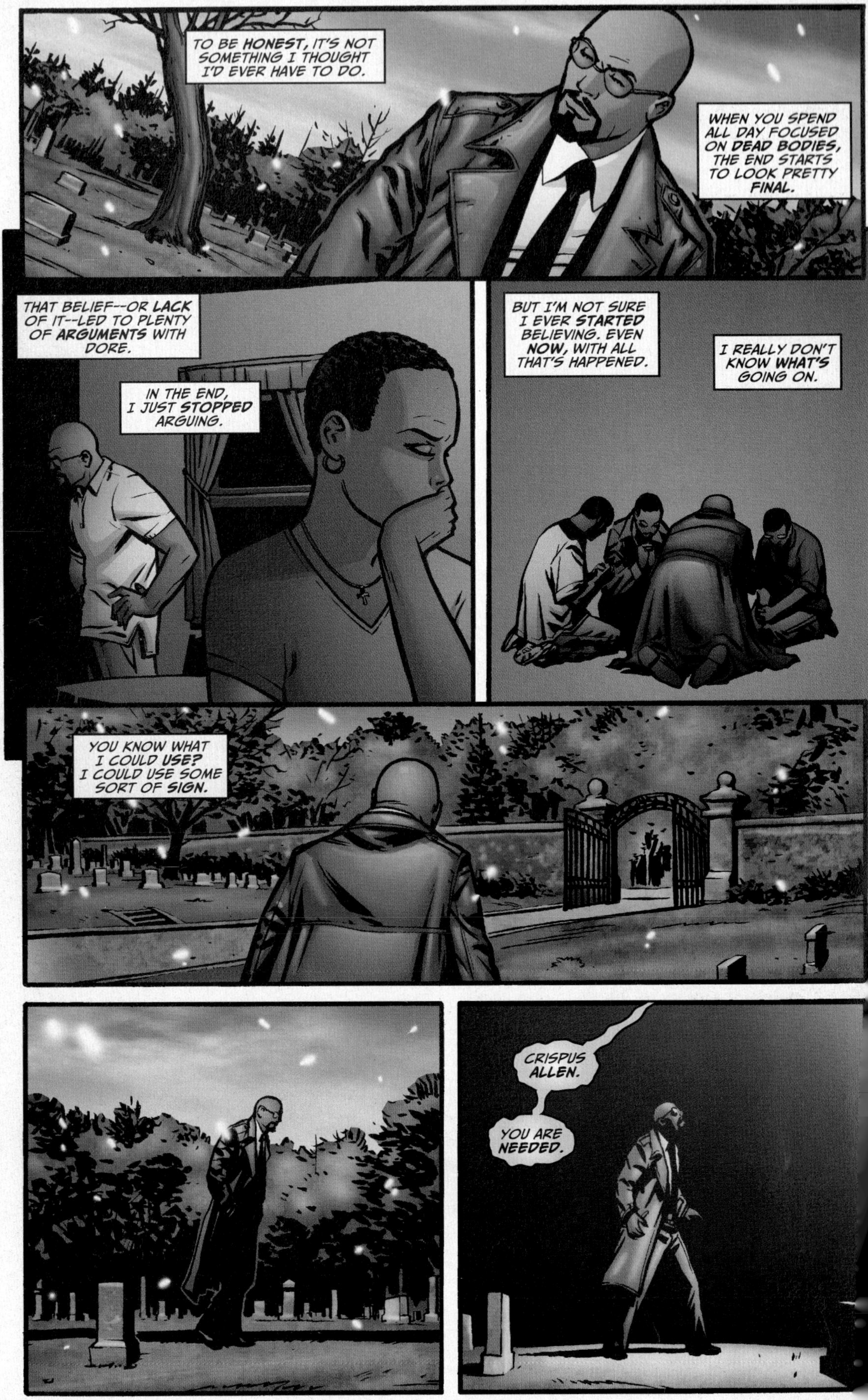
TO BE HONEST, IT'S NOT SOMETHING I THOUGHT I'D EVER HAVE TO DO.
WHEN YOU SPEND ALL DAY FOCUSED ON DEAD BODIES, THE END STARTS TO LOOK PRETTY FINAL.
THAT BELIEF--OR LACK OF IT--LED TO PLENTY OF ARGUMENTS WITH DORE.
IN THE END, I JUST STOPPED ARGUING.
BUT I'M NOT SURE I EVER STARTED BELIEVING. EVEN NOW, WITH ALL THAT'S HAPPENED.
I REALLY DON'T KNOW WHAT'S GOING ON.
YOU KNOW WHAT I COULD USE? I COULD USE SOME SORT OF SIGN.
CRISPUS ALLEN.
YOU ARE NEEDED.

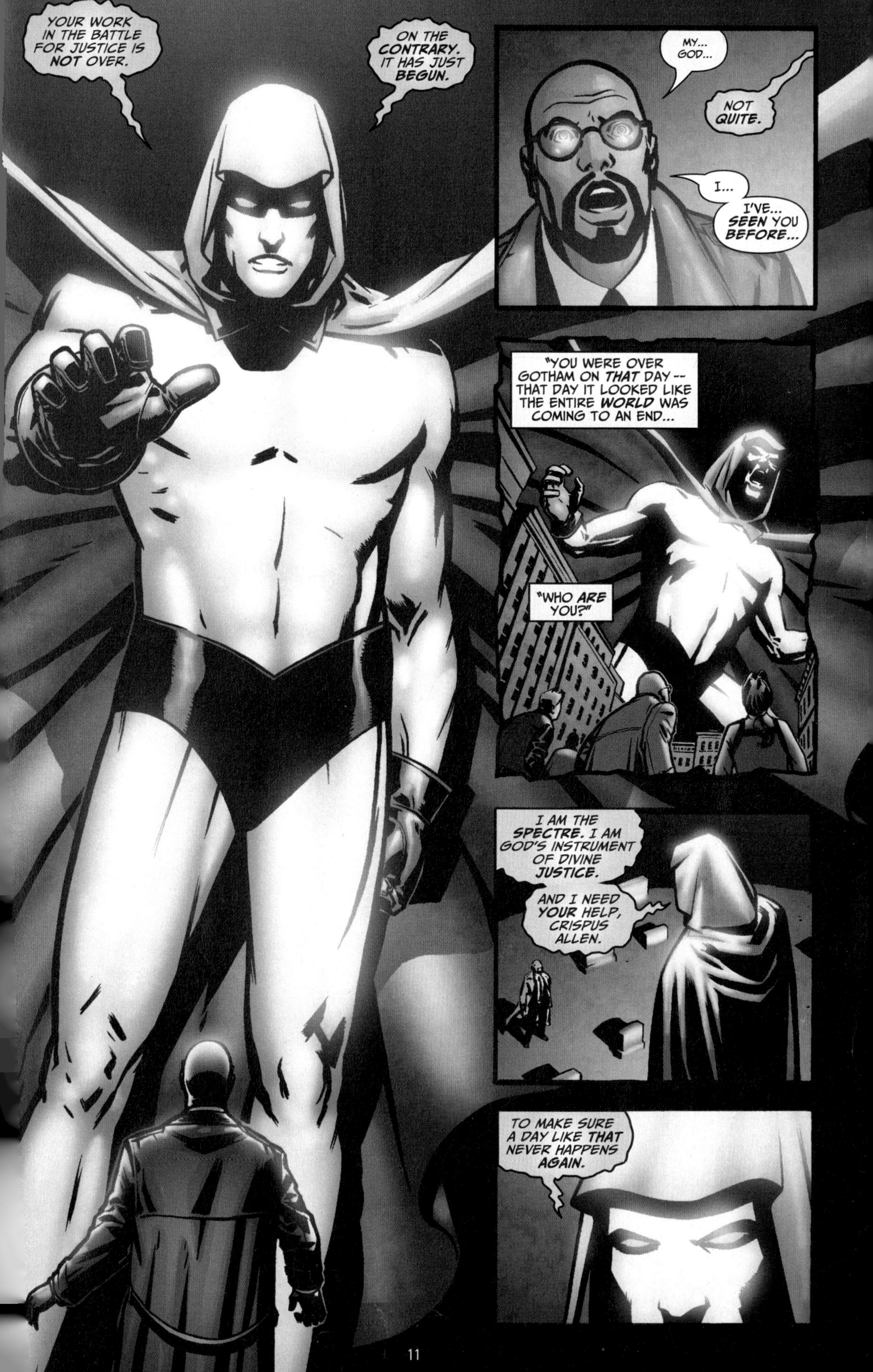
YOUR WORK IN THE BATTLE FOR JUSTICE IS NOT OVER.
ON THE CONTRARY. IT HAS JUST BEGUN.
MY... GOD...
NOT QUITE.
I...
I'VE... SEEN YOU BEFORE...
"YOU WERE OVER GOTHAM ON THAT DAY -- THAT DAY IT LOOKED LIKE THE ENTIRE WORLD WAS COMING TO AN END...
"WHO ARE YOU?"
I AM THE SPECTRE. I AM GOD'S INSTRUMENT OF DIVINE JUSTICE.
AND I NEED YOUR HELP, CRISPUS ALLEN.
TO MAKE SURE A DAY LIKE THAT NEVER HAPPENS AGAIN.

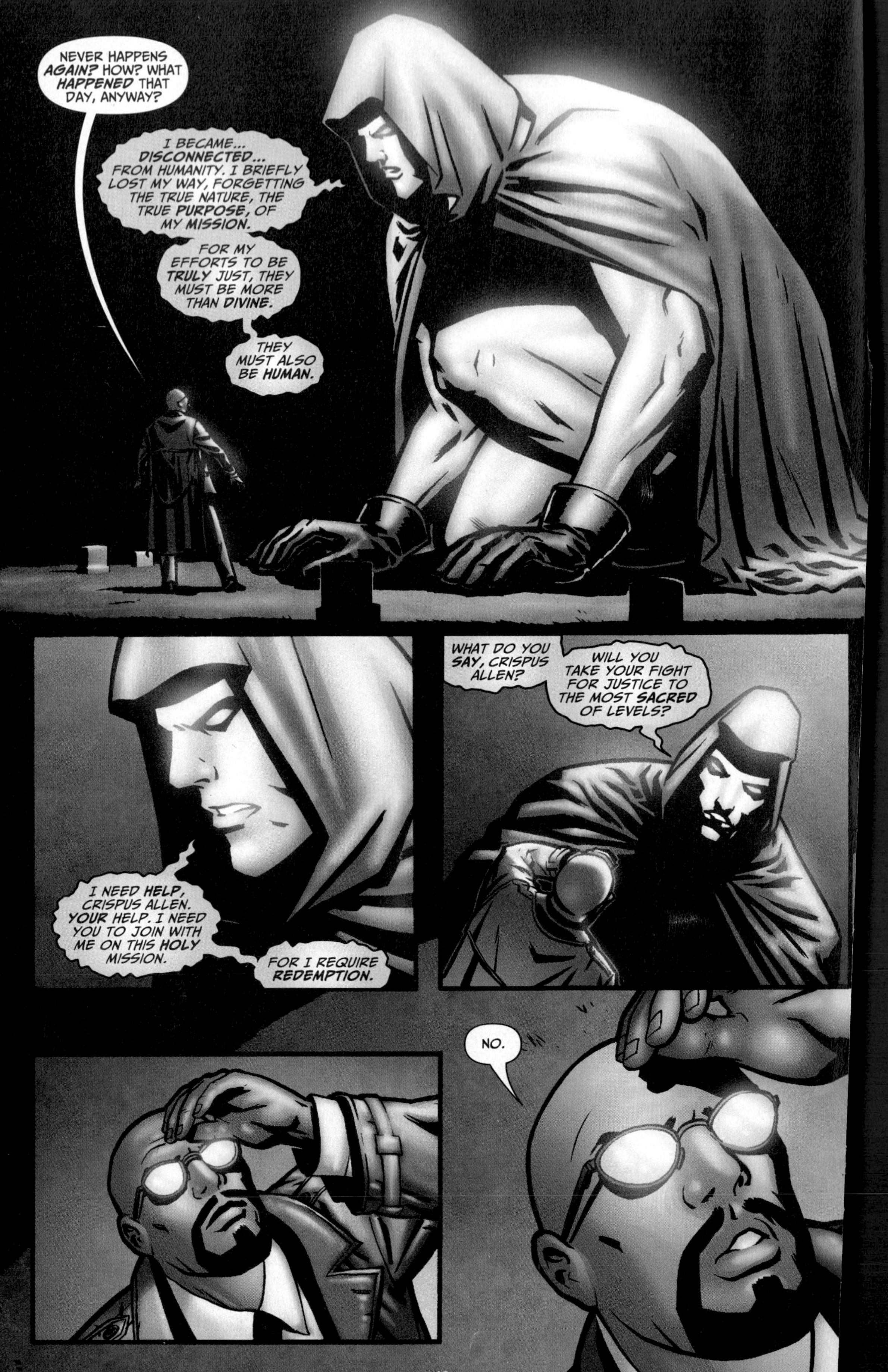
NEVER HAPPENS AGAIN? HOW? WHAT HAPPENED THAT DAY, ANYWAY?
I BECAME... DISCONNECTED... FROM HUMANITY. I BRIEFLY LOST MY WAY, FORGETTING THE TRUE NATURE, THE TRUE PURPOSE, OF MY MISSION.
FOR MY EFFORTS TO BE TRULY JUST, THEY MUST BE MORE THAN DIVINE.
THEY MUST ALSO BE HUMAN.
I NEED HELP, CRISPUS ALLEN. YOUR HELP. I NEED YOU TO JOIN WITH ME ON THIS HOLY MISSION.
FOR I REQUIRE REDEMPTION.
WHAT DO YOU SAY, CRISPUS ALLEN?
WILL YOU TAKE YOUR FIGHT FOR JUSTICE TO THE MOST SACRED OF LEVELS?
NO.

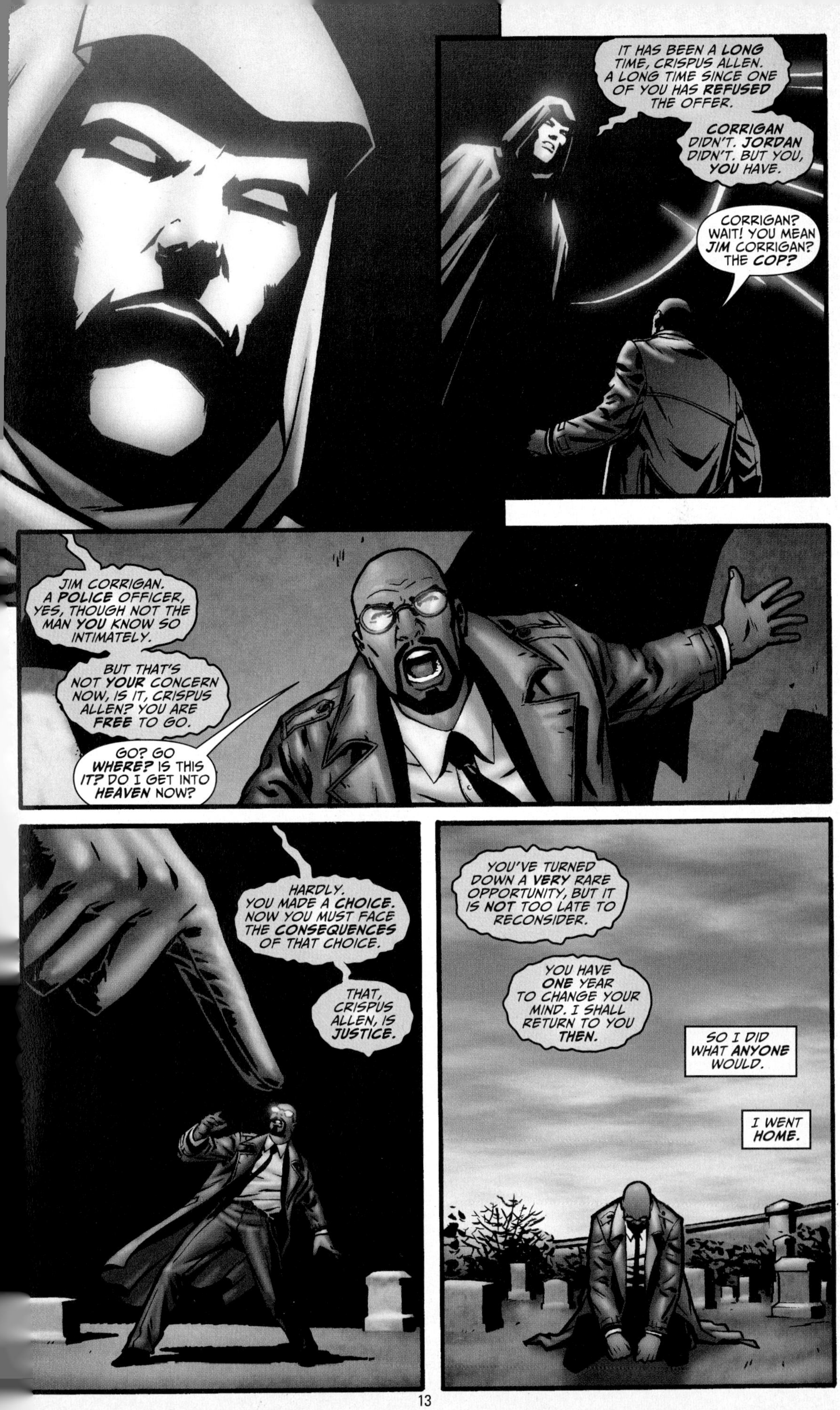
IT HAS BEEN A LONG TIME, CRISPUS ALLEN. A LONG TIME SINCE ONE OF YOU HAS REFUSED THE OFFER.
CORRIGAN DIDN'T. JORDAN DIDN'T. BUT YOU, YOU HAVE.
CORRIGAN? WAIT! YOU MEAN JIM CORRIGAN? THE COP?
JIM CORRIGAN. A POLICE OFFICER, YES, THOUGH NOT THE MAN YOU KNOW SO INTIMATELY.
BUT THAT'S NOT YOUR CONCERN NOW, IS IT, CRISPUS ALLEN? YOU ARE FREE TO GO.
GO? GO WHERE? IS THIS IT? DO I GET INTO HEAVEN NOW?
HARDLY. YOU MADE A CHOICE. NOW YOU MUST FACE THE CONSEQUENCES OF THAT CHOICE.
THAT, CRISPUS ALLEN, IS JUSTICE.
YOU'VE TURNED DOWN A VERY RARE OPPORTUNITY, BUT IT IS NOT TOO LATE TO RECONSIDER.
YOU HAVE ONE YEAR TO CHANGE YOUR MIND. I SHALL RETURN TO YOU THEN.
SO I DID WHAT ANYONE WOULD.
I WENT HOME.

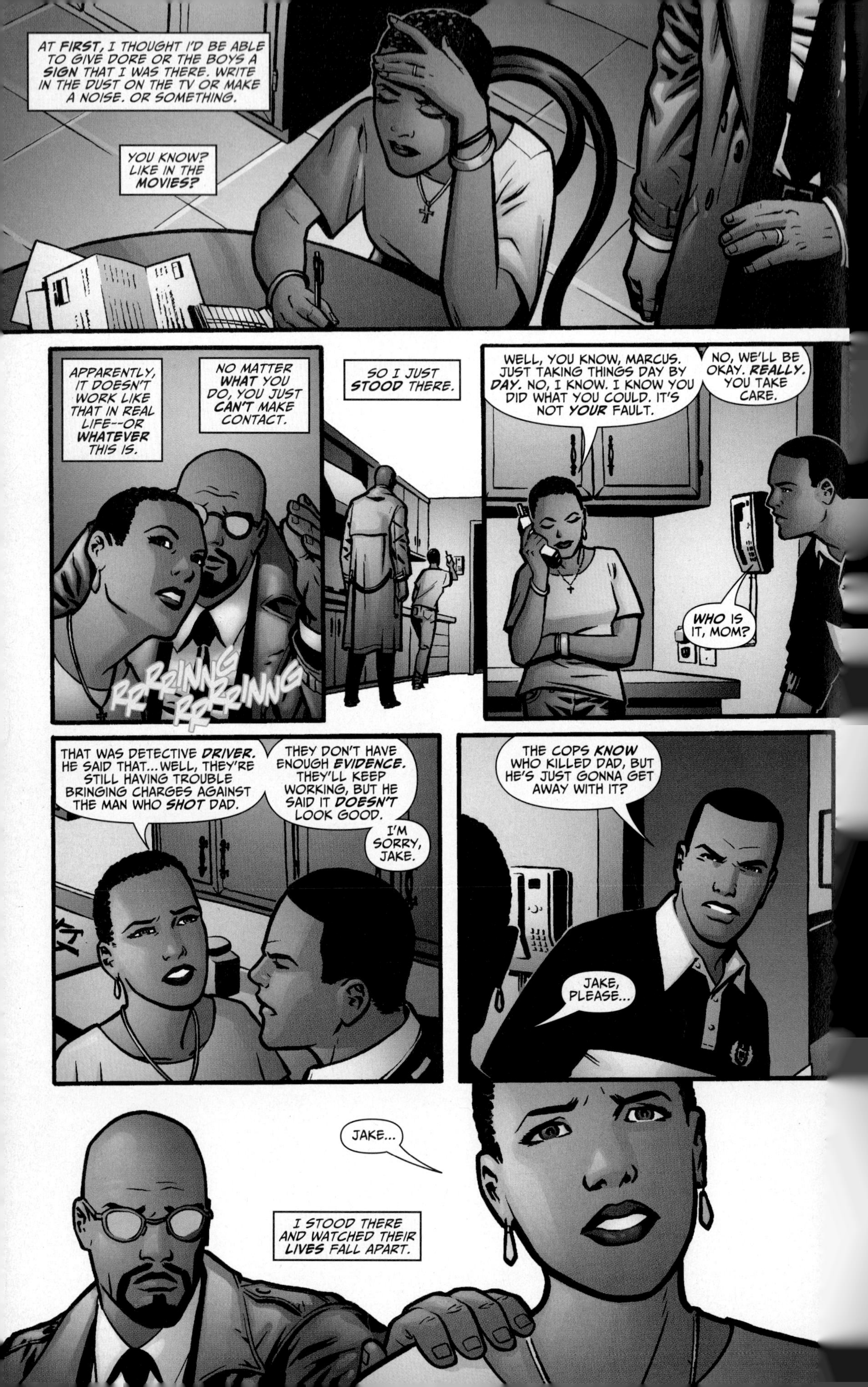

AT FIRST, I THOUGHT I'D BE ABLE TO GIVE DORE OR THE BOYS A SIGN THAT I WAS THERE. WRITE IN THE DUST ON THE TV OR MAKE A NOISE. OR SOMETHING.
YOU KNOW? LIKE IN THE MOVIES?
APPARENTLY, IT DOESN'T WORK LIKE THAT IN REAL LIFE--OR WHATEVER THIS IS.
NO MATTER WHAT YOU DO, YOU JUST CAN'T MAKE CONTACT.
RRRRINNG RRRRINNG
SO I JUST STOOD THERE.
WELL, YOU KNOW, MARCUS. JUST TAKING THINGS DAY BY DAY. NO, I KNOW. I KNOW YOU DID WHAT YOU COULD. IT'S NOT YOUR FAULT.
NO, WE'LL BE OKAY. REALLY. YOU TAKE CARE.
WHO IS IT, MOM?
THAT WAS DETECTIVE DRIVER. HE SAID THAT...WELL, THEY'RE STILL HAVING TROUBLE BRINGING CHARGES AGAINST THE MAN WHO SHOT DAD.
THEY DON'T HAVE ENOUGH EVIDENCE. THEY'LL KEEP WORKING, BUT HE SAID IT DOESN'T LOOK GOOD.
I'M SORRY, JAKE.
THE COPS KNOW WHO KILLED DAD, BUT HE'S JUST GONNA GET AWAY WITH IT?
JAKE, PLEASE...
JAKE...
I STOOD THERE AND WATCHED THEIR LIVES FALL APART.

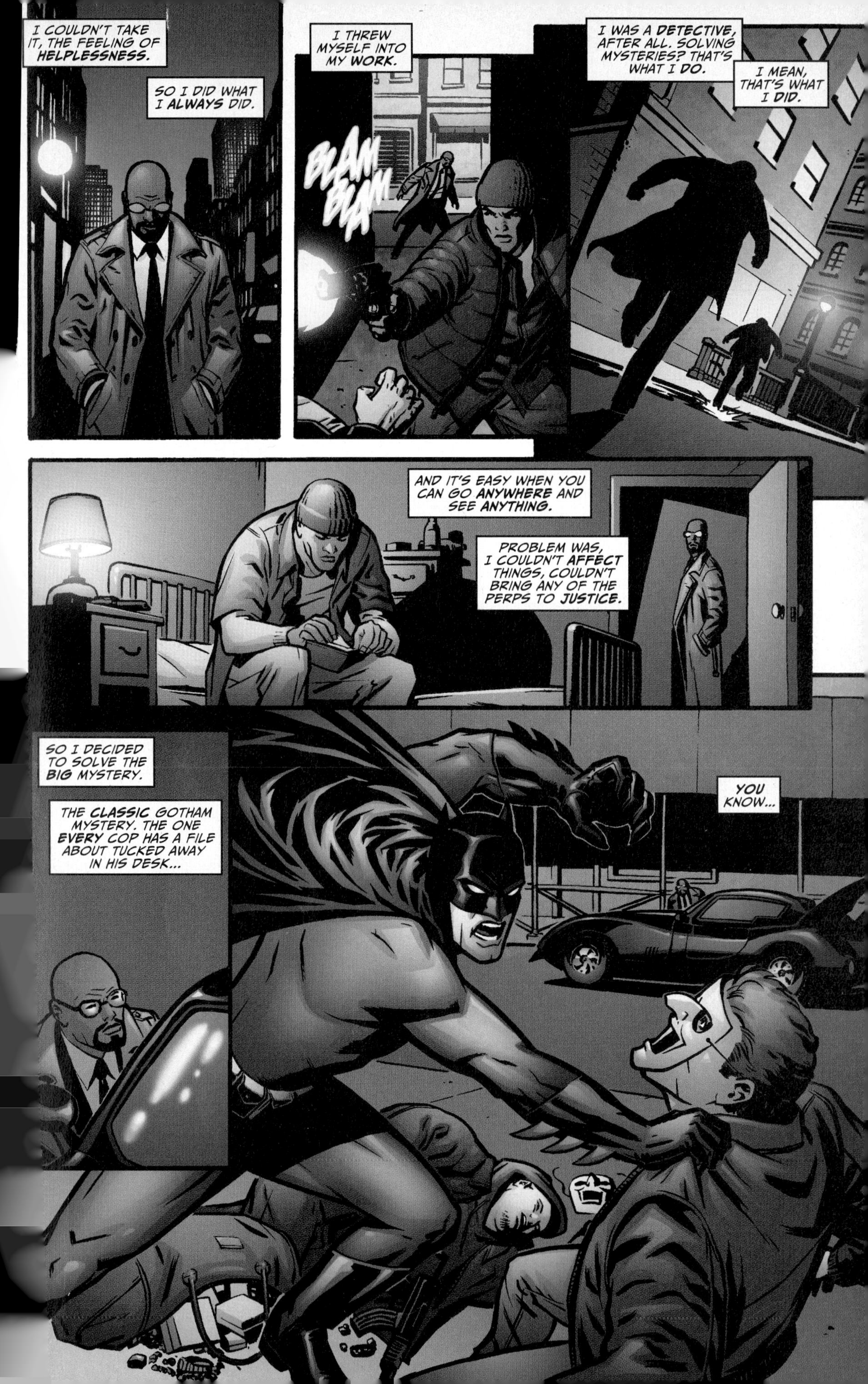
I COULDN'T TAKE IT, THE FEELING OF HELPLESSNESS.
SO I DID WHAT I ALWAYS DID.
I THREW MYSELF INTO MY WORK.
BLAM BLAM BLAM
I WAS A DETECTIVE, AFTER ALL. SOLVING MYSTERIES? THAT'S WHAT I DO.
I MEAN, THAT'S WHAT I DID.
AND IT'S EASY WHEN YOU CAN GO ANYWHERE AND SEE ANYTHING.
PROBLEM WAS, I COULDN'T AFFECT THINGS, COULDN'T BRING ANY OF THE PERPS TO JUSTICE.
SO I DECIDED TO SOLVE THE BIG MYSTERY.
THE CLASSIC GOTHAM MYSTERY. THE ONE EVERY COP HAS A FILE ABOUT TUCKED AWAY IN HIS DESK...
YOU KNOW...

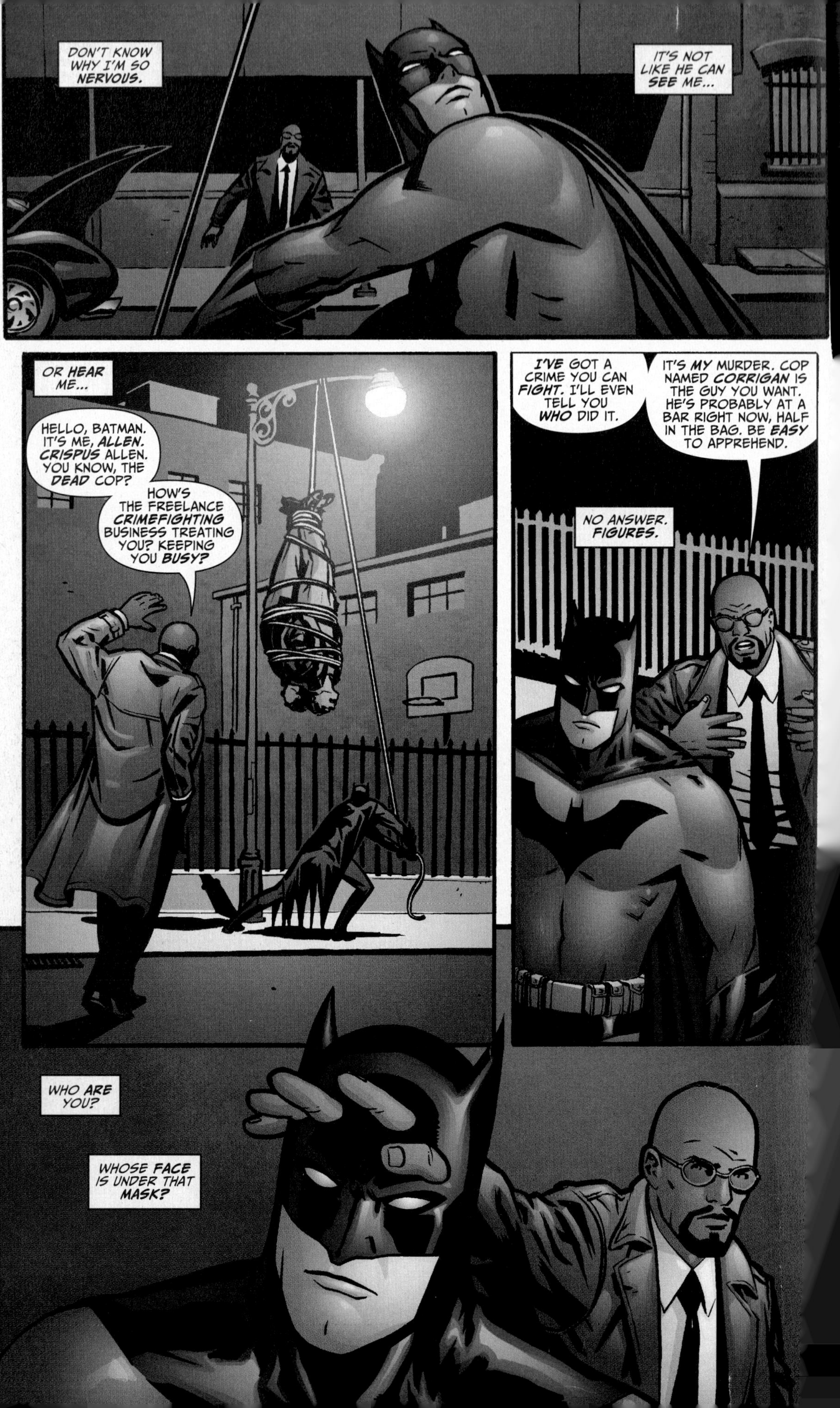
DON'T KNOW WHY I'M SO NERVOUS.
IT'S NOT LIKE HE CAN SEE ME...
OR HEAR ME...
HELLO, BATMAN. IT'S ME, ALLEN. CRISPUS ALLEN. YOU KNOW, THE DEAD COP?
HOW'S THE FREELANCE CRIMEFIGHTING BUSINESS TREATING YOU? KEEPING YOU BUSY?
I'VE GOT A CRIME YOU CAN FIGHT. I'LL EVEN TELL YOU WHO DID IT.
IT'S MY MURDER. COP NAMED CORRIGAN IS THE GUY YOU WANT. HE'S PROBABLY AT A BAR RIGHT NOW, HALF IN THE BAG. BE EASY TO APPREHEND.
NO ANSWER. FIGURES.
WHO ARE YOU?
WHOSE FACE IS UNDER THAT MASK?

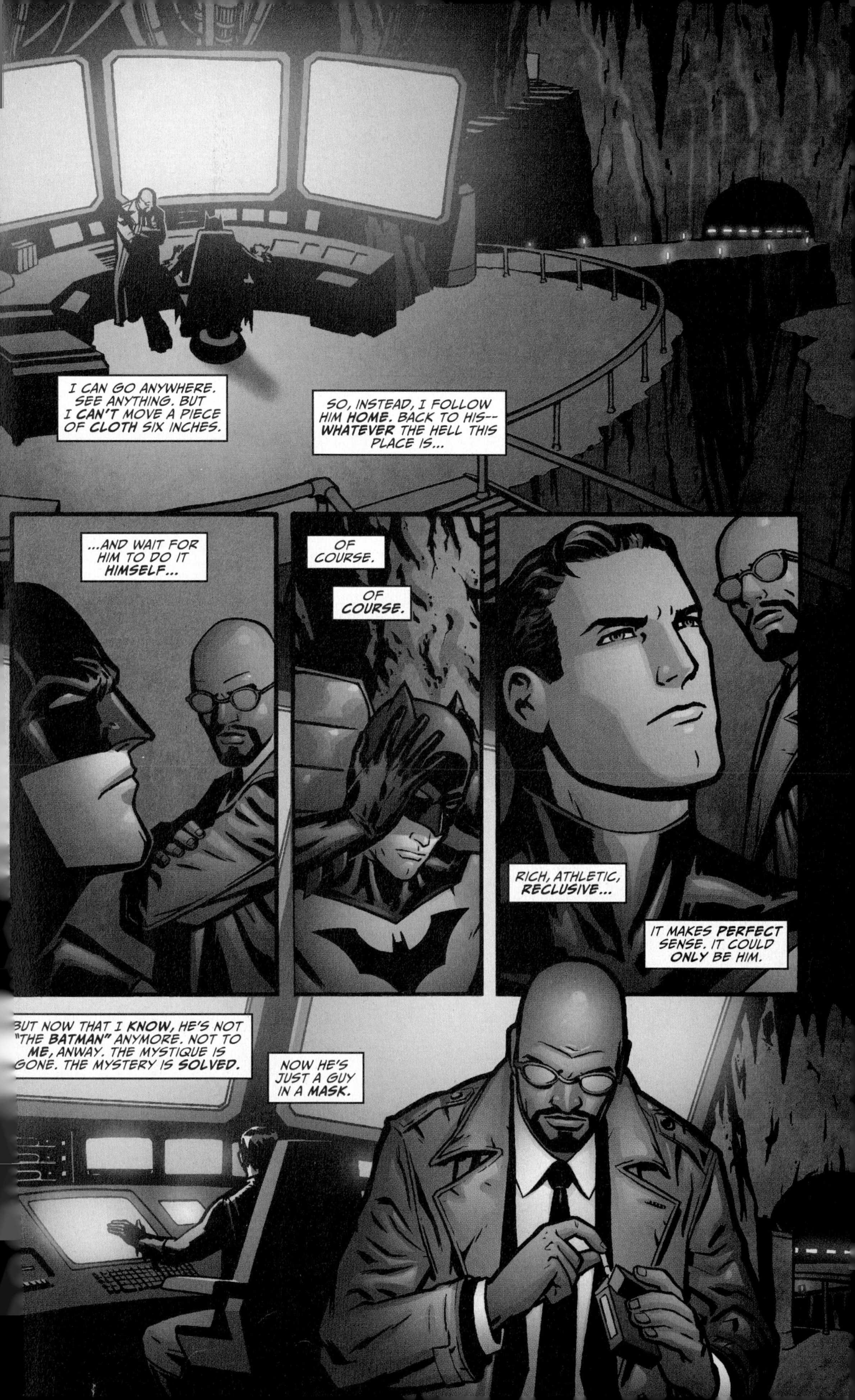
I CAN GO ANYWHERE. SEE ANYTHING. BUT I CAN'T MOVE A PIECE OF CLOTH SIX INCHES.
SO, INSTEAD, I FOLLOW HIM HOME. BACK TO HIS-- WHATEVER THE HELL THIS PLACE IS...
...AND WAIT FOR HIM TO DO IT HIMSELF...
OF COURSE.
OF COURSE.
RICH, ATHLETIC, RECLUSIVE...
IT MAKES PERFECT SENSE. IT COULD ONLY BE HIM.
BUT NOW THAT I KNOW, HE'S NOT "THE BATMAN" ANYMORE. NOT TO ME, ANWAY. THE MYSTIQUE IS GONE. THE MYSTERY IS SOLVED.
NOW HE'S JUST A GUY IN A MASK.

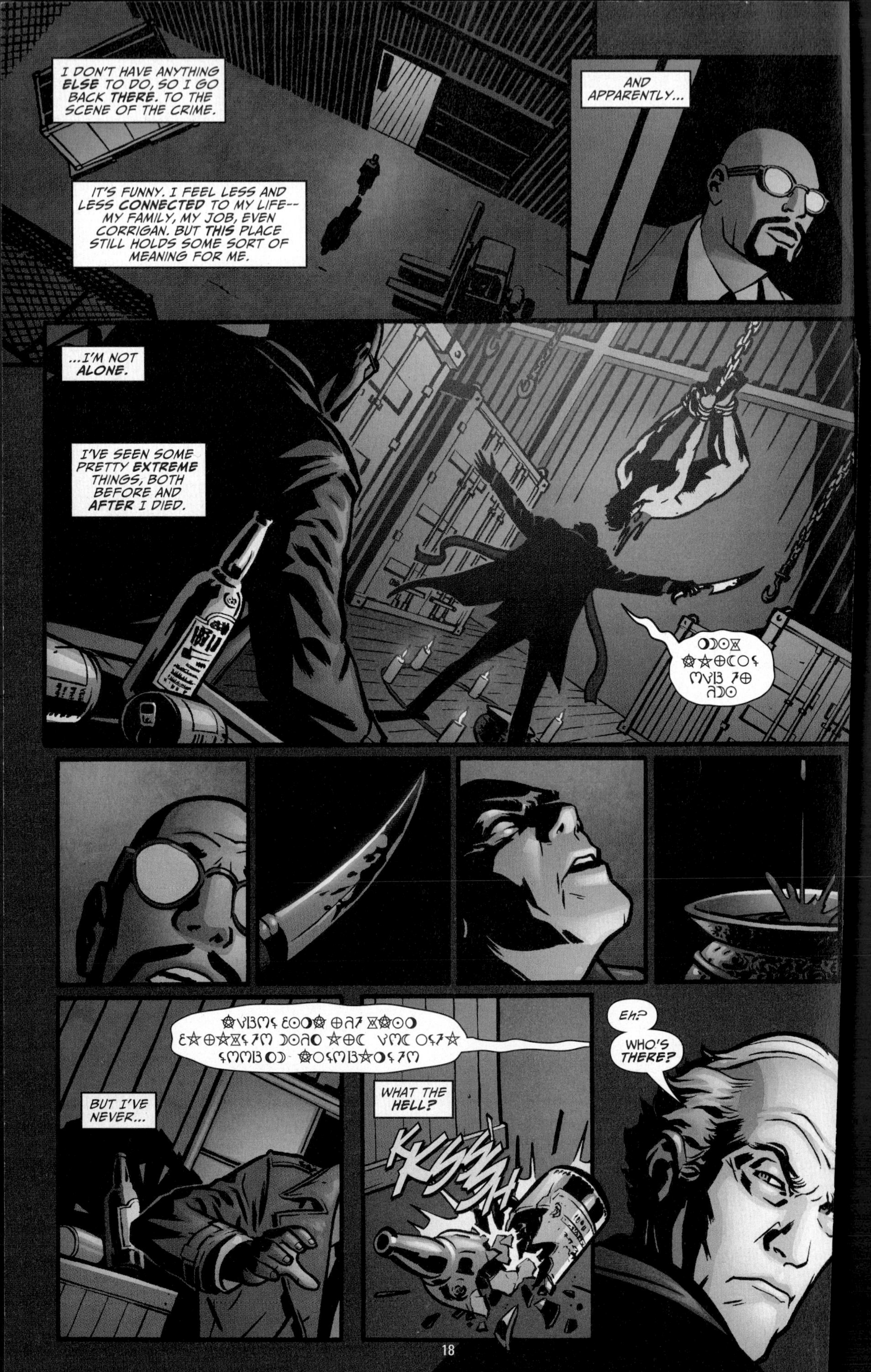

I DON'T HAVE ANYTHING ELSE TO DO, SO I GO BACK THERE. TO THE SCENE OF THE CRIME.
IT'S FUNNY. I FEEL LESS AND LESS CONNECTED TO MY LIFE-- MY FAMILY, MY JOB, EVEN CORRIGAN. BUT THIS PLACE STILL HOLDS SOME SORT OF MEANING FOR ME.
AND APPARENTLY...
...I'M NOT ALONE.
I'VE SEEN SOME PRETTY EXTREME THINGS, BOTH BEFORE AND AFTER I DIED.
BUT I'VE NEVER...
WHAT THE HELL?
KKSSHH
Eh?
WHO'S THERE?

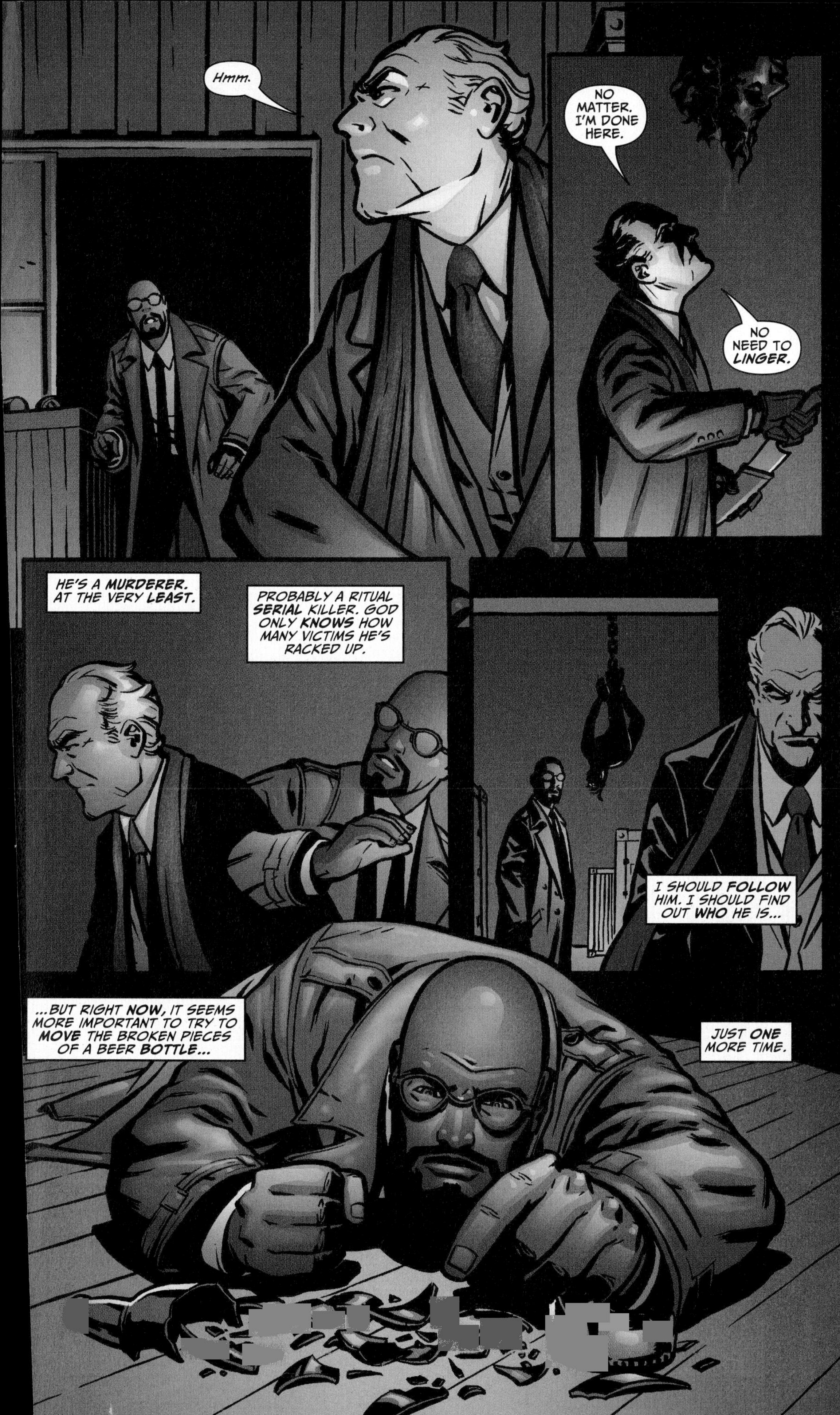
Hmm.
NO MATTER. I'M DONE HERE.
NO NEED TO LINGER.
HE'S A MURDERER. AT THE VERY LEAST.
PROBABLY A RITUAL SERIAL KILLER. GOD ONLY KNOWS HOW MANY VICTIMS HE'S RACKED UP.
I SHOULD FOLLOW HIM. I SHOULD FIND OUT WHO HE IS...
...BUT RIGHT NOW, IT SEEMS MORE IMPORTANT TO TRY TO MOVE THE BROKEN PIECES OF A BEER BOTTLE...
JUST ONE MORE TIME.

COULDN'T DO IT, THOUGH. NO MATTER **HOW** HARD I TRIED.

I FIGURED MAYBE IT HAD SOMETHING TO DO WITH THE **KILLER**, SO I CAUGHT UP WITH HIM AND STUCK LIKE GLUE. FOR **WEEKS.**

WARM UP YOUR **COFFEE,** MR. WEISS?

THANK YOU, CARLA.

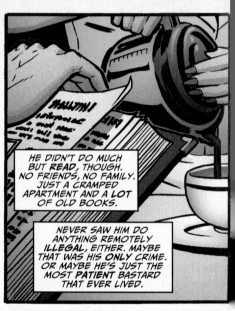

HE DIDN'T DO MUCH BUT **READ,** THOUGH. NO FRIENDS, NO FAMILY. JUST A CRAMPED APARTMENT AND A **LOT** OF OLD BOOKS.

NEVER SAW HIM DO ANYTHING REMOTELY **ILLEGAL,** EITHER. MAYBE THAT WAS HIS **ONLY** CRIME. OR MAYBE HE'S JUST THE MOST **PATIENT** BASTARD THAT EVER LIVED.

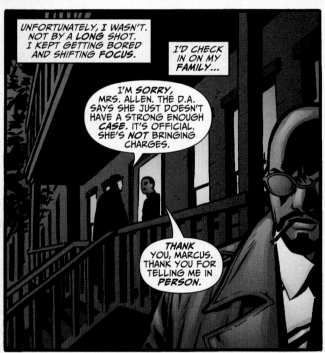

UNFORTUNATELY, I WASN'T. NOT BY A **LONG** SHOT. I KEPT GETTING BORED AND SHIFTING **FOCUS.**

I'D CHECK IN ON MY **FAMILY...**

I'M **SORRY,** MRS. ALLEN. THE D.A. SAYS SHE JUST DOESN'T HAVE A STRONG ENOUGH **CASE.** IT'S OFFICIAL. SHE'S **NOT** BRINGING CHARGES.

THANK YOU, MARCUS. THANK YOU FOR TELLING ME IN **PERSON.**

THEN I'D CHECK IN ON **WEISS.**

JUST LIKE ALWAYS, I SPLIT MY TIME BETWEEN **WORK...**

AND, AFTER THE **BREAK,** WE'LL FIND OUT WHICH CLIP WINS THE $10,000 **GRAND** PRIZE! YOU'VE WAITED **ALL** SEASON TO FIND OUT, SO **DON'T** MISS IT!

...AND **HOME.**

SO HE'S **NOT** GOING TO JAIL? HE'S NOT EVEN GOING TO GET **ARRESTED?**

NO, MAL. BUT HE'LL PAY EVENTUALLY. HE **WILL.**

WHOEVER DID THIS, HONEY, WHOEVER DID THIS TO **DAD...**

WELL, SOMEDAY, **HE'S** GOING TO HAVE TO ANSWER TO **GOD.**

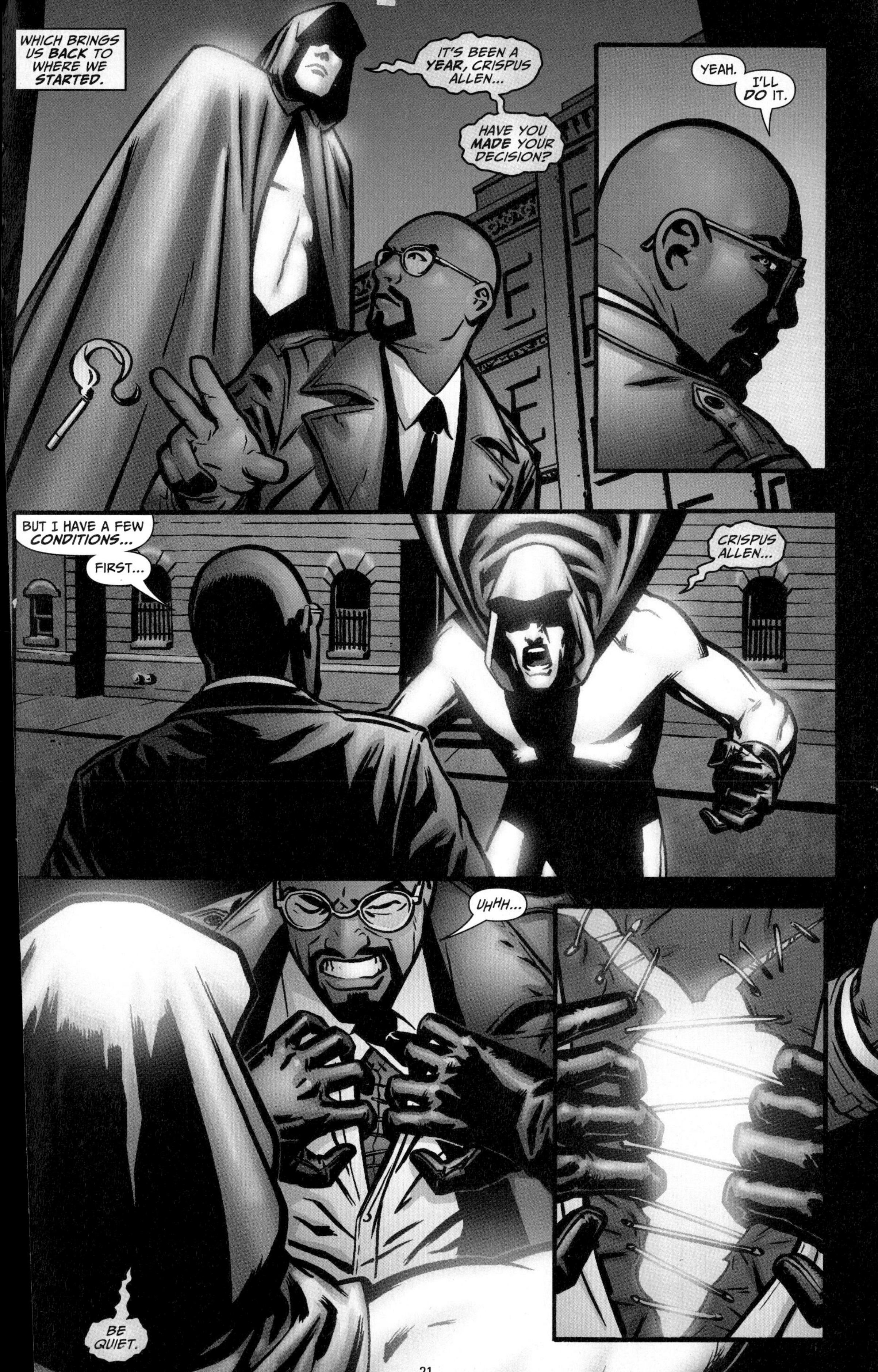
WHICH BRINGS US BACK TO WHERE WE STARTED.
IT'S BEEN A YEAR, CRISPUS ALLEN...
HAVE YOU MADE YOUR DECISION?
YEAH.
I'LL DO IT.
BUT I HAVE A FEW CONDITIONS...
FIRST...
CRISPUS ALLEN...
UHHH...
BE QUIET.

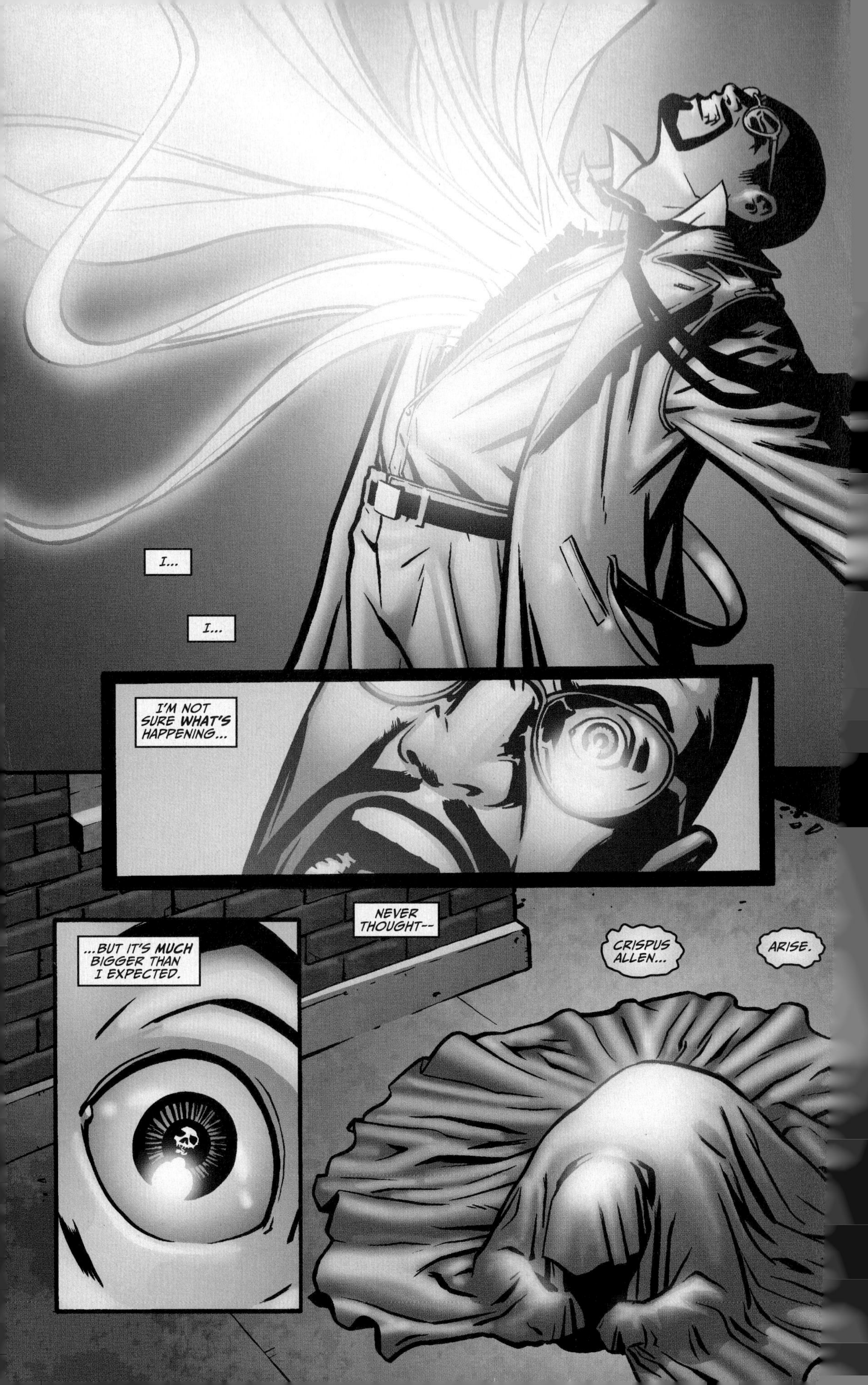
I...
I...
I'M NOT SURE WHAT'S HAPPENING...
NEVER THOUGHT--
...BUT IT'S MUCH BIGGER THAN I EXPECTED.
CRISPUS ALLEN...
ARISE.

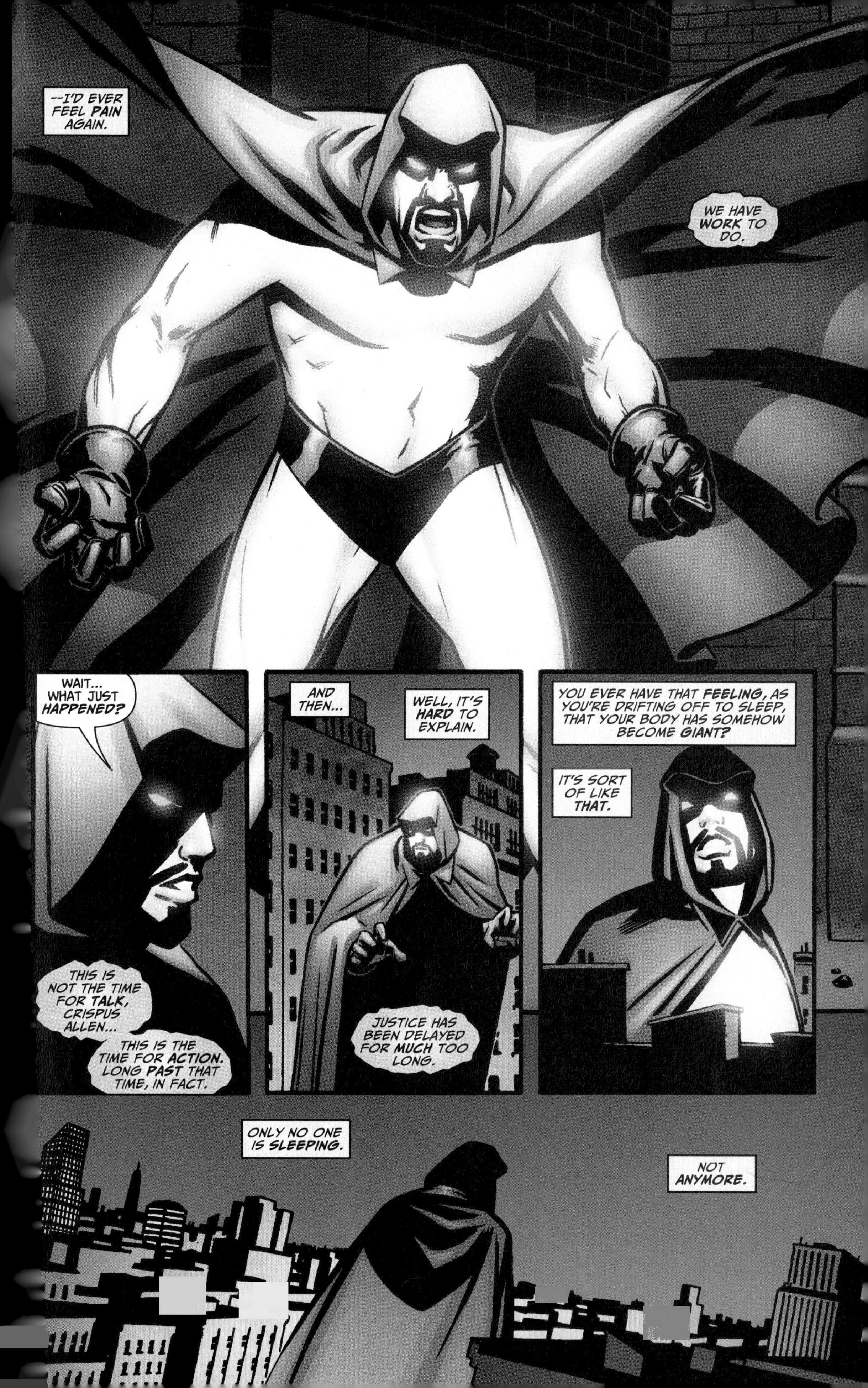
--I'D EVER FEEL PAIN AGAIN.
WE HAVE WORK TO DO.
WAIT... WHAT JUST HAPPENED?
THIS IS NOT THE TIME FOR TALK, CRISPUS ALLEN...
THIS IS THE TIME FOR ACTION. LONG PAST THAT TIME, IN FACT.
AND THEN...
WELL, IT'S HARD TO EXPLAIN.
JUSTICE HAS BEEN DELAYED FOR MUCH TOO LONG.
YOU EVER HAVE THAT FEELING, AS YOU'RE DRIFTING OFF TO SLEEP, THAT YOUR BODY HAS SOMEHOW BECOME GIANT?
IT'S SORT OF LIKE THAT.
ONLY NO ONE IS SLEEPING.
NOT ANYMORE.

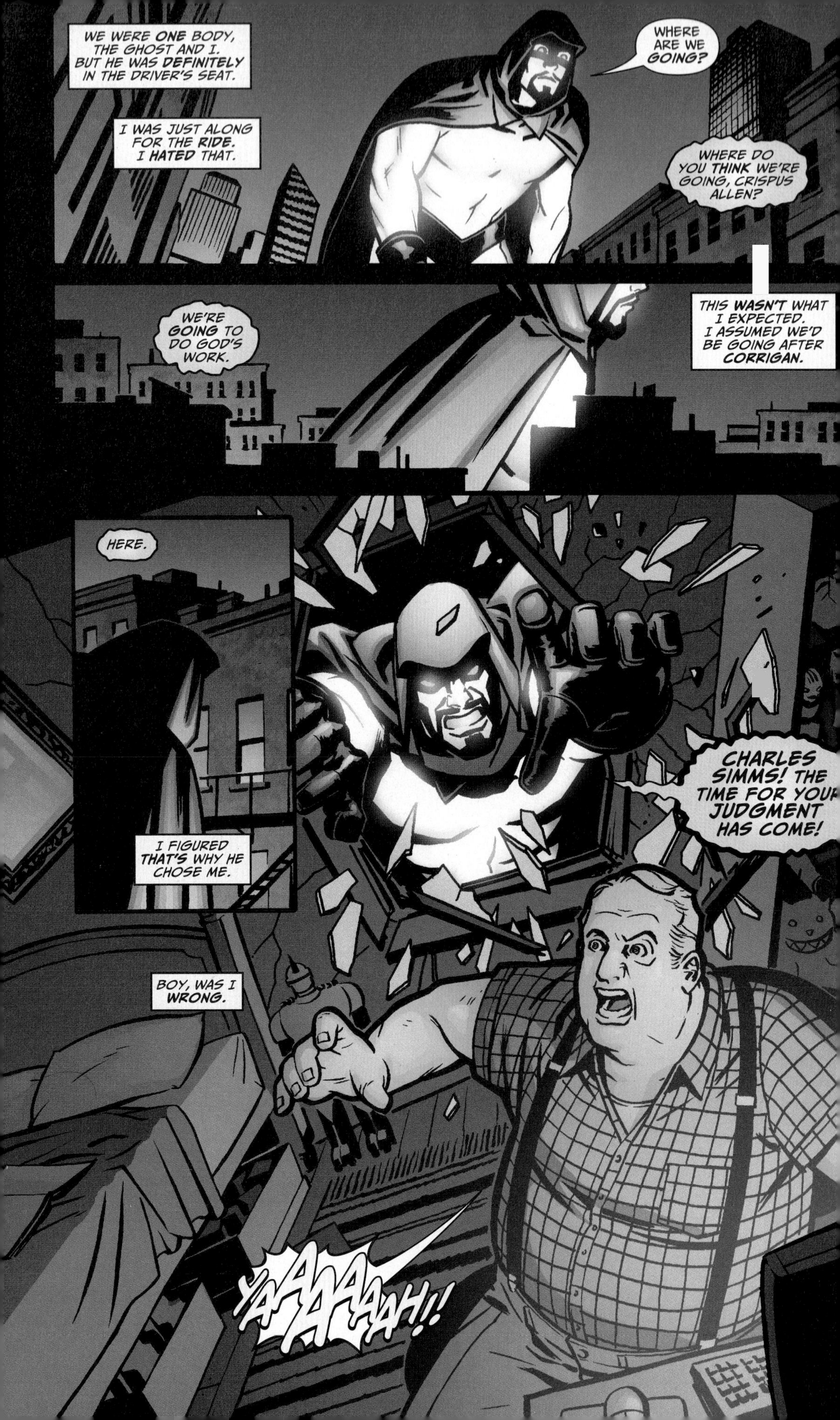
WE WERE ONE BODY, THE GHOST AND I. BUT HE WAS DEFINITELY IN THE DRIVER'S SEAT.
WHERE ARE WE GOING?
I WAS JUST ALONG FOR THE RIDE. I HATED THAT.
WHERE DO YOU THINK WE'RE GOING, CRISPUS ALLEN?
WE'RE GOING TO DO GOD'S WORK.
THIS WASN'T WHAT I EXPECTED. I ASSUMED WE'D BE GOING AFTER CORRIGAN.
HERE.
I FIGURED THAT'S WHY HE CHOSE ME.
CHARLES SIMMS! THE TIME FOR YOUR JUDGMENT HAS COME!
BOY, WAS I WRONG.
YAAAAAAAH!!

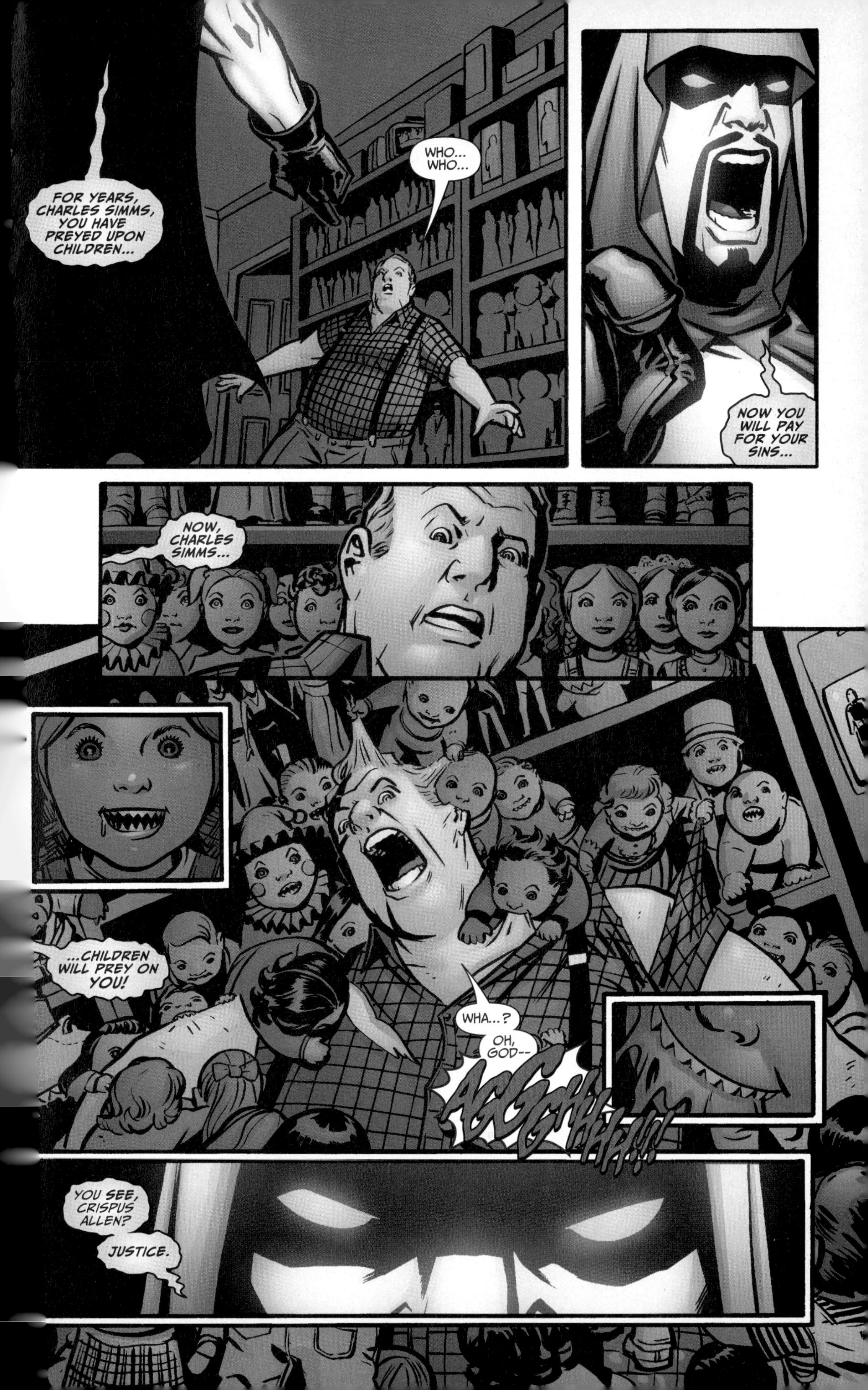

FOR YEARS, CHARLES SIMMS, YOU HAVE PREYED UPON CHILDREN...
WHO... WHO...
NOW YOU WILL PAY FOR YOUR SINS...
NOW, CHARLES SIMMS...
...CHILDREN WILL PREY ON YOU!
WHA...?
OH, GOD--
AGGHHH!!
YOU SEE, CRISPUS ALLEN?
JUSTICE.

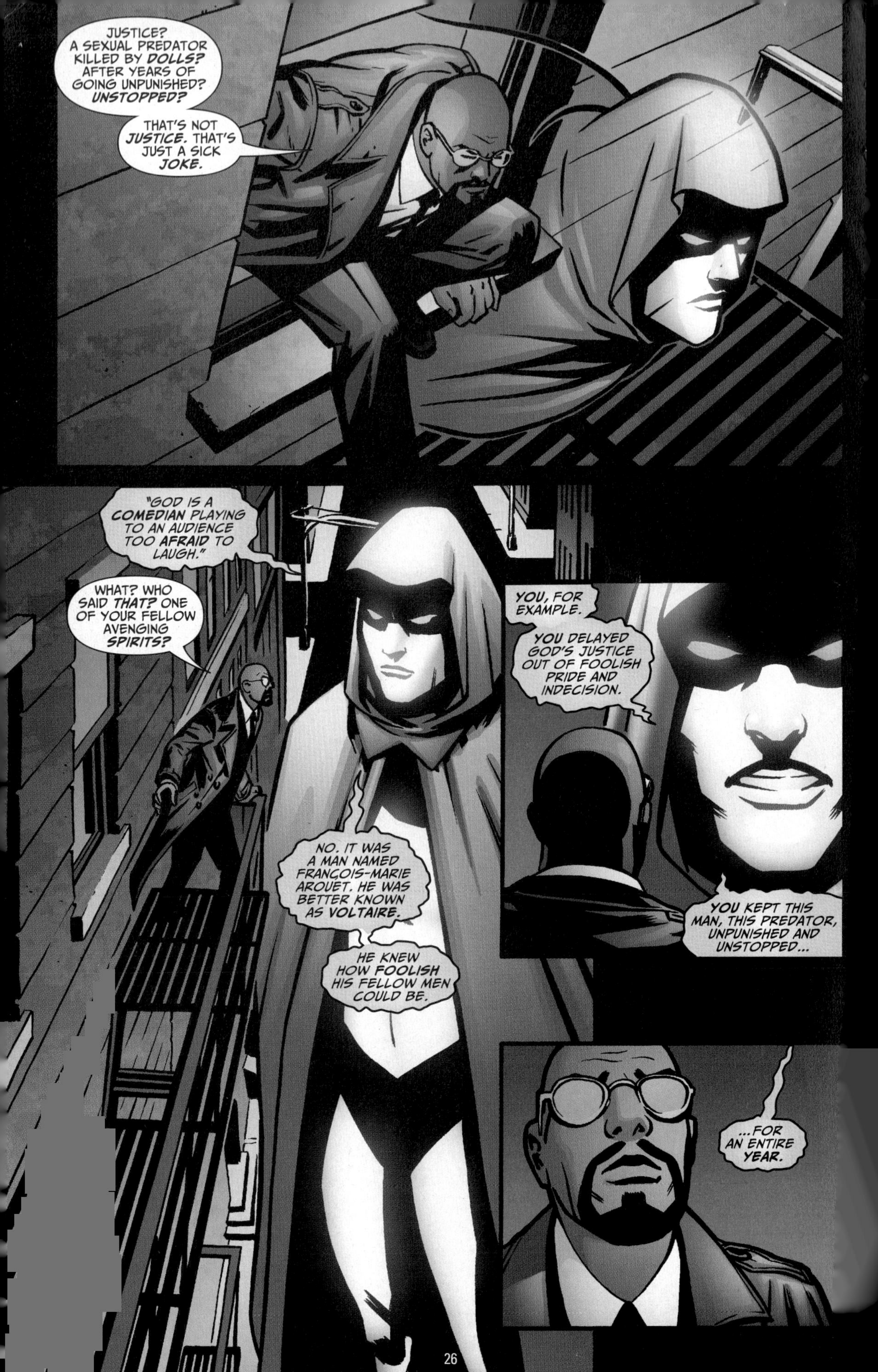
JUSTICE? A SEXUAL PREDATOR KILLED BY DOLLS? AFTER YEARS OF GOING UNPUNISHED? UNSTOPPED?
THAT'S NOT JUSTICE. THAT'S JUST A SICK JOKE.
"GOD IS A COMEDIAN PLAYING TO AN AUDIENCE TOO AFRAID TO LAUGH."
WHAT? WHO SAID THAT? ONE OF YOUR FELLOW AVENGING SPIRITS?
NO. IT WAS A MAN NAMED FRANÇOIS-MARIE AROUET. HE WAS BETTER KNOWN AS VOLTAIRE.
HE KNEW HOW FOOLISH HIS FELLOW MEN COULD BE.
YOU, FOR EXAMPLE.
YOU DELAYED GOD'S JUSTICE OUT OF FOOLISH PRIDE AND INDECISION.
YOU KEPT THIS MAN, THIS PREDATOR, UNPUNISHED AND UNSTOPPED...
...FOR AN ENTIRE YEAR.

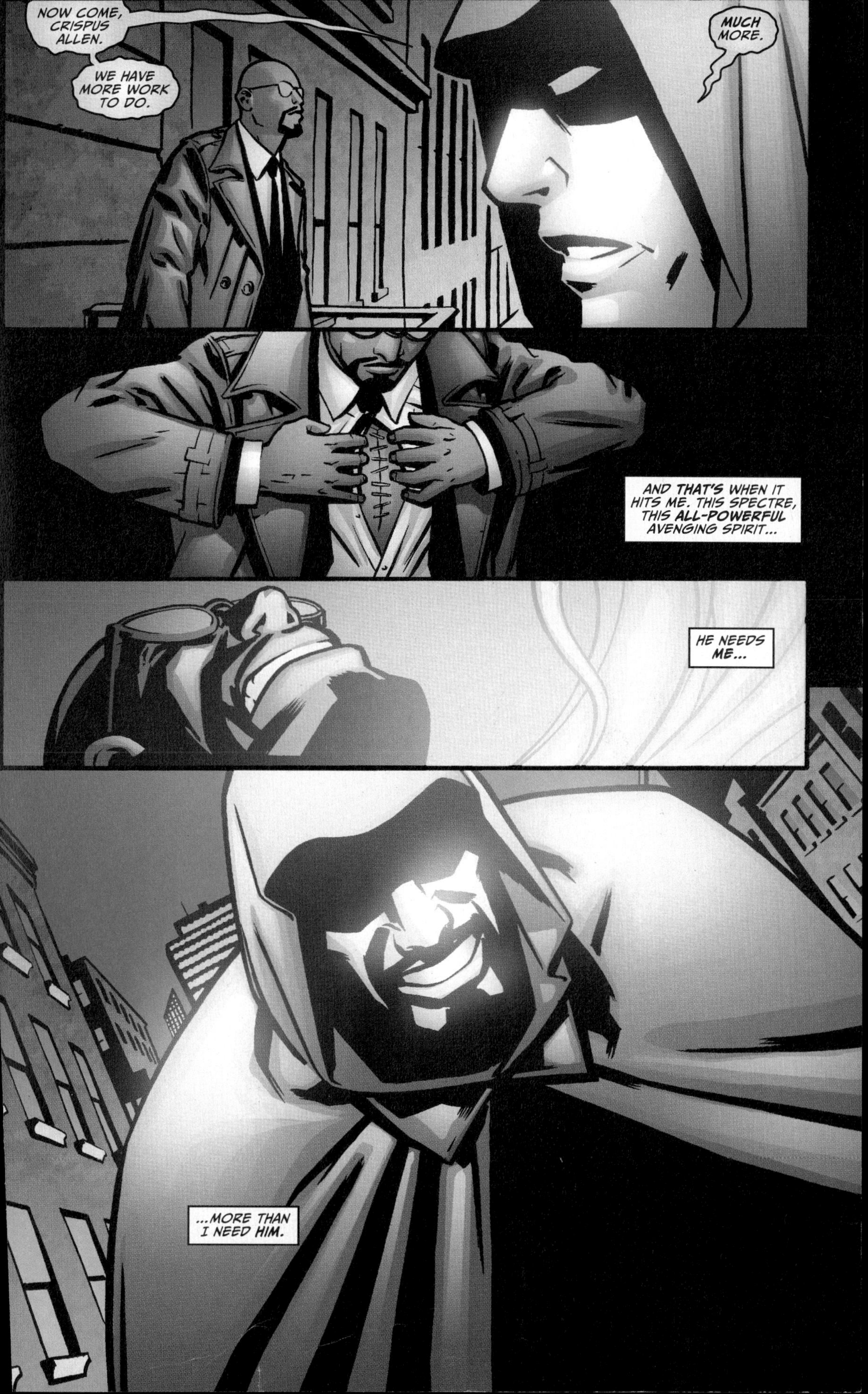
NOW COME, CRISPUS ALLEN.
WE HAVE MORE WORK TO DO.
MUCH MORE.
AND **THAT'S** WHEN IT HITS ME. THIS SPECTRE, THIS **ALL-POWERFUL** AVENGING SPIRIT...
HE NEEDS **ME**...
...MORE THAN I NEED **HIM**.

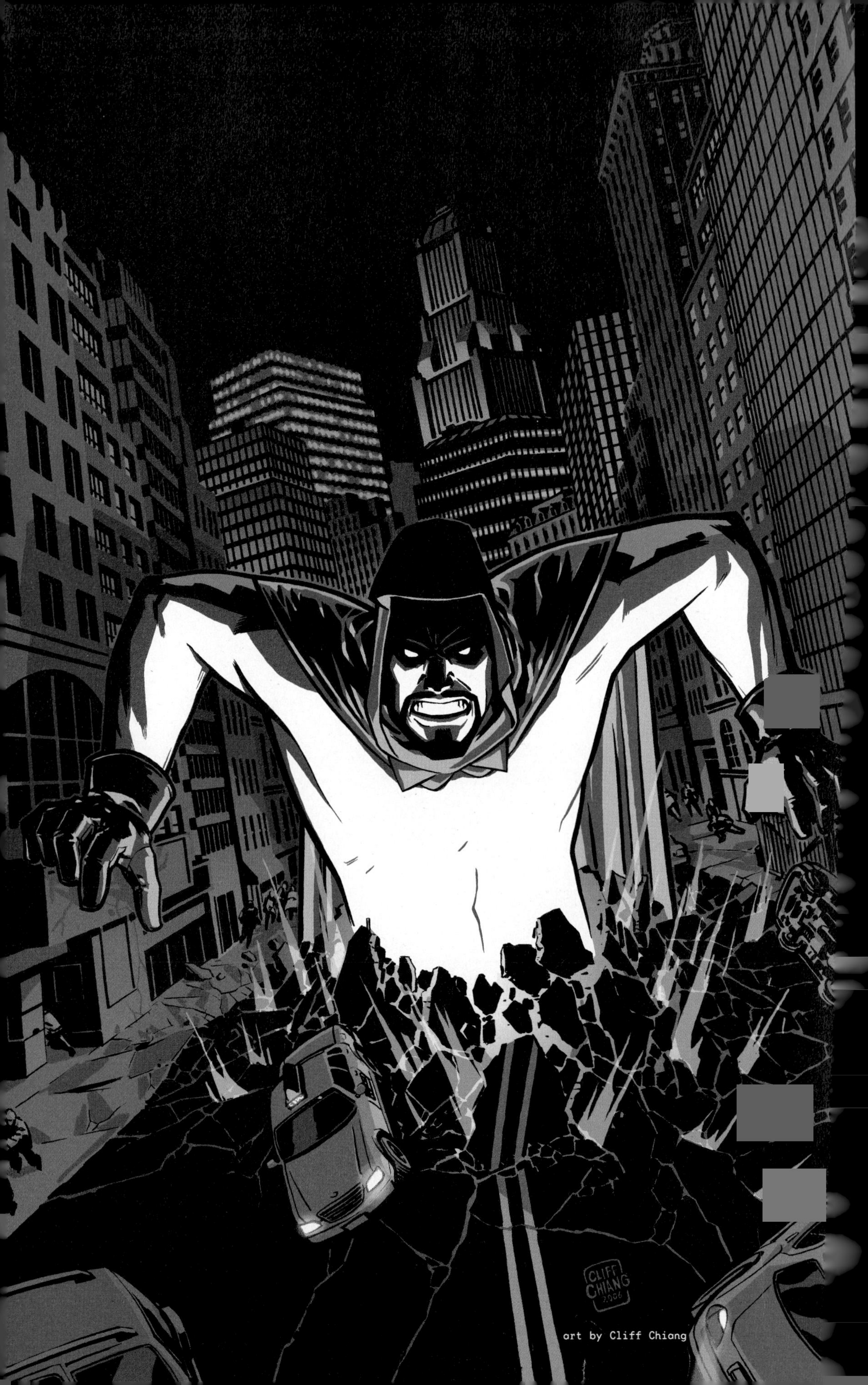
CLIFF CHIANG 2006
art by Cliff Chiang

COPS--LIKE I WAS, NOT SO LONG AGO--WE SEE A LOT. THINGS THAT NORMAL PEOPLE-- PEOPLE LIKE YOU--NEVER SEE.

ASSAULT. RAPE. MURDER. SUICIDE. PEOPLE AT THEIR ABSOLUTE WORST. BUT HERE'S THE THING...

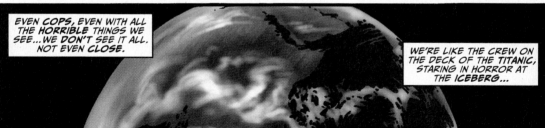

EVEN COPS, EVEN WITH ALL THE HORRIBLE THINGS WE SEE...WE DON'T SEE IT ALL. NOT EVEN CLOSE.

WE'RE LIKE THE CREW ON THE DECK OF THE TITANIC, STARING IN HORROR AT THE ICEBERG...

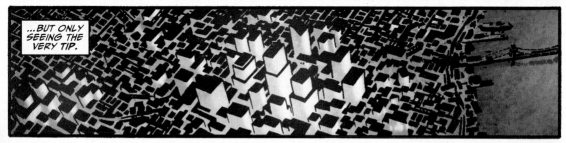

...BUT ONLY SEEING THE VERY TIP.

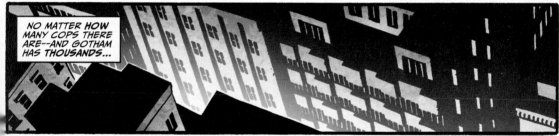

NO MATTER HOW MANY COPS THERE ARE--AND GOTHAM HAS THOUSANDS...

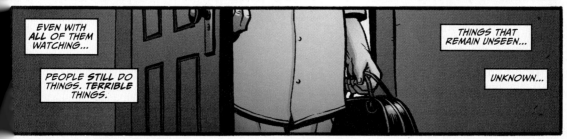

EVEN WITH ALL OF THEM WATCHING...

THINGS THAT REMAIN UNSEEN...

PEOPLE STILL DO THINGS. TERRIBLE THINGS.

UNKNOWN...

UNPUNISHED.

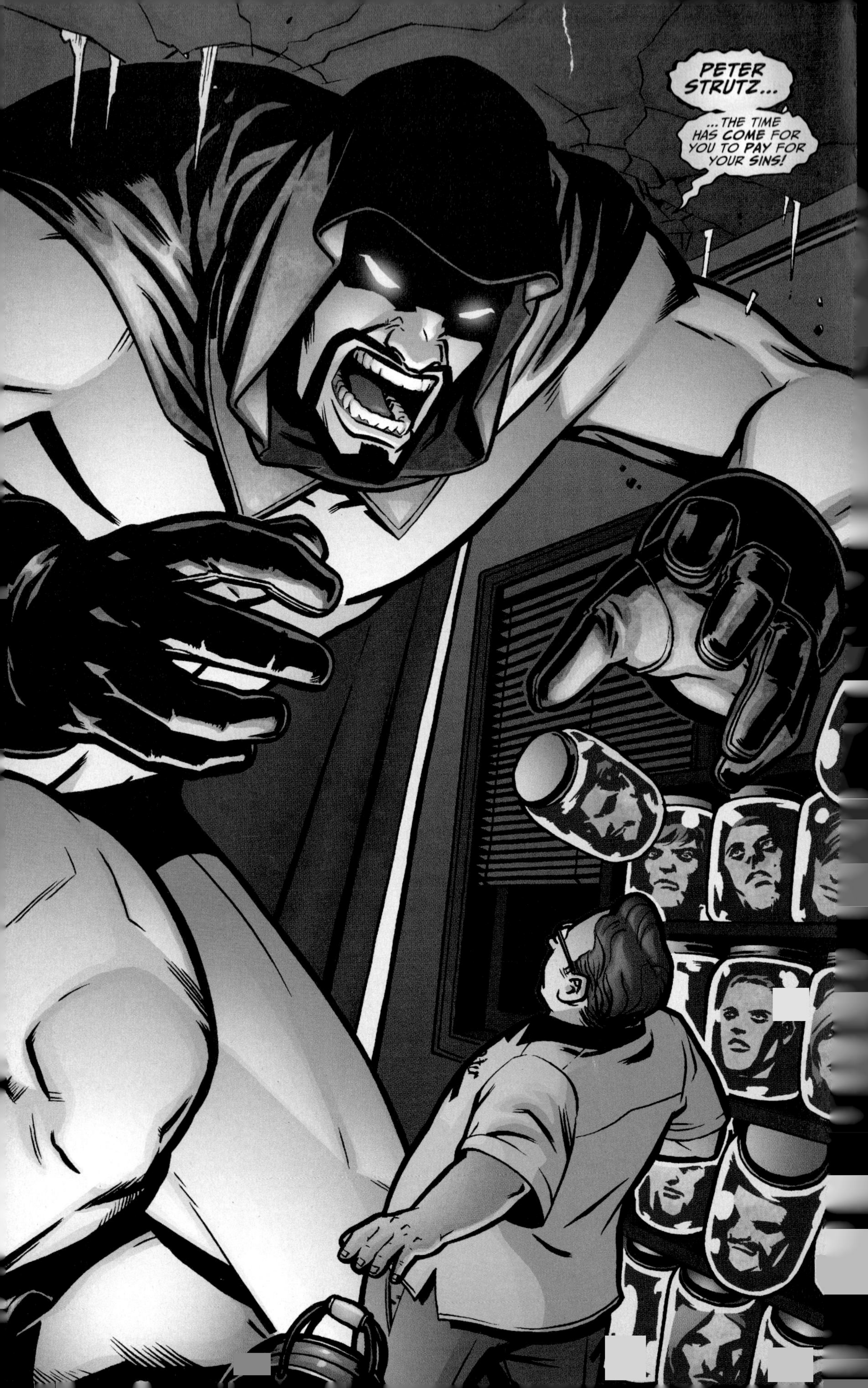
PETER STRUTZ...
...THE TIME HAS COME FOR YOU TO PAY FOR YOUR SINS!

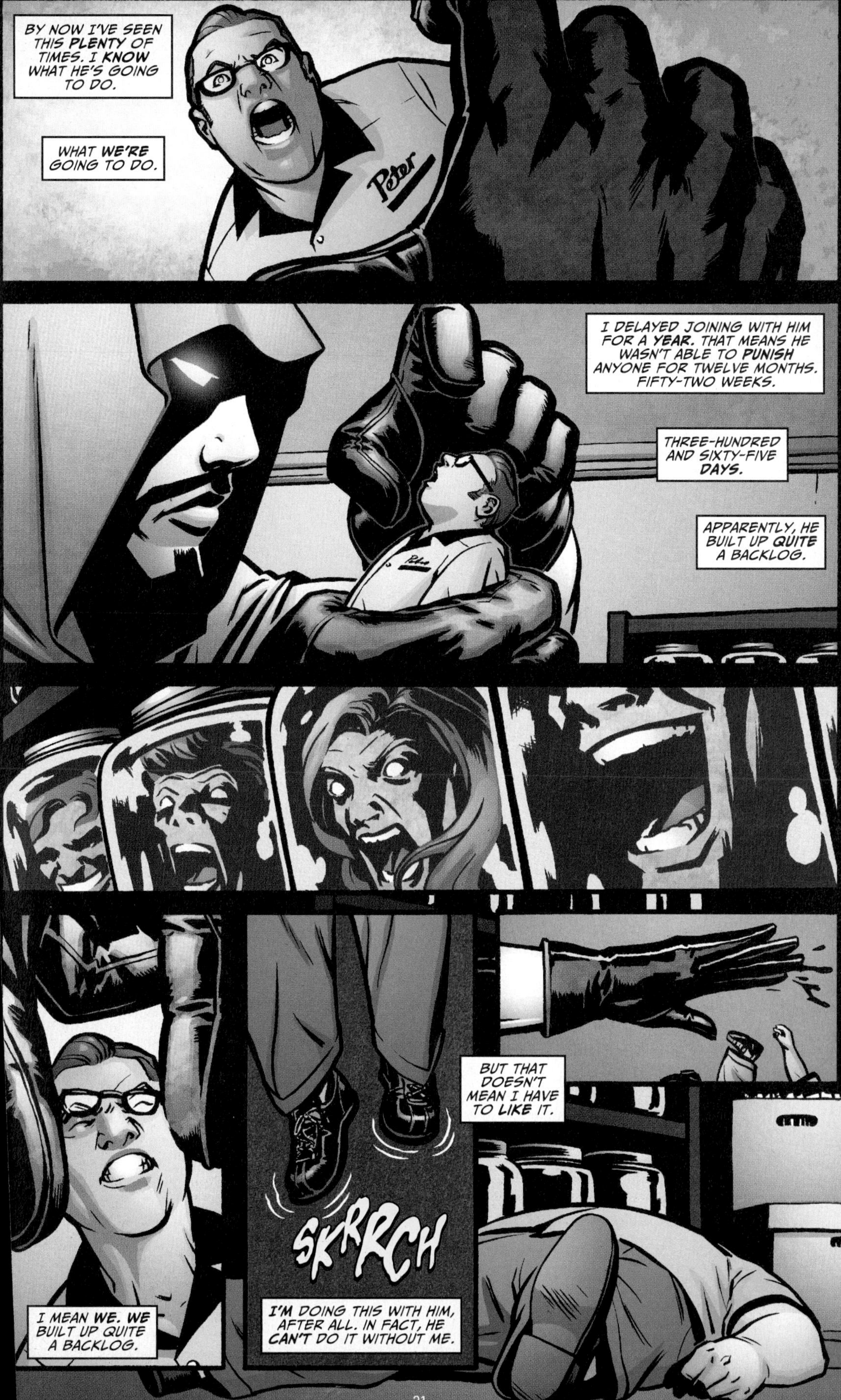

BY NOW I'VE SEEN THIS PLENTY OF TIMES. I KNOW WHAT HE'S GOING TO DO.
WHAT WE'RE GOING TO DO.
Peter
I DELAYED JOINING WITH HIM FOR A YEAR. THAT MEANS HE WASN'T ABLE TO PUNISH ANYONE FOR TWELVE MONTHS. FIFTY-TWO WEEKS.
THREE-HUNDRED AND SIXTY-FIVE DAYS.
APPARENTLY, HE BUILT UP QUITE A BACKLOG.
I MEAN WE. WE BUILT UP QUITE A BACKLOG.
SKRRCH
I'M DOING THIS WITH HIM, AFTER ALL. IN FACT, HE CAN'T DO IT WITHOUT ME.
BUT THAT DOESN'T MEAN I HAVE TO LIKE IT.

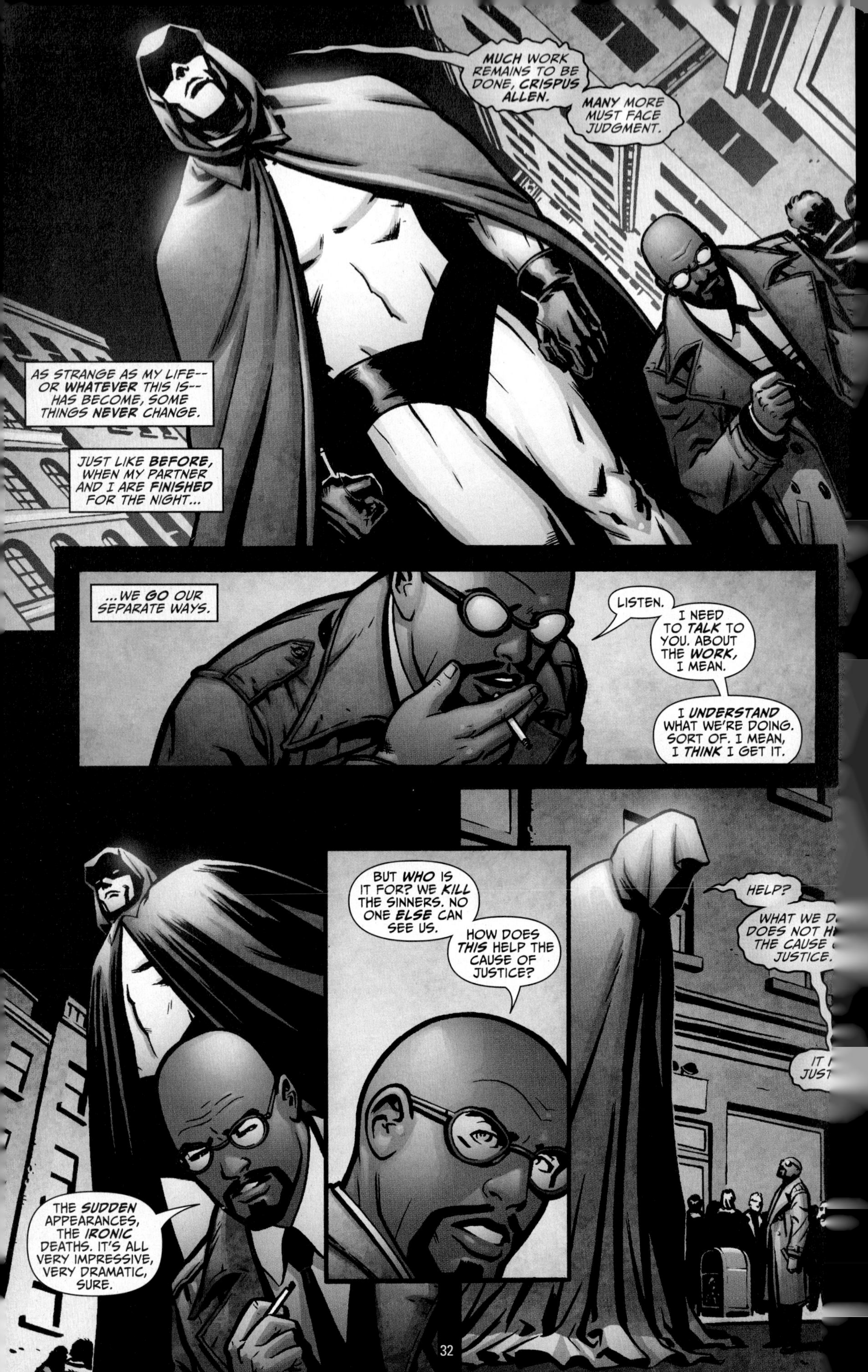
MUCH WORK REMAINS TO BE DONE, CRISPUS ALLEN.
MANY MORE MUST FACE JUDGMENT.
AS STRANGE AS MY LIFE-- OR WHATEVER THIS IS-- HAS BECOME, SOME THINGS NEVER CHANGE.
JUST LIKE BEFORE, WHEN MY PARTNER AND I ARE FINISHED FOR THE NIGHT...
...WE GO OUR SEPARATE WAYS.
LISTEN.
I NEED TO TALK TO YOU. ABOUT THE WORK, I MEAN.
I UNDERSTAND WHAT WE'RE DOING. SORT OF. I MEAN, I THINK I GET IT.
THE SUDDEN APPEARANCES, THE IRONIC DEATHS. IT'S ALL VERY IMPRESSIVE, VERY DRAMATIC, SURE.
BUT WHO IS IT FOR? WE KILL THE SINNERS. NO ONE ELSE CAN SEE US.
HOW DOES THIS HELP THE CAUSE OF JUSTICE?
HELP?

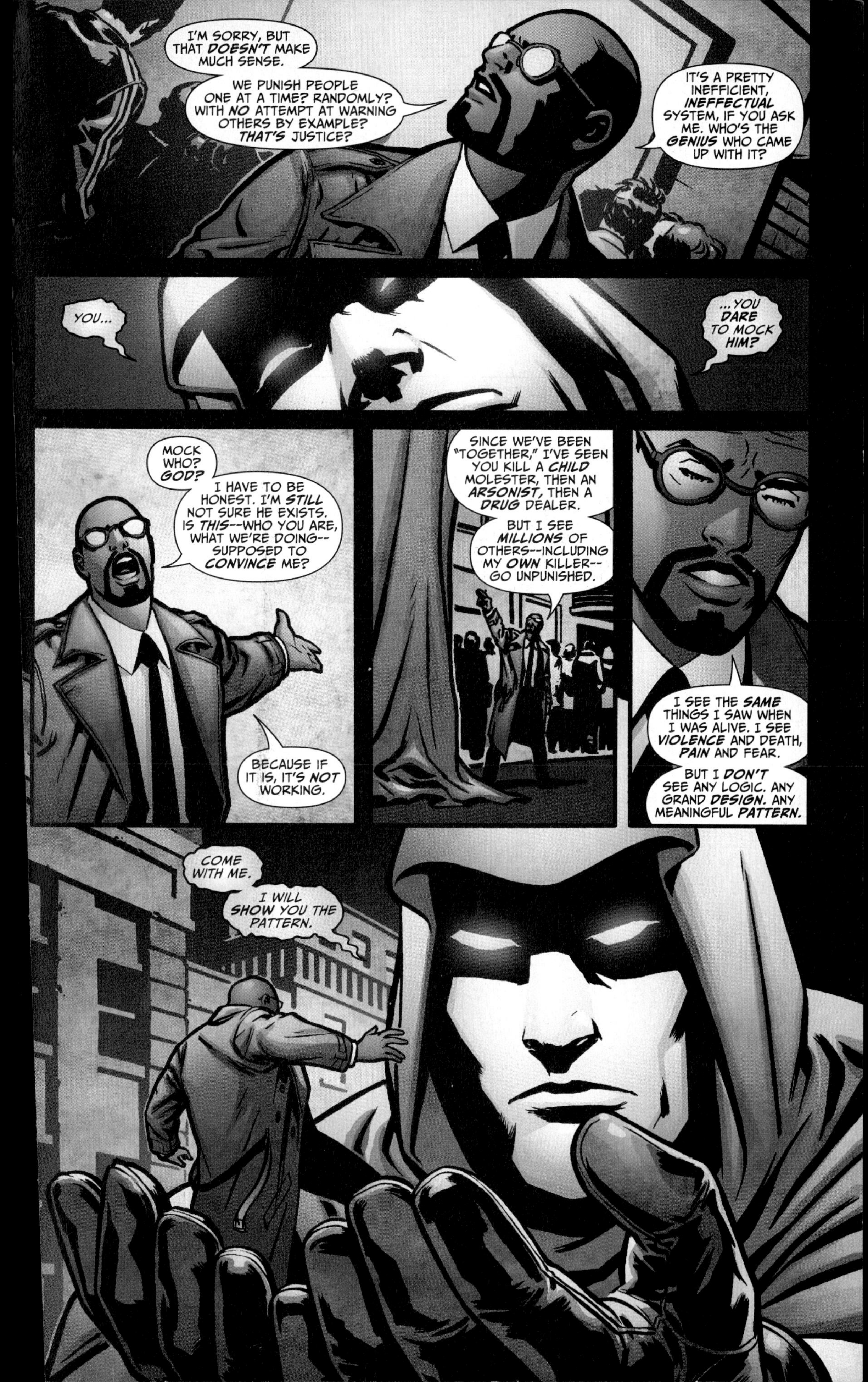
I'M SORRY, BUT THAT DOESN'T MAKE MUCH SENSE.
WE PUNISH PEOPLE ONE AT A TIME? RANDOMLY? WITH NO ATTEMPT AT WARNING OTHERS BY EXAMPLE? THAT'S JUSTICE?
IT'S A PRETTY INEFFICIENT, INEFFECTUAL SYSTEM, IF YOU ASK ME. WHO'S THE GENIUS WHO CAME UP WITH IT?
YOU...
...YOU DARE TO MOCK HIM?
MOCK WHO? GOD?
I HAVE TO BE HONEST. I'M STILL NOT SURE HE EXISTS. IS THIS--WHO YOU ARE, WHAT WE'RE DOING--SUPPOSED TO CONVINCE ME?
BECAUSE IF IT IS, IT'S NOT WORKING.
SINCE WE'VE BEEN "TOGETHER," I'VE SEEN YOU KILL A CHILD MOLESTER, THEN AN ARSONIST, THEN A DRUG DEALER.
BUT I SEE MILLIONS OF OTHERS--INCLUDING MY OWN KILLER--GO UNPUNISHED.
I SEE THE SAME THINGS I SAW WHEN I WAS ALIVE. I SEE VIOLENCE AND DEATH, PAIN AND FEAR.
BUT I DON'T SEE ANY LOGIC. ANY GRAND DESIGN. ANY MEANINGFUL PATTERN.
COME WITH ME.
I WILL SHOW YOU THE PATTERN.

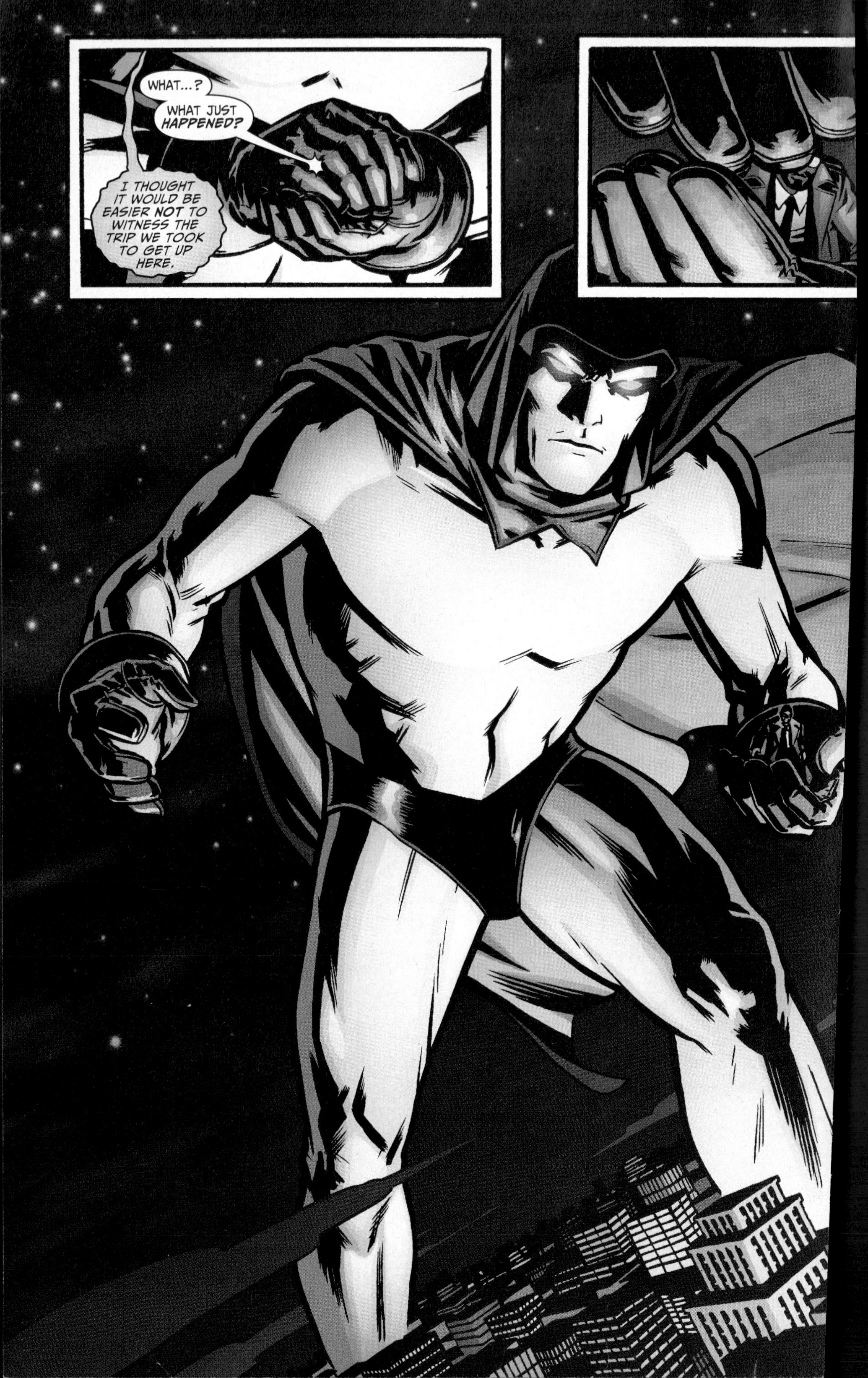

WHAT...?
WHAT JUST HAPPENED?
I THOUGHT IT WOULD BE EASIER NOT TO WITNESS THE TRIP WE TOOK TO GET UP HERE.

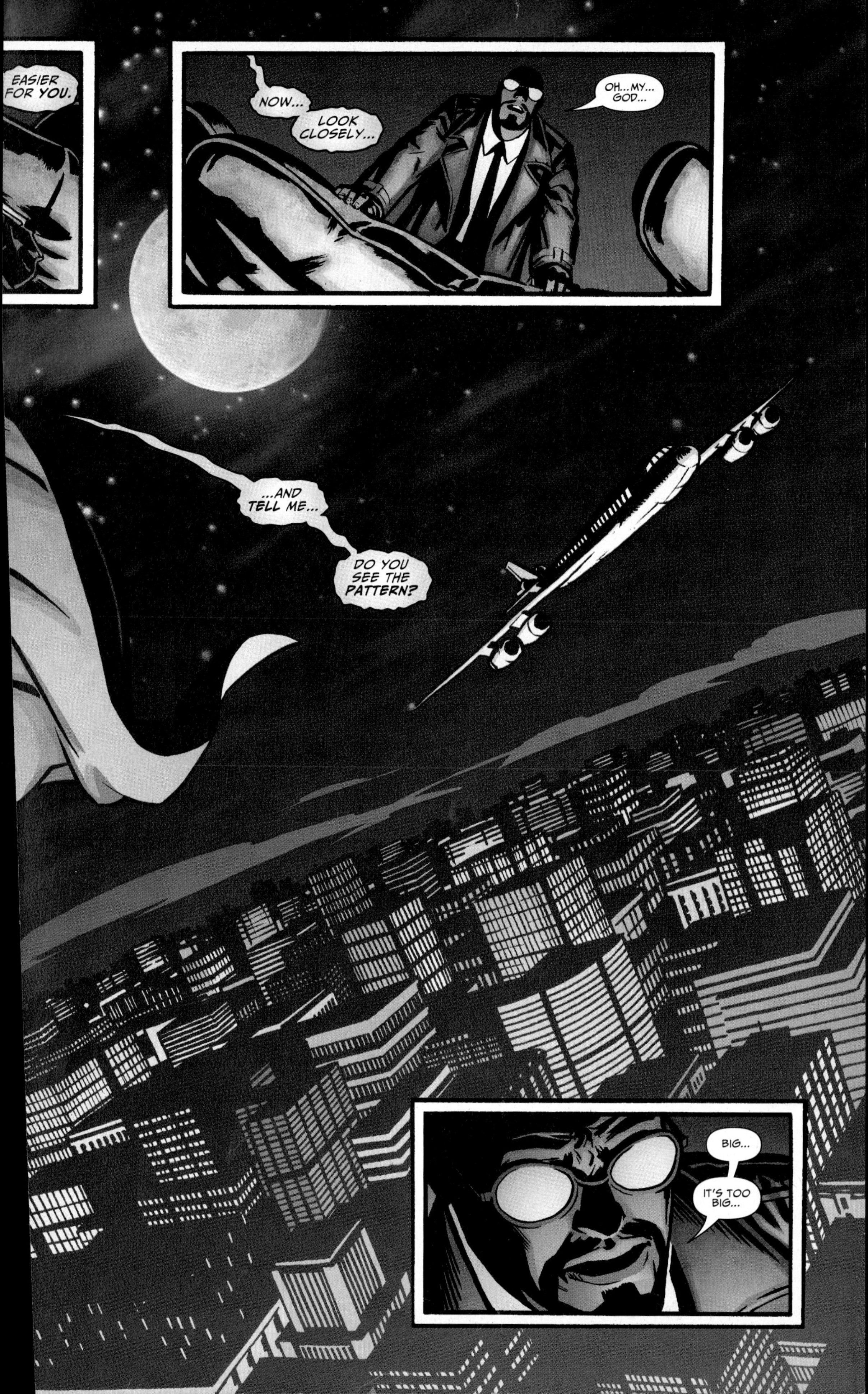
EASIER FOR YOU.
NOW...
LOOK CLOSELY...
OH...MY... GOD...
...AND TELL ME...
DO YOU SEE THE PATTERN?
BIG...
IT'S TOO BIG...

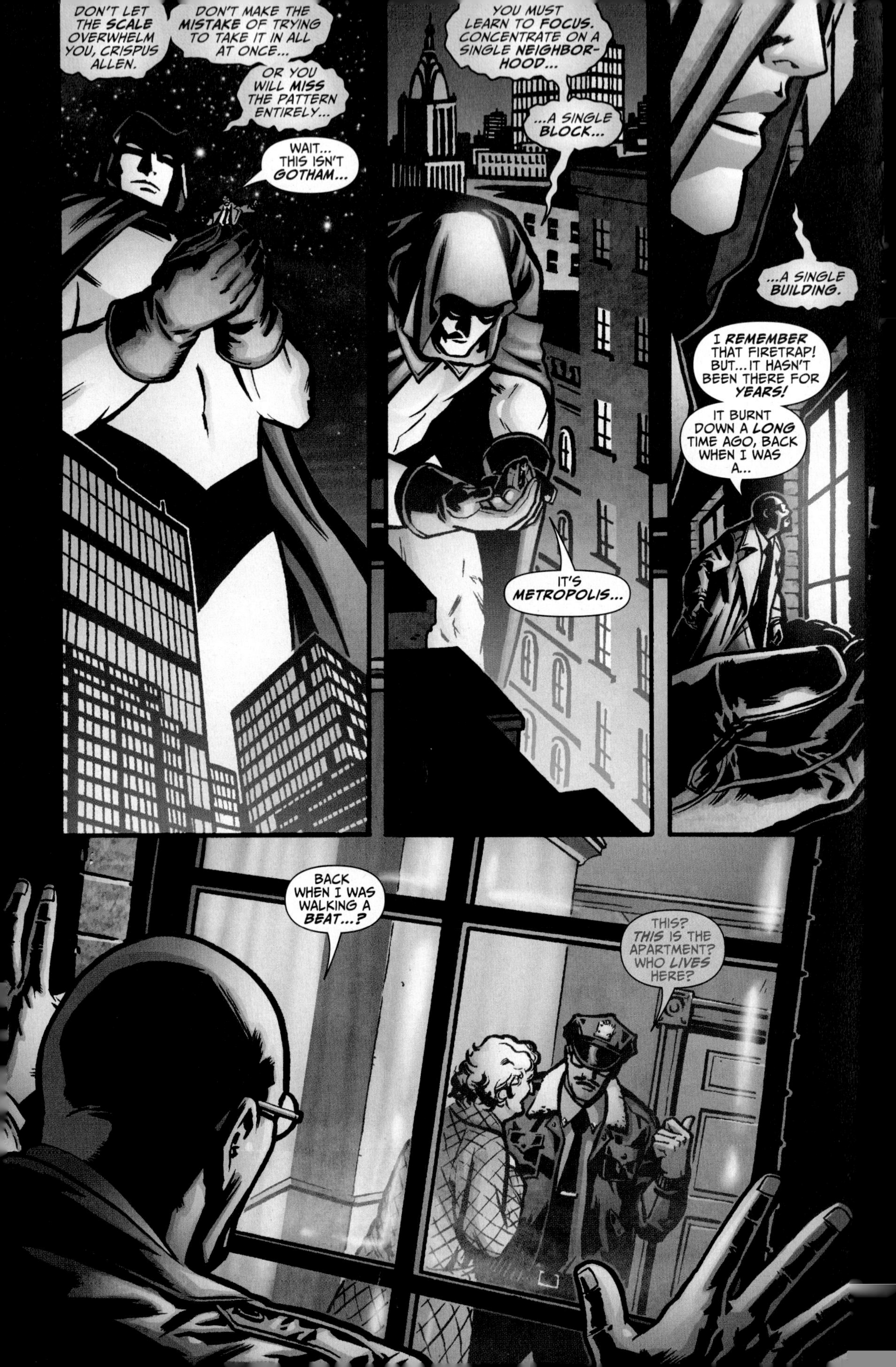
DON'T LET THE SCALE OVERWHELM YOU, CRISPUS ALLEN.
DON'T MAKE THE MISTAKE OF TRYING TO TAKE IT IN ALL AT ONCE...
OR YOU WILL MISS THE PATTERN ENTIRELY...
WAIT... THIS ISN'T GOTHAM...
YOU MUST LEARN TO FOCUS. CONCENTRATE ON A SINGLE NEIGHBOR-HOOD...
...A SINGLE BLOCK...
IT'S METROPOLIS...
...A SINGLE BUILDING.
I REMEMBER THAT FIRETRAP! BUT...IT HASN'T BEEN THERE FOR YEARS!
IT BURNT DOWN A LONG TIME AGO, BACK WHEN I WAS A...
BACK WHEN I WAS WALKING A BEAT...?
THIS? THIS IS THE APARTMENT? WHO LIVES HERE?

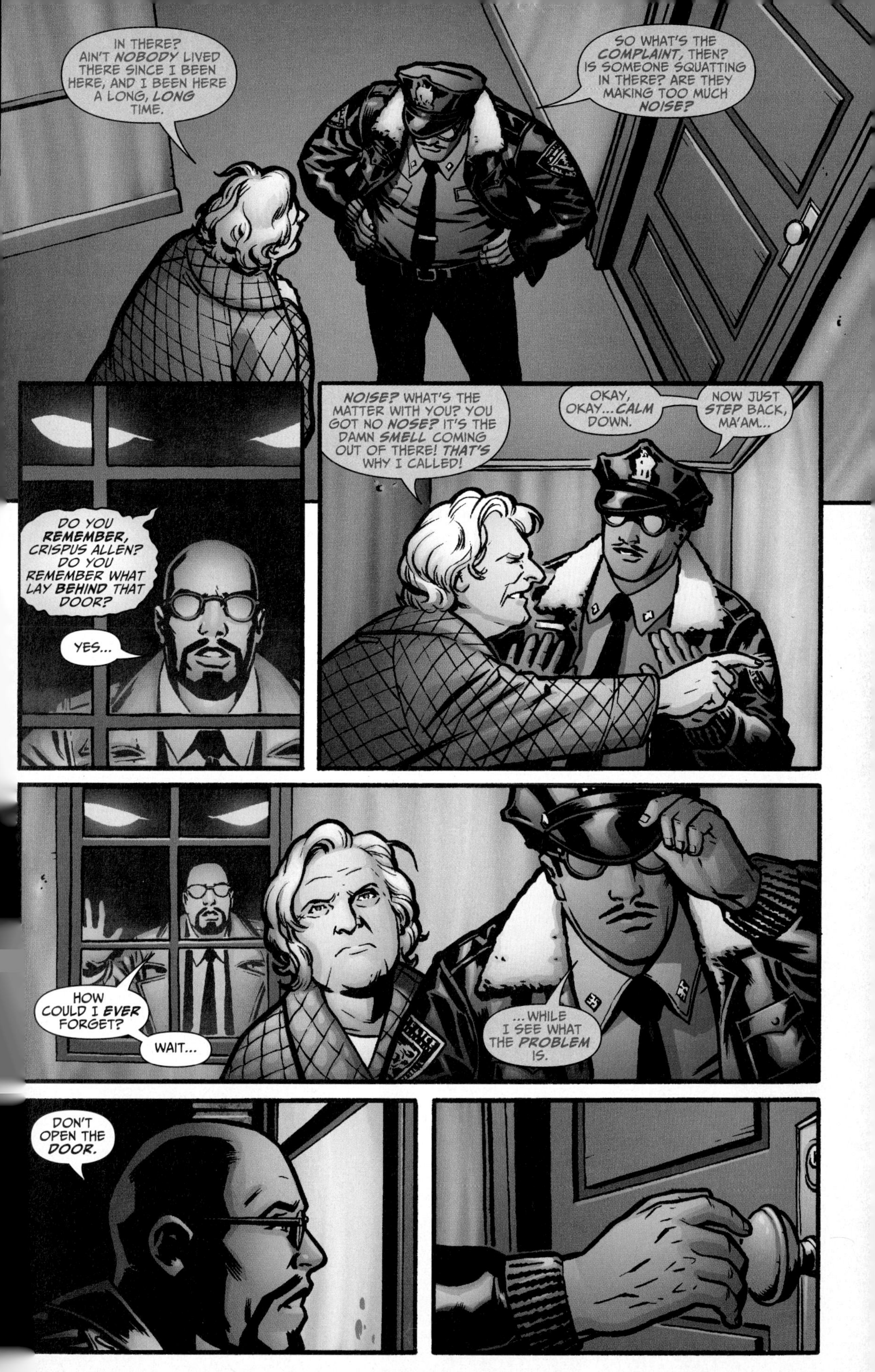
IN THERE? AIN'T NOBODY LIVED THERE SINCE I BEEN HERE, AND I BEEN HERE A LONG, LONG TIME.
SO WHAT'S THE COMPLAINT, THEN? IS SOMEONE SQUATTING IN THERE? ARE THEY MAKING TOO MUCH NOISE?
DO YOU REMEMBER, CRISPUS ALLEN? DO YOU REMEMBER WHAT LAY BEHIND THAT DOOR?
YES...
NOISE? WHAT'S THE MATTER WITH YOU? YOU GOT NO NOSE? IT'S THE DAMN SMELL COMING OUT OF THERE! THAT'S WHY I CALLED!
OKAY, OKAY...CALM DOWN.
NOW JUST STEP BACK, MA'AM...
HOW COULD I EVER FORGET?
WAIT...
...WHILE I SEE WHAT THE PROBLEM IS.
DON'T OPEN THE DOOR.

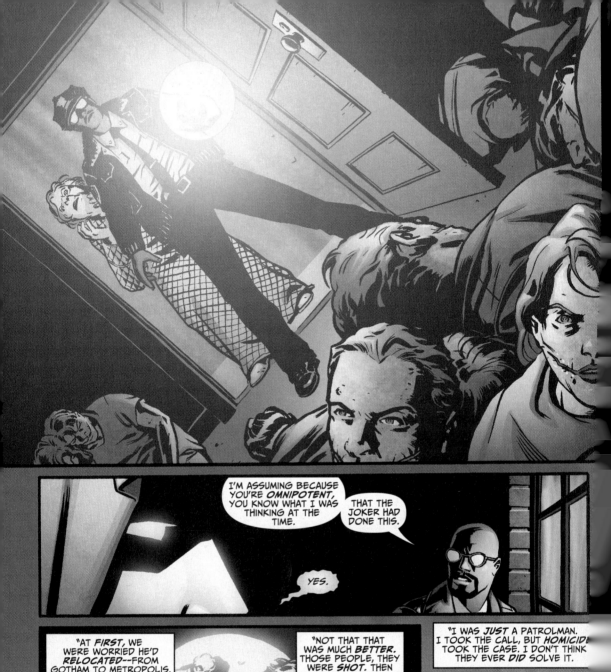

I'M ASSUMING BECAUSE YOU'RE *OMNIPOTENT,* YOU KNOW WHAT I WAS THINKING AT THE TIME.

THAT THE JOKER HAD DONE THIS.

YES.

"AT *FIRST,* WE WERE WORRIED HE'D *RELOCATED*--FROM GOTHAM TO METROPOLIS. BUT *THIS* WAS JUST A WANNABE, A COPYCAT...

"NOT THAT THAT WAS MUCH *BETTER.* THOSE PEOPLE, THEY WERE *SHOT.* THEN THEIR MOUTHS... HE *CARVED*...

"I WAS *JUST* A PATROLMAN. I TOOK THE CALL, BUT *HOMICIDE* TOOK THE CASE. I DON'T THINK THEY EVER *DID* SOLVE IT.

"IT'S AN OLD STORY. CRIME, NO *PUNISHME*.

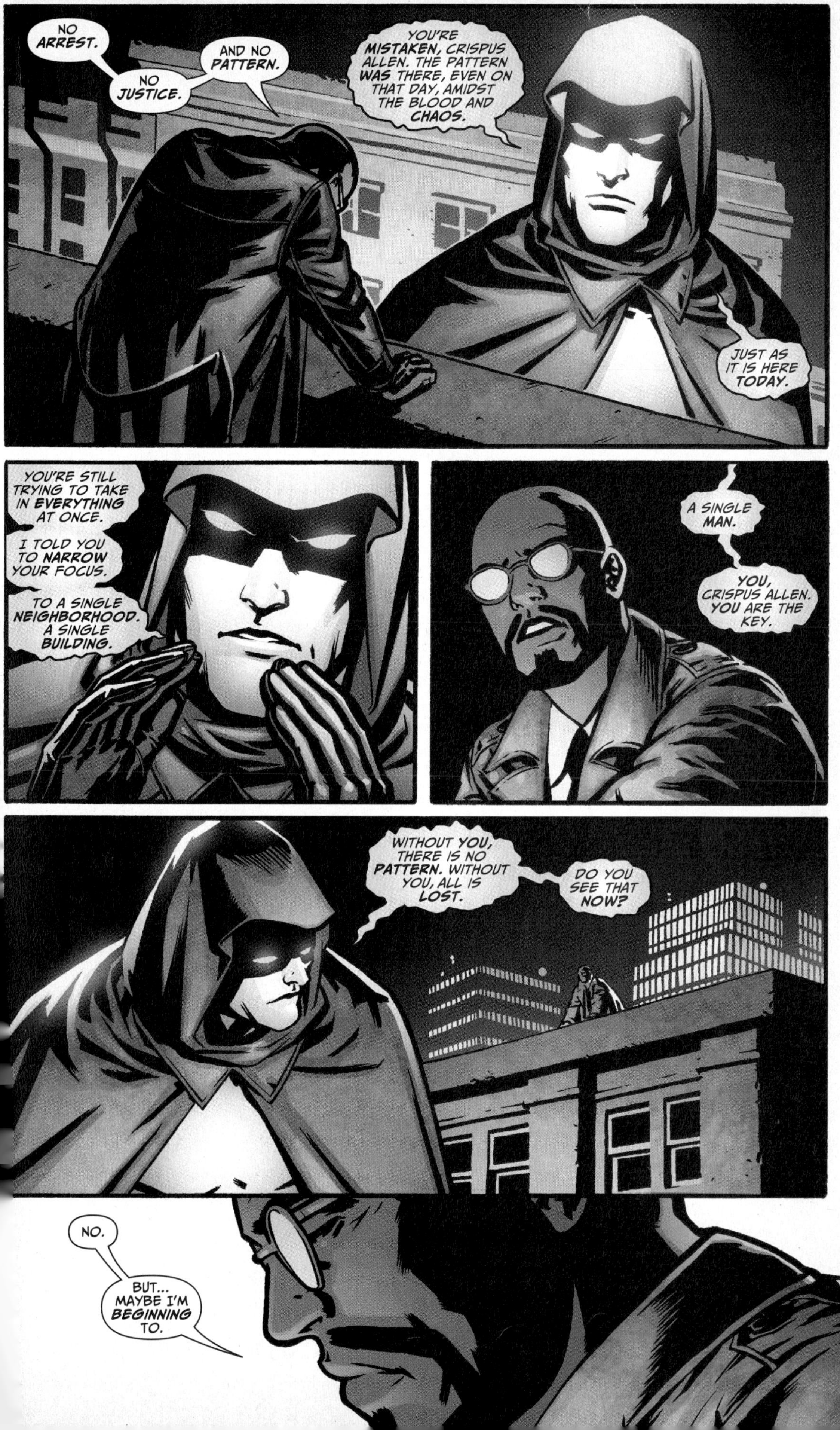
NO ARREST.
NO JUSTICE.
AND NO PATTERN.
YOU'RE MISTAKEN, CRISPUS ALLEN. THE PATTERN WAS THERE, EVEN ON THAT DAY, AMIDST THE BLOOD AND CHAOS.
JUST AS IT IS HERE TODAY.
YOU'RE STILL TRYING TO TAKE IN EVERYTHING AT ONCE.
I TOLD YOU TO NARROW YOUR FOCUS.
TO A SINGLE NEIGHBORHOOD. A SINGLE BUILDING.
A SINGLE MAN.
YOU, CRISPUS ALLEN. YOU ARE THE KEY.
WITHOUT YOU, THERE IS NO PATTERN. WITHOUT YOU, ALL IS LOST.
DO YOU SEE THAT NOW?
NO.
BUT... MAYBE I'M BEGINNING TO.

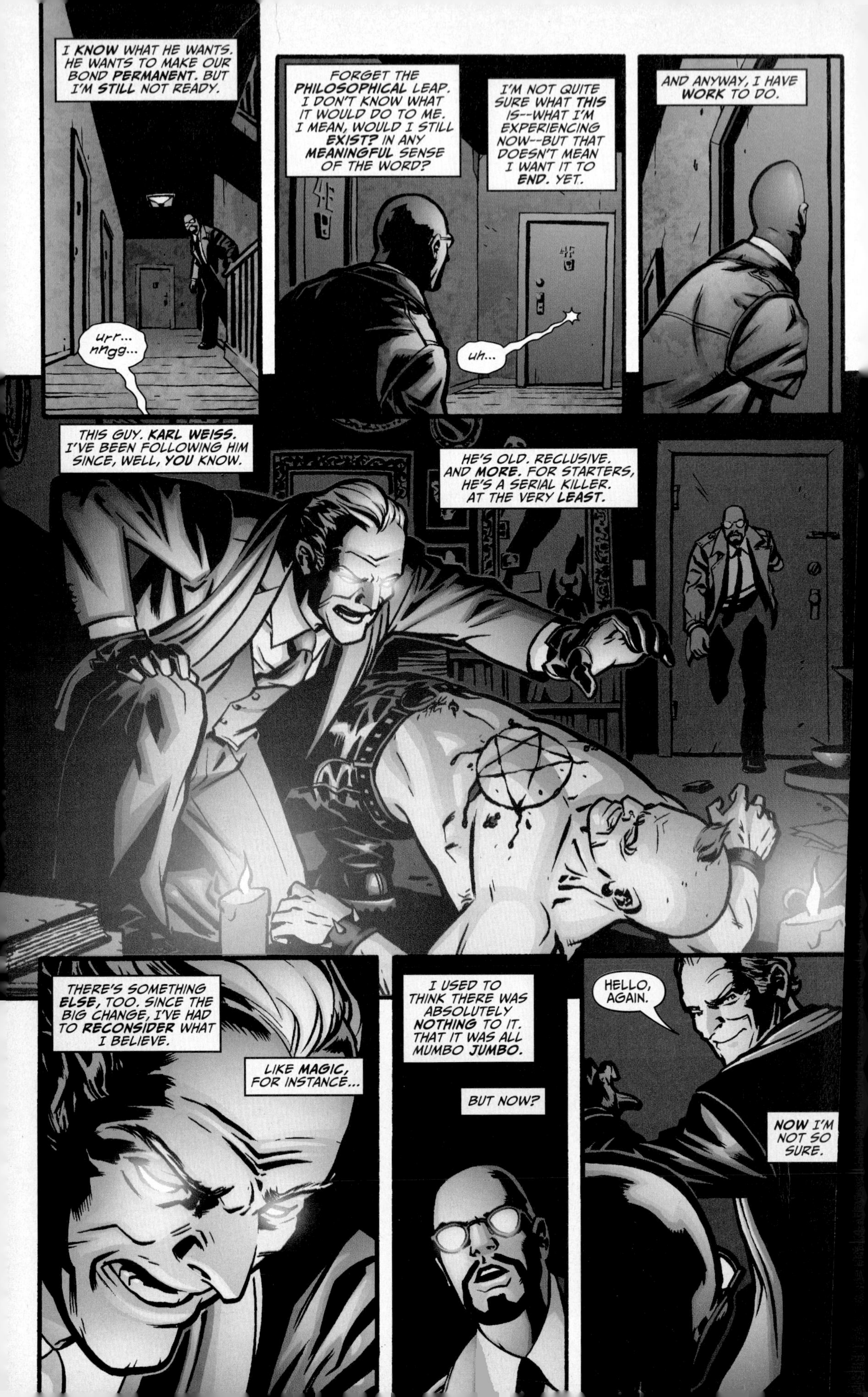
I KNOW WHAT HE WANTS. HE WANTS TO MAKE OUR BOND PERMANENT. BUT I'M STILL NOT READY.
urr... nngg...
FORGET THE PHILOSOPHICAL LEAP. I DON'T KNOW WHAT IT WOULD DO TO ME. I MEAN, WOULD I STILL EXIST? IN ANY MEANINGFUL SENSE OF THE WORD?
I'M NOT QUITE SURE WHAT THIS IS--WHAT I'M EXPERIENCING NOW--BUT THAT DOESN'T MEAN I WANT IT TO END. YET.
uh...
AND ANYWAY, I HAVE WORK TO DO.
THIS GUY. KARL WEISS. I'VE BEEN FOLLOWING HIM SINCE, WELL, YOU KNOW.
HE'S OLD. RECLUSIVE. AND MORE. FOR STARTERS, HE'S A SERIAL KILLER. AT THE VERY LEAST.
THERE'S SOMETHING ELSE, TOO. SINCE THE BIG CHANGE, I'VE HAD TO RECONSIDER WHAT I BELIEVE.
LIKE MAGIC, FOR INSTANCE...
I USED TO THINK THERE WAS ABSOLUTELY NOTHING TO IT. THAT IT WAS ALL MUMBO JUMBO.
BUT NOW?
HELLO, AGAIN.
NOW I'M NOT SO SURE.

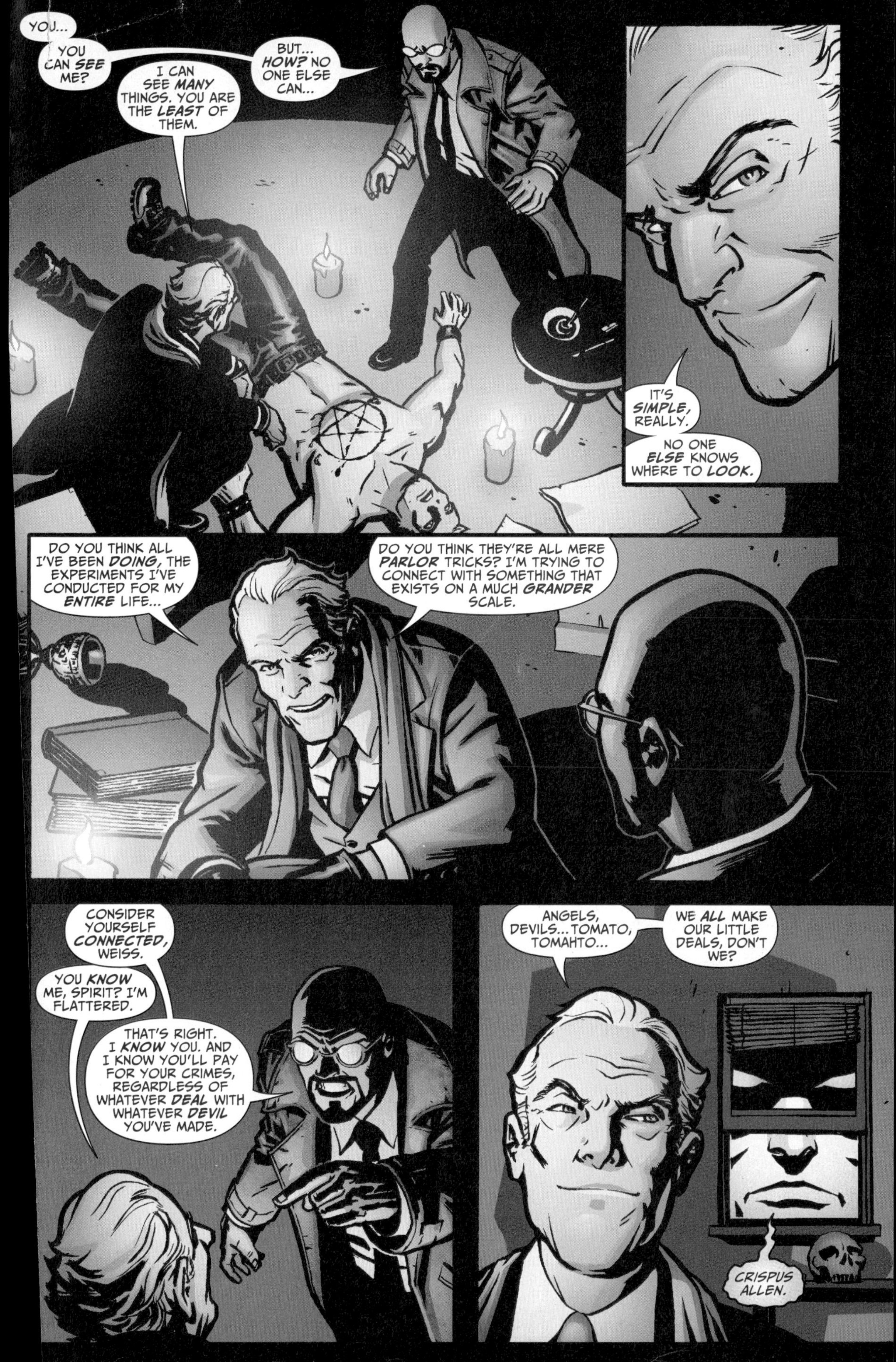
YOU...
YOU CAN SEE ME?
BUT... HOW? NO ONE ELSE CAN...
I CAN SEE MANY THINGS. YOU ARE THE LEAST OF THEM.
IT'S SIMPLE, REALLY.
NO ONE ELSE KNOWS WHERE TO LOOK.
DO YOU THINK ALL I'VE BEEN DOING, THE EXPERIMENTS I'VE CONDUCTED FOR MY ENTIRE LIFE...
DO YOU THINK THEY'RE ALL MERE PARLOR TRICKS? I'M TRYING TO CONNECT WITH SOMETHING THAT EXISTS ON A MUCH GRANDER SCALE.
CONSIDER YOURSELF CONNECTED, WEISS.
YOU KNOW ME, SPIRIT? I'M FLATTERED.
THAT'S RIGHT. I KNOW YOU. AND I KNOW YOU'LL PAY FOR YOUR CRIMES, REGARDLESS OF WHATEVER DEAL WITH WHATEVER DEVIL YOU'VE MADE.
ANGELS, DEVILS... TOMATO, TOMAHTO...
WE ALL MAKE OUR LITTLE DEALS, DON'T WE?
CRISPUS ALLEN.

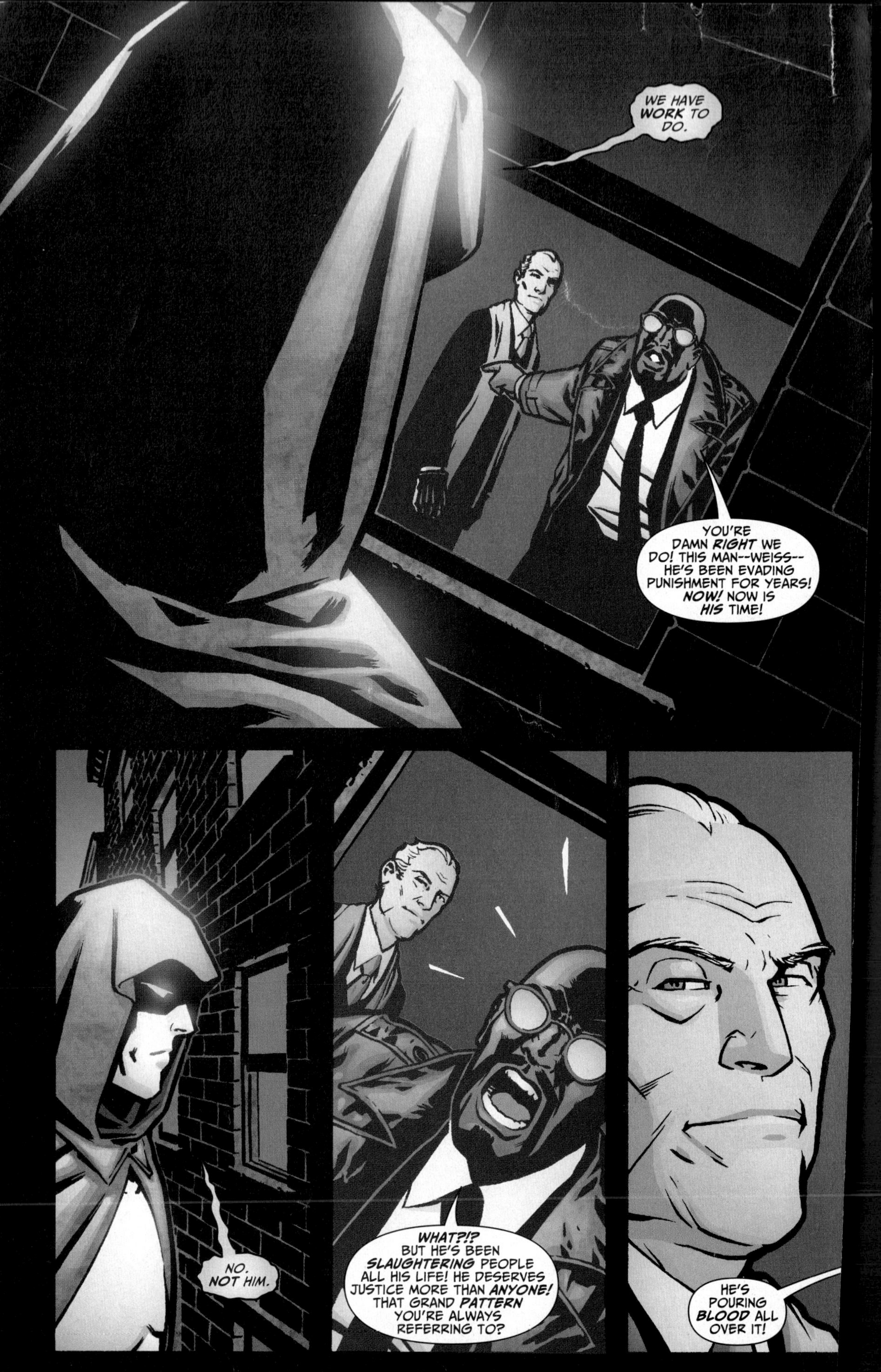
WE HAVE WORK TO DO.
YOU'RE DAMN RIGHT WE DO! THIS MAN--WEISS-- HE'S BEEN EVADING PUNISHMENT FOR YEARS! NOW! NOW IS HIS TIME!
NO. NOT HIM.
WHAT?!? BUT HE'S BEEN SLAUGHTERING PEOPLE ALL HIS LIFE! HE DESERVES JUSTICE MORE THAN ANYONE! THAT GRAND PATTERN YOU'RE ALWAYS REFERRING TO?
HE'S POURING BLOOD ALL OVER IT!

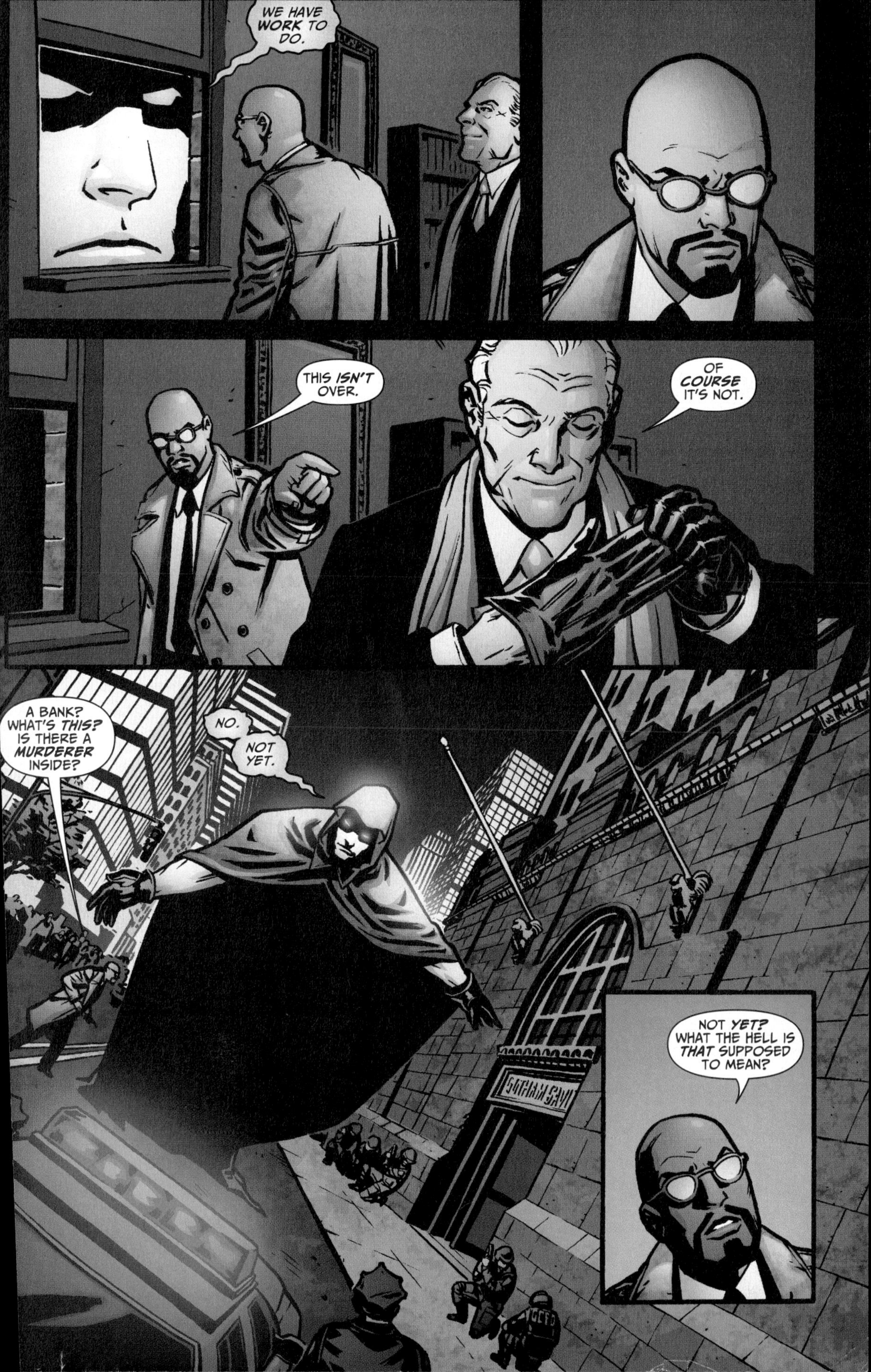

WE HAVE WORK TO DO.
THIS ISN'T OVER.
OF COURSE IT'S NOT.
A BANK? WHAT'S THIS? IS THERE A MURDERER INSIDE?
NO.
NOT YET.
NOT YET? WHAT THE HELL IS THAT SUPPOSED TO MEAN?

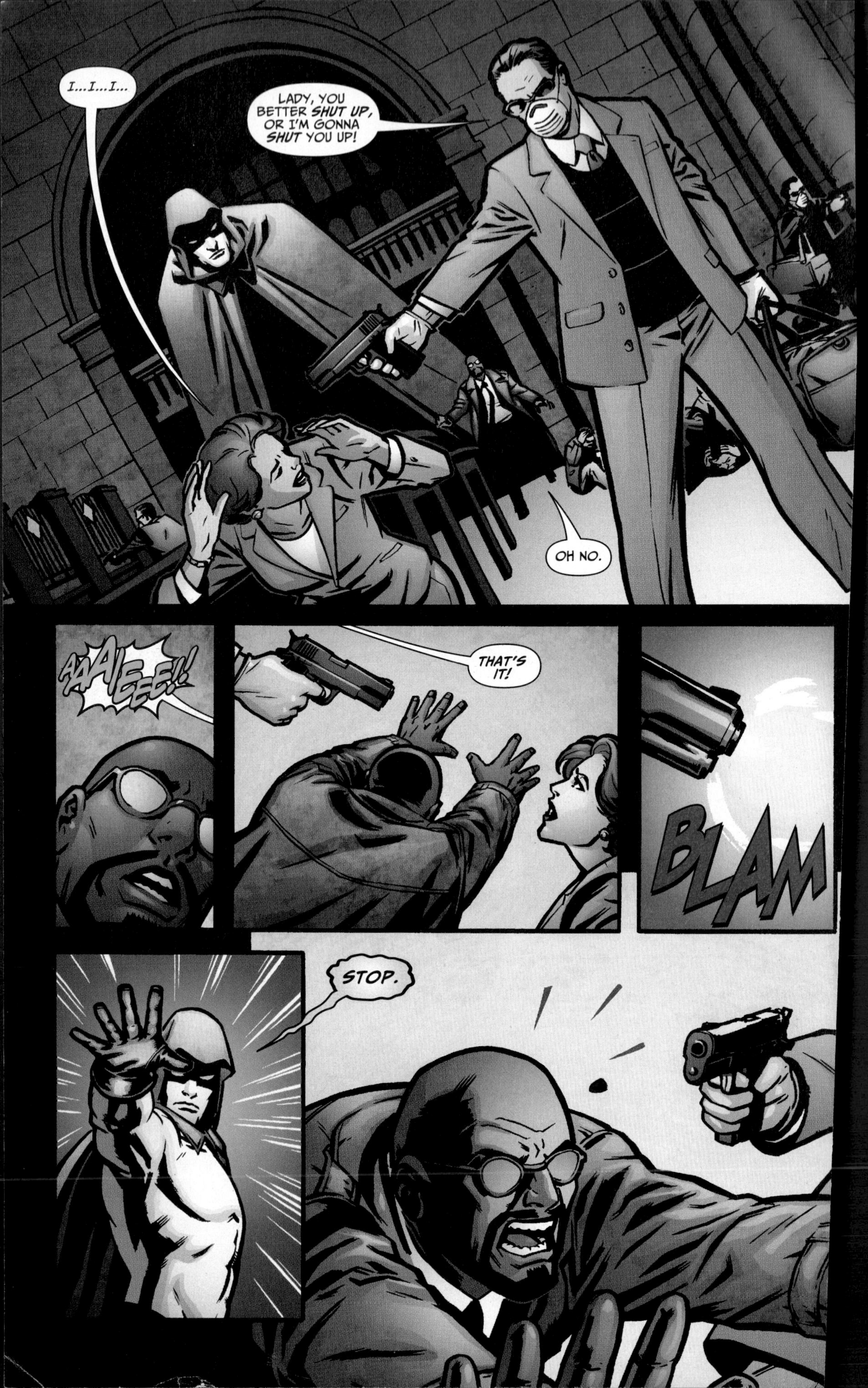
I...I...I...
LADY, YOU BETTER SHUT UP, OR I'M GONNA SHUT YOU UP!
OH NO.
AAAIEEEE!!
THAT'S IT!
BLAM
STOP.

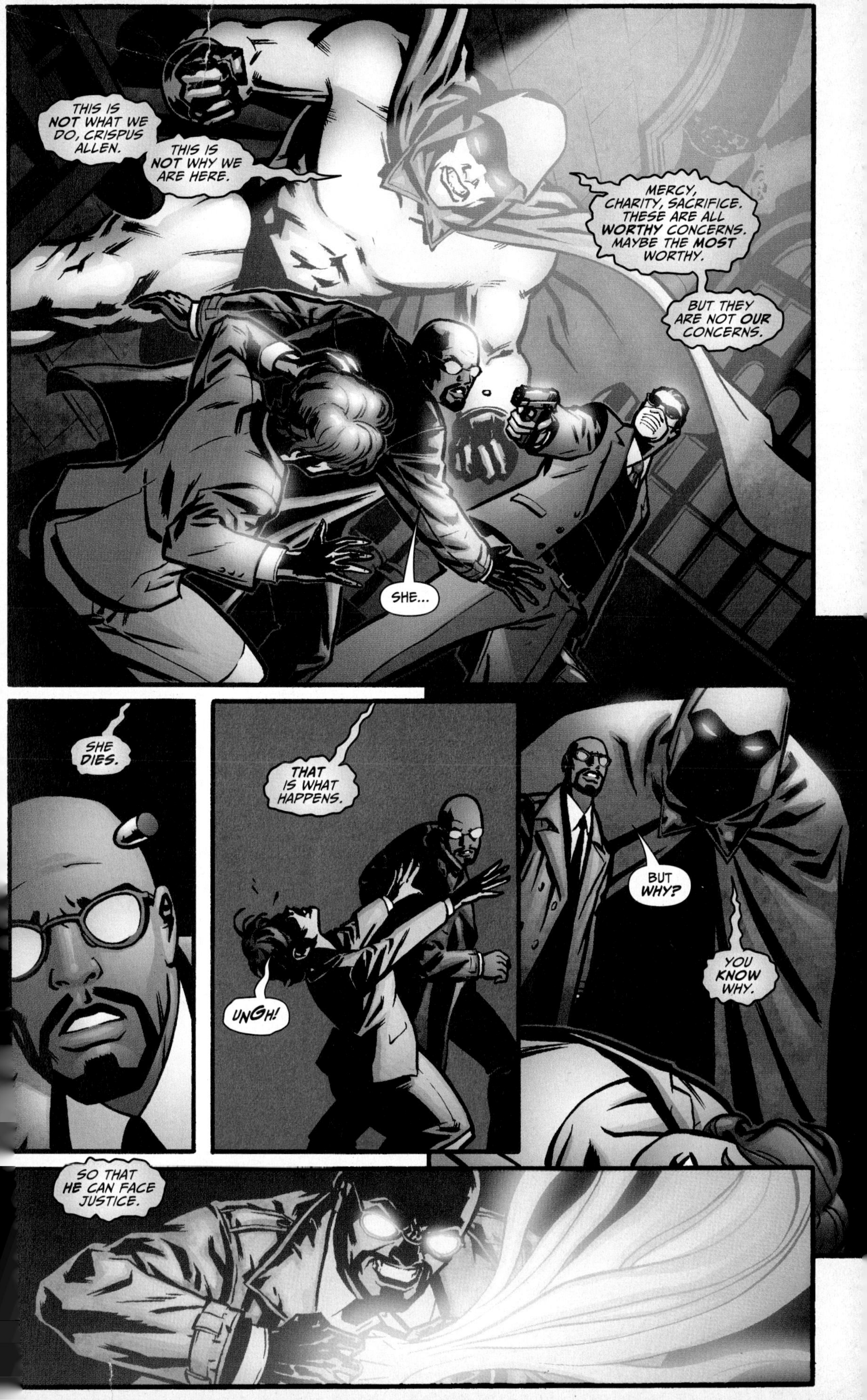
THIS IS NOT WHAT WE DO, CRISPUS ALLEN.
THIS IS NOT WHY WE ARE HERE.
MERCY, CHARITY, SACRIFICE. THESE ARE ALL WORTHY CONCERNS. MAYBE THE MOST WORTHY.
BUT THEY ARE NOT OUR CONCERNS.
SHE...
SHE DIES.
THAT IS WHAT HAPPENS.
UNGH!
BUT WHY?
YOU KNOW WHY.
SO THAT HE CAN FACE JUSTICE.

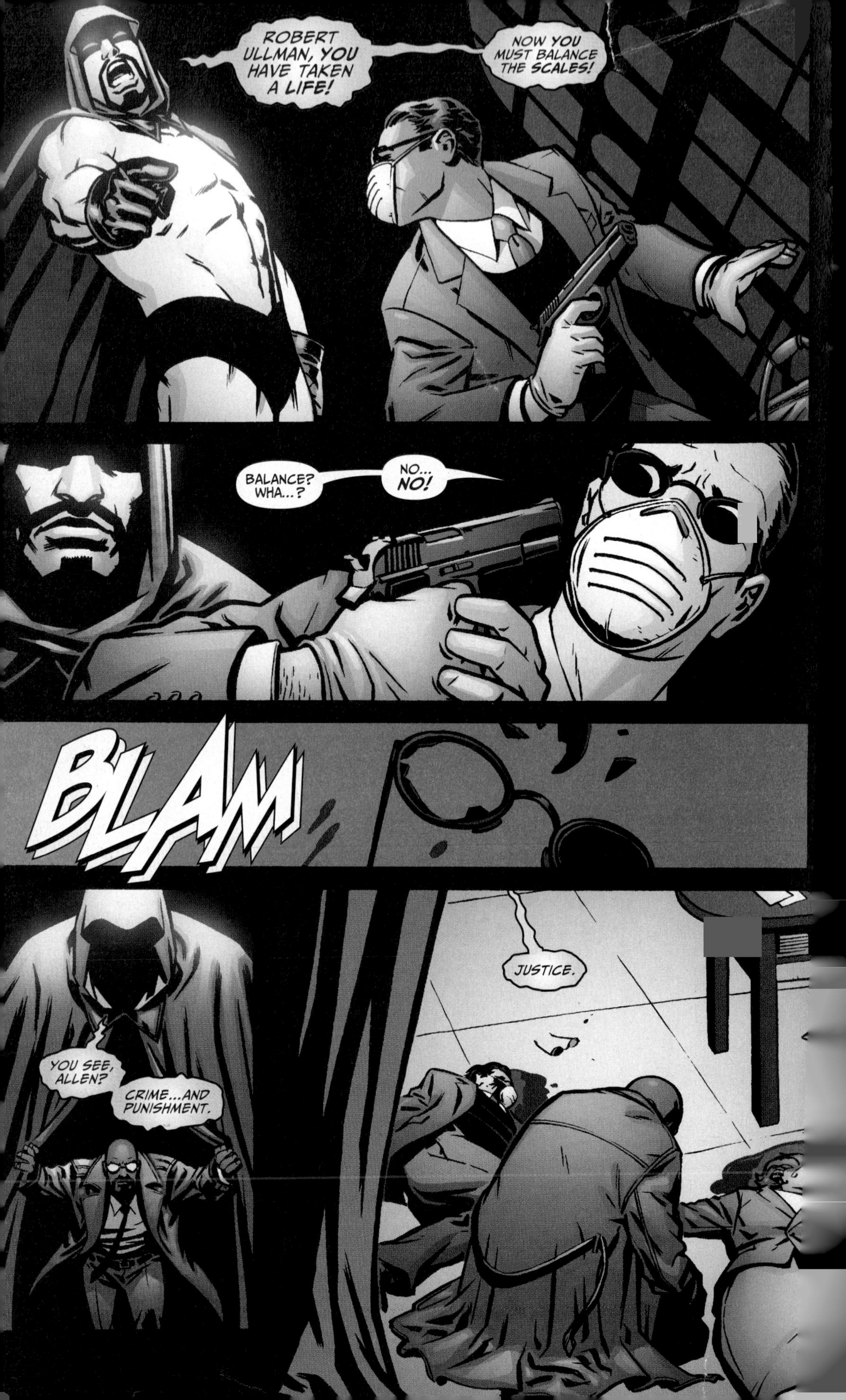
ROBERT ULLMAN, YOU HAVE TAKEN A LIFE!
NOW YOU MUST BALANCE THE SCALES!
BALANCE? WHA...?
NO... NO!
BLAM
JUSTICE.
YOU SEE, ALLEN?
CRIME...AND PUNISHMENT.

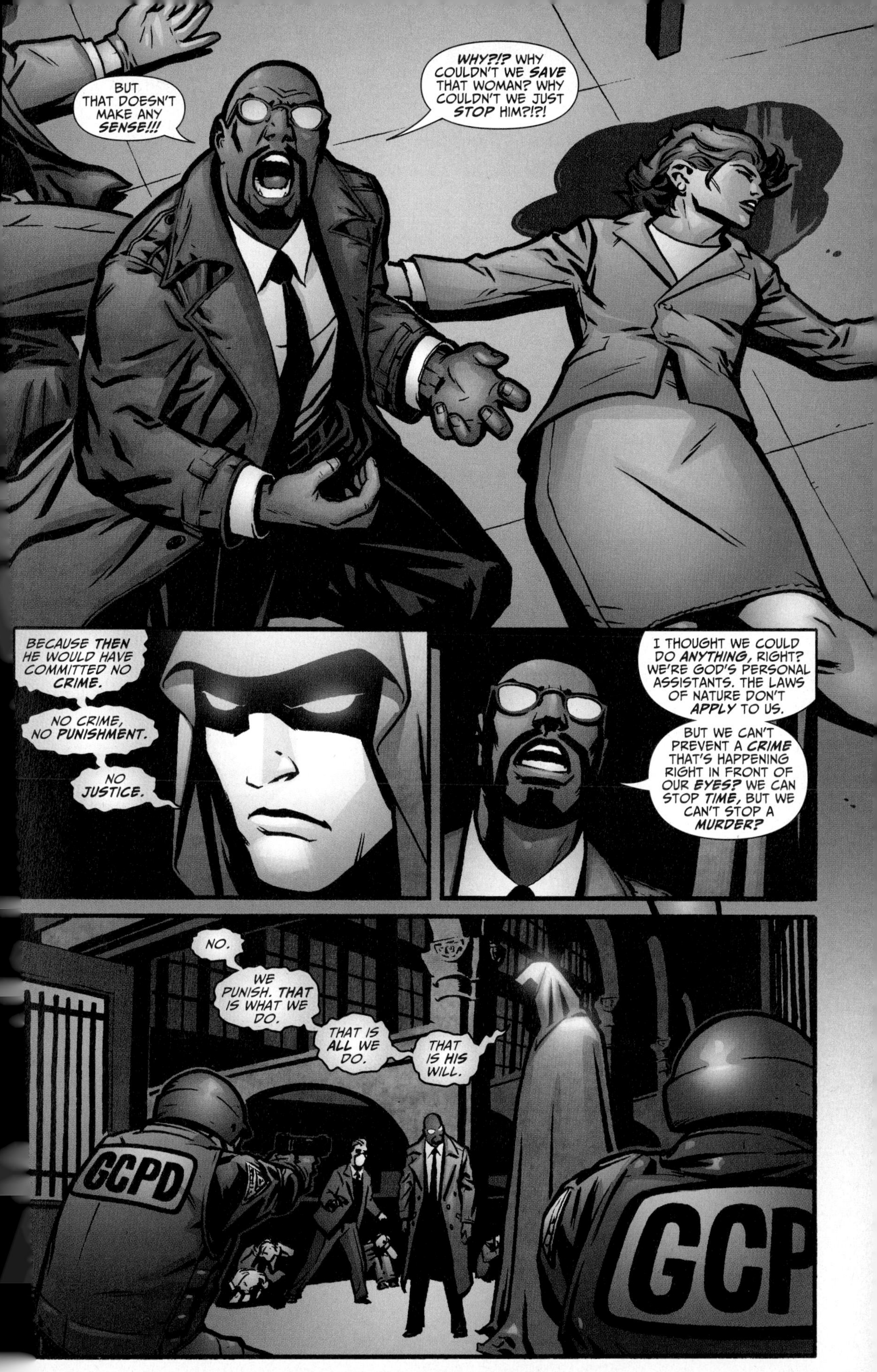

BUT THAT DOESN'T MAKE ANY SENSE!!!
WHY?!? WHY COULDN'T WE SAVE THAT WOMAN? WHY COULDN'T WE JUST STOP HIM?!?!
BECAUSE THEN HE WOULD HAVE COMMITTED NO CRIME.
NO CRIME, NO PUNISHMENT.
NO JUSTICE.
I THOUGHT WE COULD DO ANYTHING, RIGHT? WE'RE GOD'S PERSONAL ASSISTANTS. THE LAWS OF NATURE DON'T APPLY TO US.
BUT WE CAN'T PREVENT A CRIME THAT'S HAPPENING RIGHT IN FRONT OF OUR EYES? WE CAN STOP TIME, BUT WE CAN'T STOP A MURDER?
NO.
WE PUNISH. THAT IS WHAT WE DO.
THAT IS ALL WE DO.
THAT IS HIS WILL.
GCPD
GCP

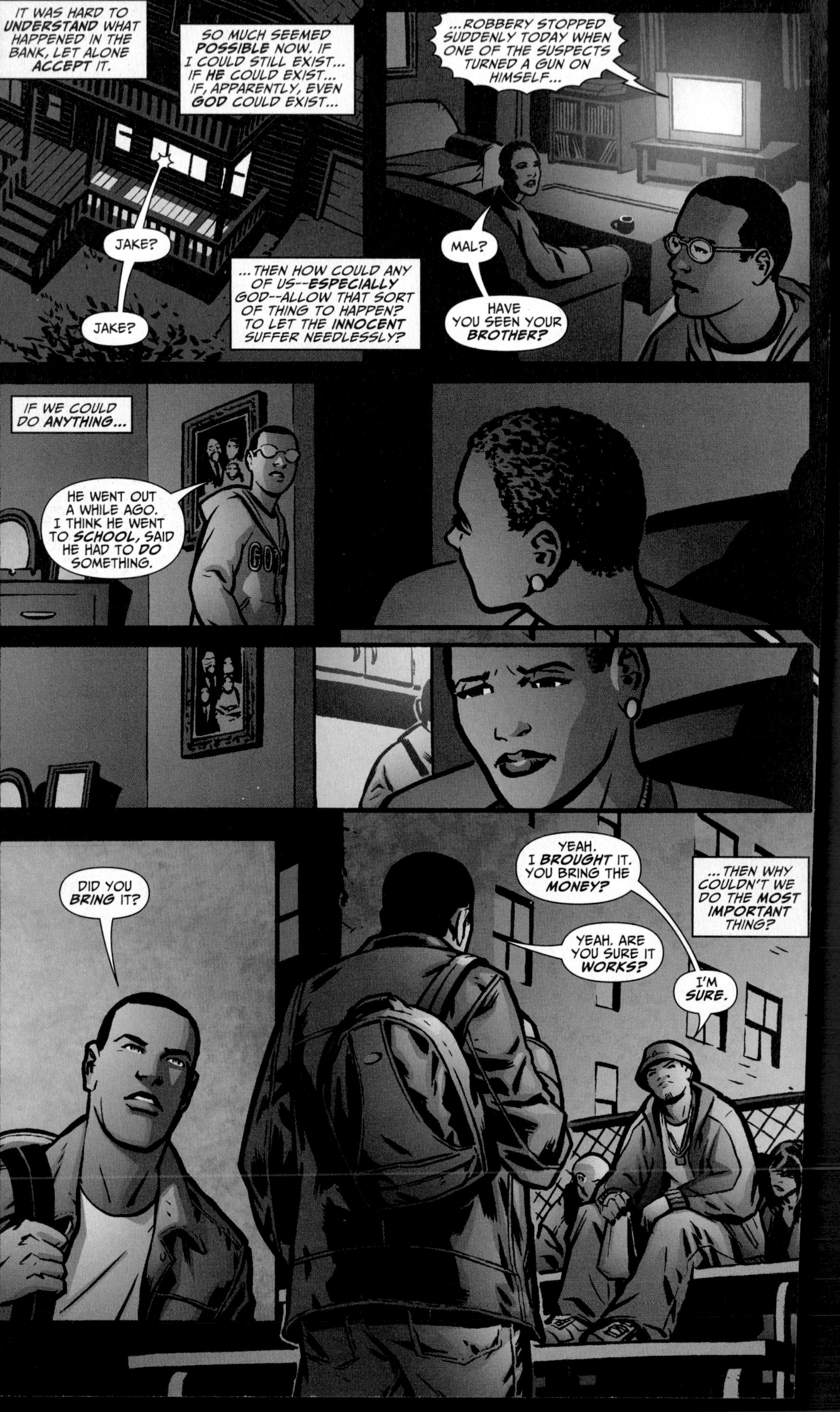
IT WAS HARD TO UNDERSTAND WHAT HAPPENED IN THE BANK, LET ALONE ACCEPT IT.
SO MUCH SEEMED POSSIBLE NOW. IF I COULD STILL EXIST... IF HE COULD EXIST... IF, APPARENTLY, EVEN GOD COULD EXIST...
JAKE?
JAKE?
...THEN HOW COULD ANY OF US--ESPECIALLY GOD--ALLOW THAT SORT OF THING TO HAPPEN? TO LET THE INNOCENT SUFFER NEEDLESSLY?
...ROBBERY STOPPED SUDDENLY TODAY WHEN ONE OF THE SUSPECTS TURNED A GUN ON HIMSELF...
MAL?
HAVE YOU SEEN YOUR BROTHER?
IF WE COULD DO ANYTHING...
HE WENT OUT A WHILE AGO. I THINK HE WENT TO SCHOOL, SAID HE HAD TO DO SOMETHING.
DID YOU BRING IT?
YEAH. I BROUGHT IT. YOU BRING THE MONEY?
YEAH. ARE YOU SURE IT WORKS?
I'M SURE.
...THEN WHY COULDN'T WE DO THE MOST IMPORTANT THING?

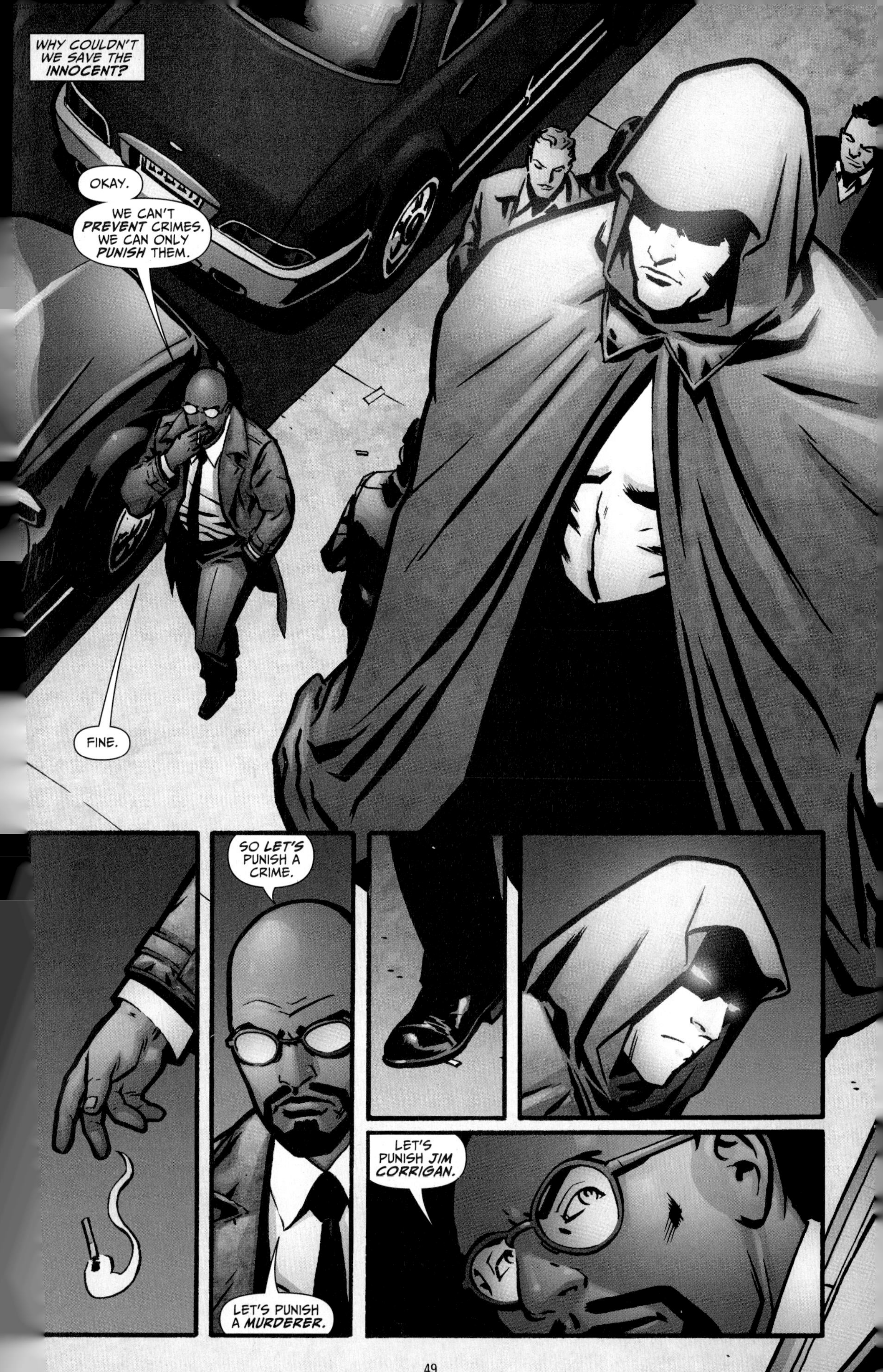
WHY COULDN'T WE SAVE THE INNOCENT?
OKAY.
WE CAN'T PREVENT CRIMES. WE CAN ONLY PUNISH THEM.
FINE.
SO LET'S PUNISH A CRIME.
LET'S PUNISH A MURDERER.
LET'S PUNISH JIM CORRIGAN.

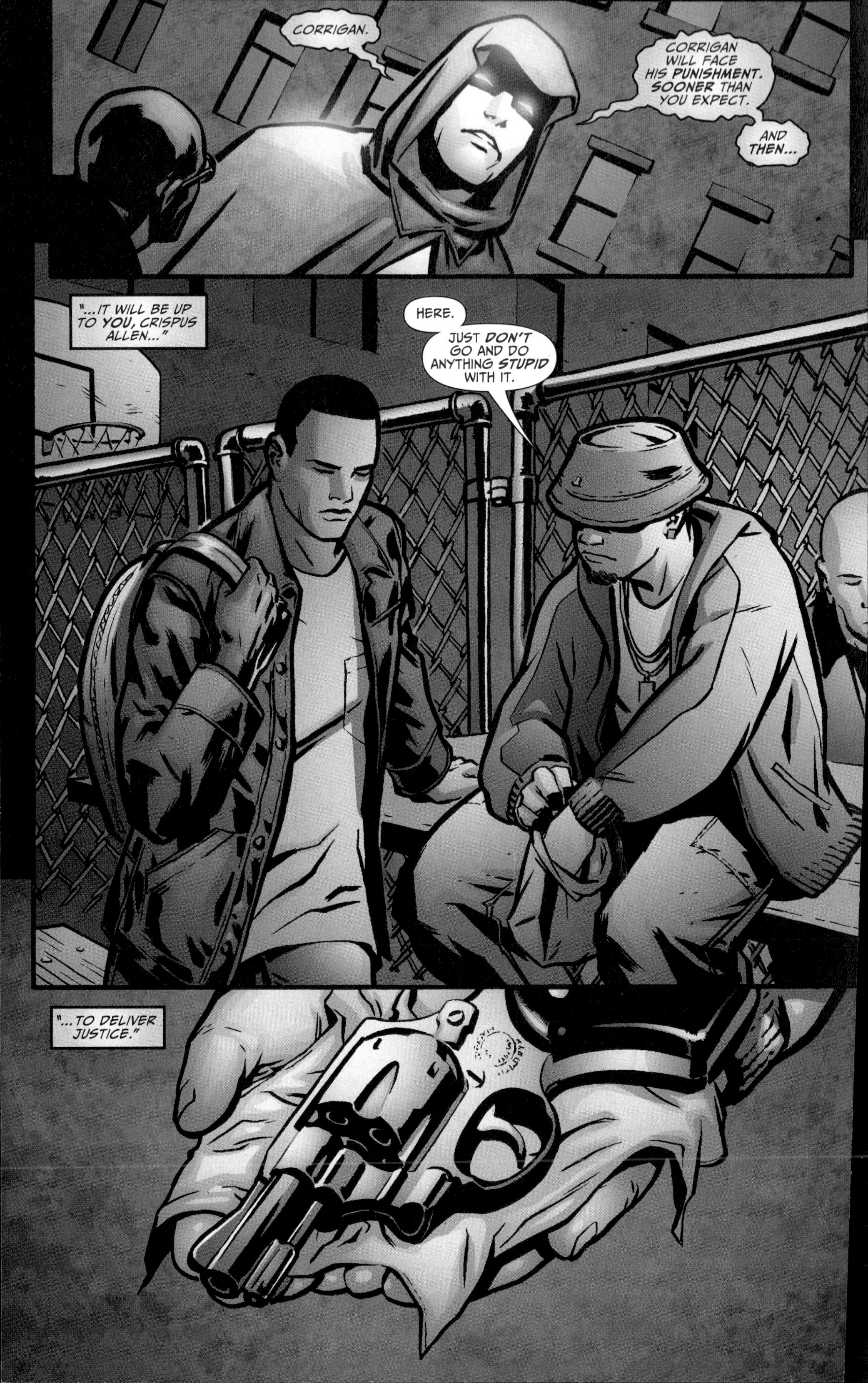
CORRIGAN.
CORRIGAN WILL FACE HIS PUNISHMENT. SOONER THAN YOU EXPECT.
AND THEN...
"...IT WILL BE UP TO YOU, CRISPUS ALLEN..."
HERE.
JUST DON'T GO AND DO ANYTHING STUPID WITH IT.
"...TO DELIVER JUSTICE."

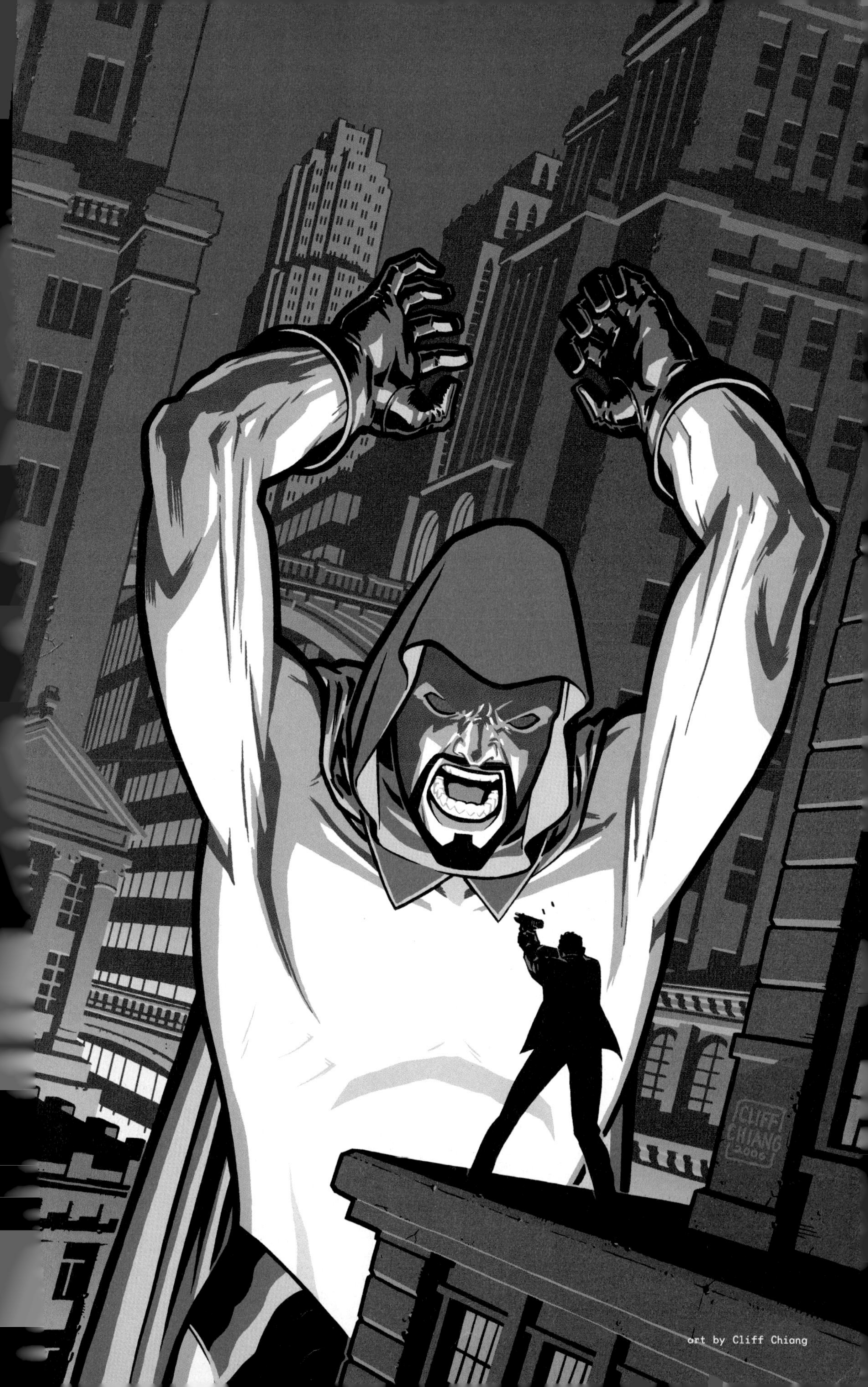
CLIFF CHIANG 2006

art by Cliff Chiang

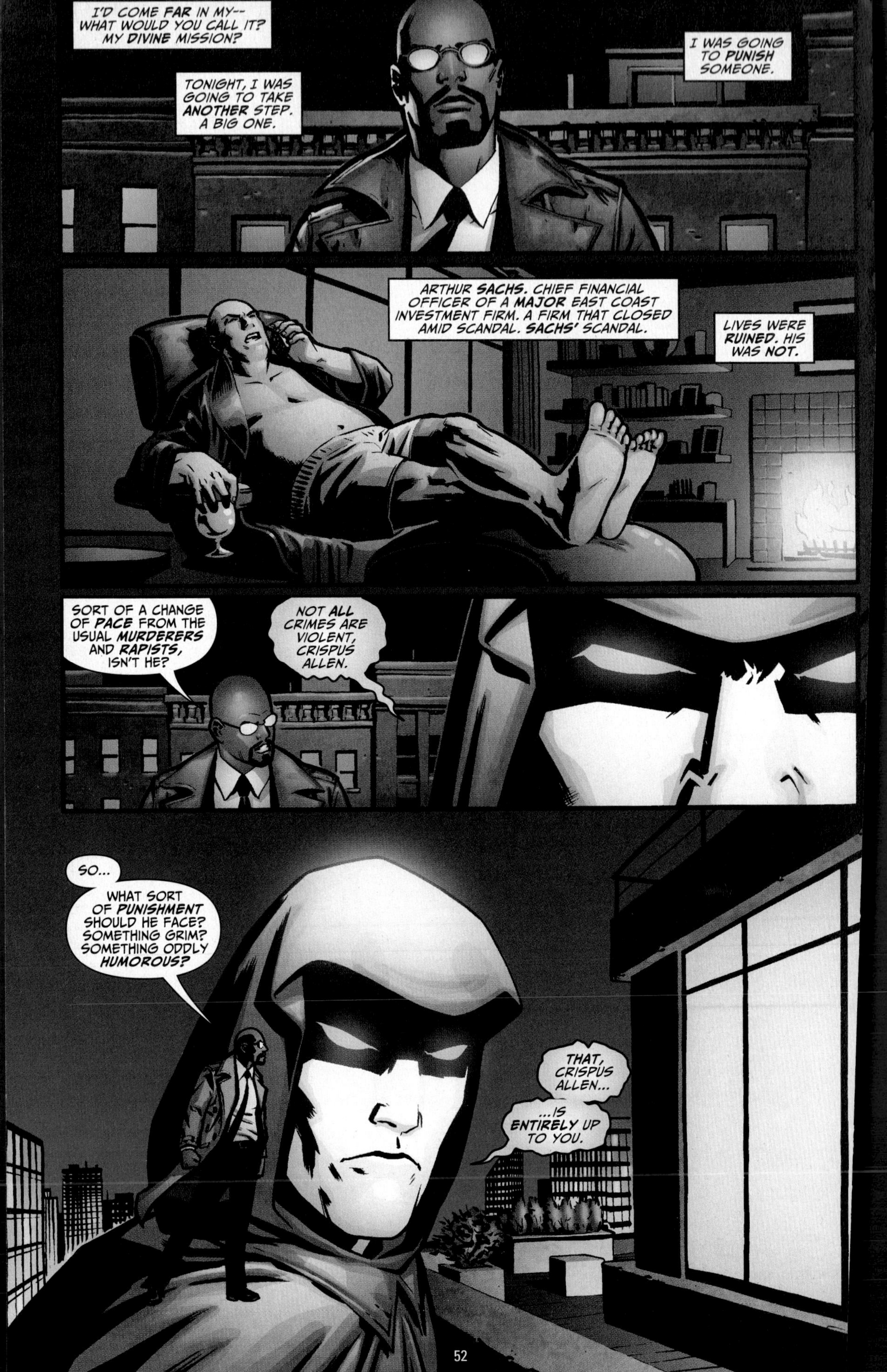
I'D COME FAR IN MY-- WHAT WOULD YOU CALL IT? MY DIVINE MISSION?
TONIGHT, I WAS GOING TO TAKE ANOTHER STEP. A BIG ONE.
I WAS GOING TO PUNISH SOMEONE.
ARTHUR SACHS. CHIEF FINANCIAL OFFICER OF A MAJOR EAST COAST INVESTMENT FIRM. A FIRM THAT CLOSED AMID SCANDAL. SACHS' SCANDAL.
LIVES WERE RUINED. HIS WAS NOT.
SORT OF A CHANGE OF PACE FROM THE USUAL MURDERERS AND RAPISTS, ISN'T HE?
NOT ALL CRIMES ARE VIOLENT, CRISPUS ALLEN.
SO...
WHAT SORT OF PUNISHMENT SHOULD HE FACE? SOMETHING GRIM? SOMETHING ODDLY HUMOROUS?
THAT, CRISPUS ALLEN...
...IS ENTIRELY UP TO YOU.

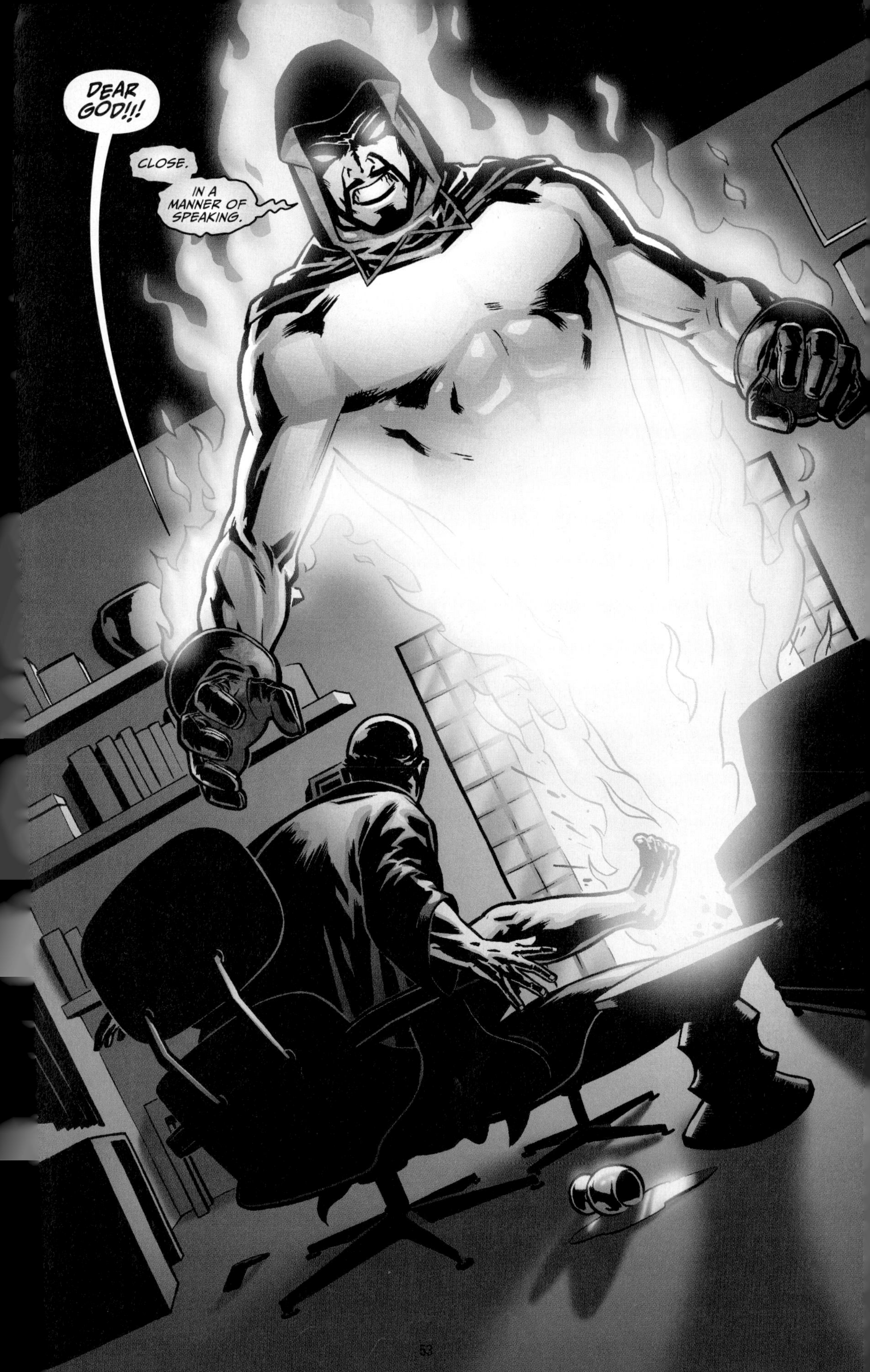
DEAR GOD!!!
CLOSE.
IN A MANNER OF SPEAKING.

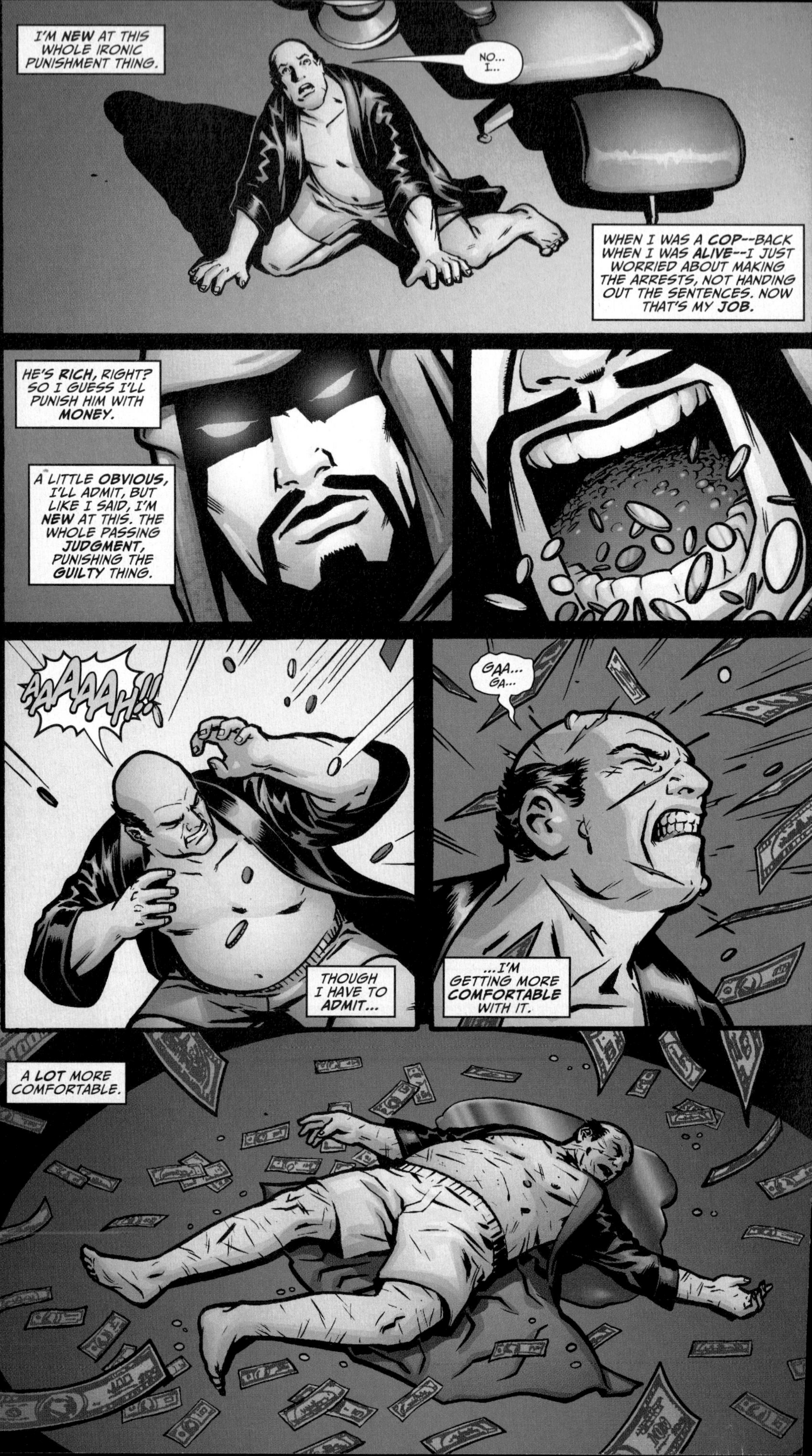
I'M NEW AT THIS WHOLE IRONIC PUNISHMENT THING.
NO... I...
WHEN I WAS A COP--BACK WHEN I WAS ALIVE--I JUST WORRIED ABOUT MAKING THE ARRESTS, NOT HANDING OUT THE SENTENCES. NOW THAT'S MY JOB.
HE'S RICH, RIGHT? SO I GUESS I'LL PUNISH HIM WITH MONEY.
A LITTLE OBVIOUS, I'LL ADMIT, BUT LIKE I SAID, I'M NEW AT THIS. THE WHOLE PASSING JUDGMENT, PUNISHING THE GUILTY THING.
AAAAAH!!!
THOUGH I HAVE TO ADMIT...
GAA... GA...
...I'M GETTING MORE COMFORTABLE WITH IT.
A LOT MORE COMFORTABLE.

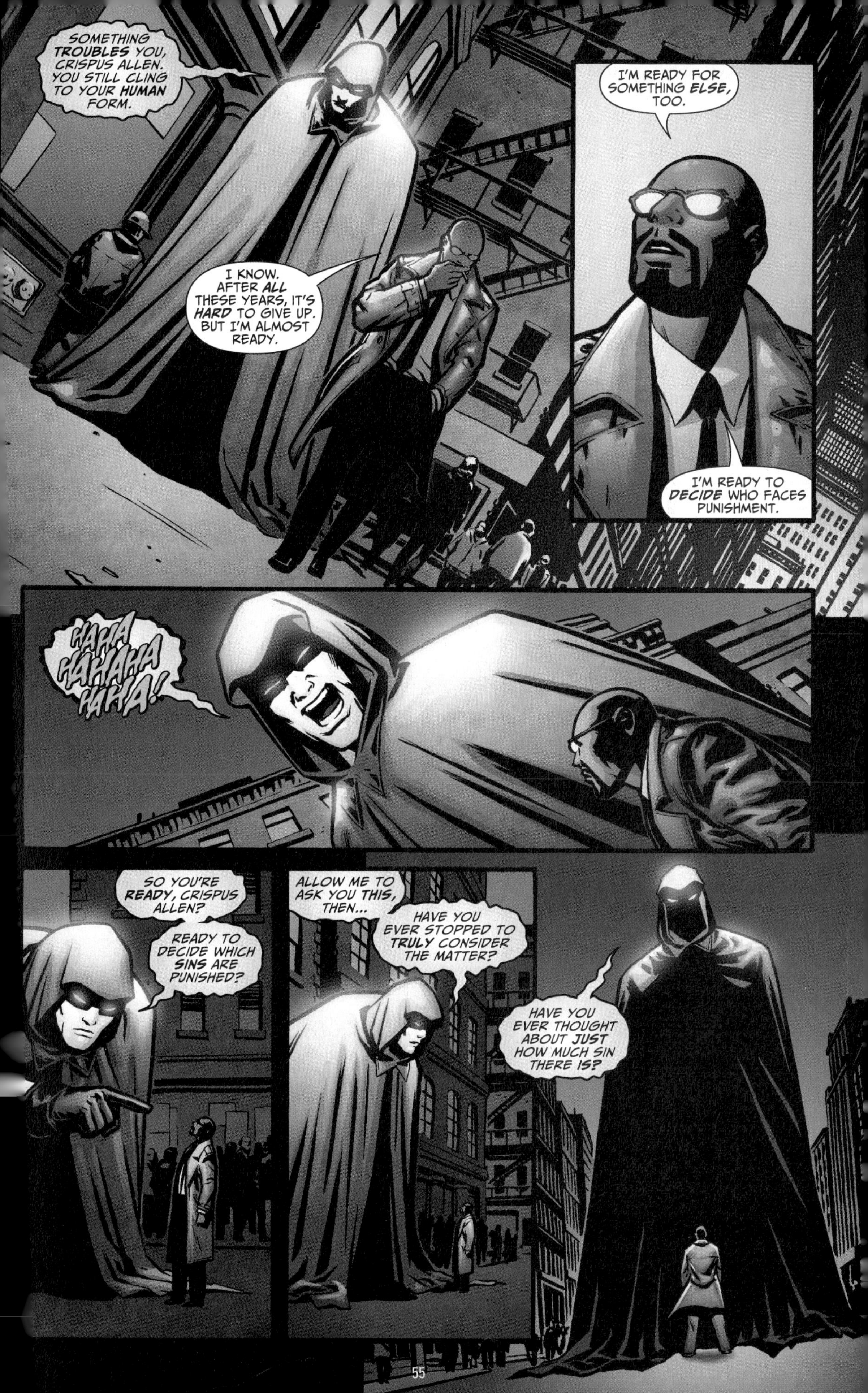
SOMETHING TROUBLES YOU, CRISPUS ALLEN. YOU STILL CLING TO YOUR HUMAN FORM.
I KNOW. AFTER ALL THESE YEARS, IT'S HARD TO GIVE UP. BUT I'M ALMOST READY.
I'M READY FOR SOMETHING ELSE, TOO.
I'M READY TO DECIDE WHO FACES PUNISHMENT.
HAHA HAHAHA HAHA!
SO YOU'RE READY, CRISPUS ALLEN?
READY TO DECIDE WHICH SINS ARE PUNISHED?
ALLOW ME TO ASK YOU THIS, THEN...
HAVE YOU EVER STOPPED TO TRULY CONSIDER THE MATTER?
HAVE YOU EVER THOUGHT ABOUT JUST HOW MUCH SIN THERE IS?

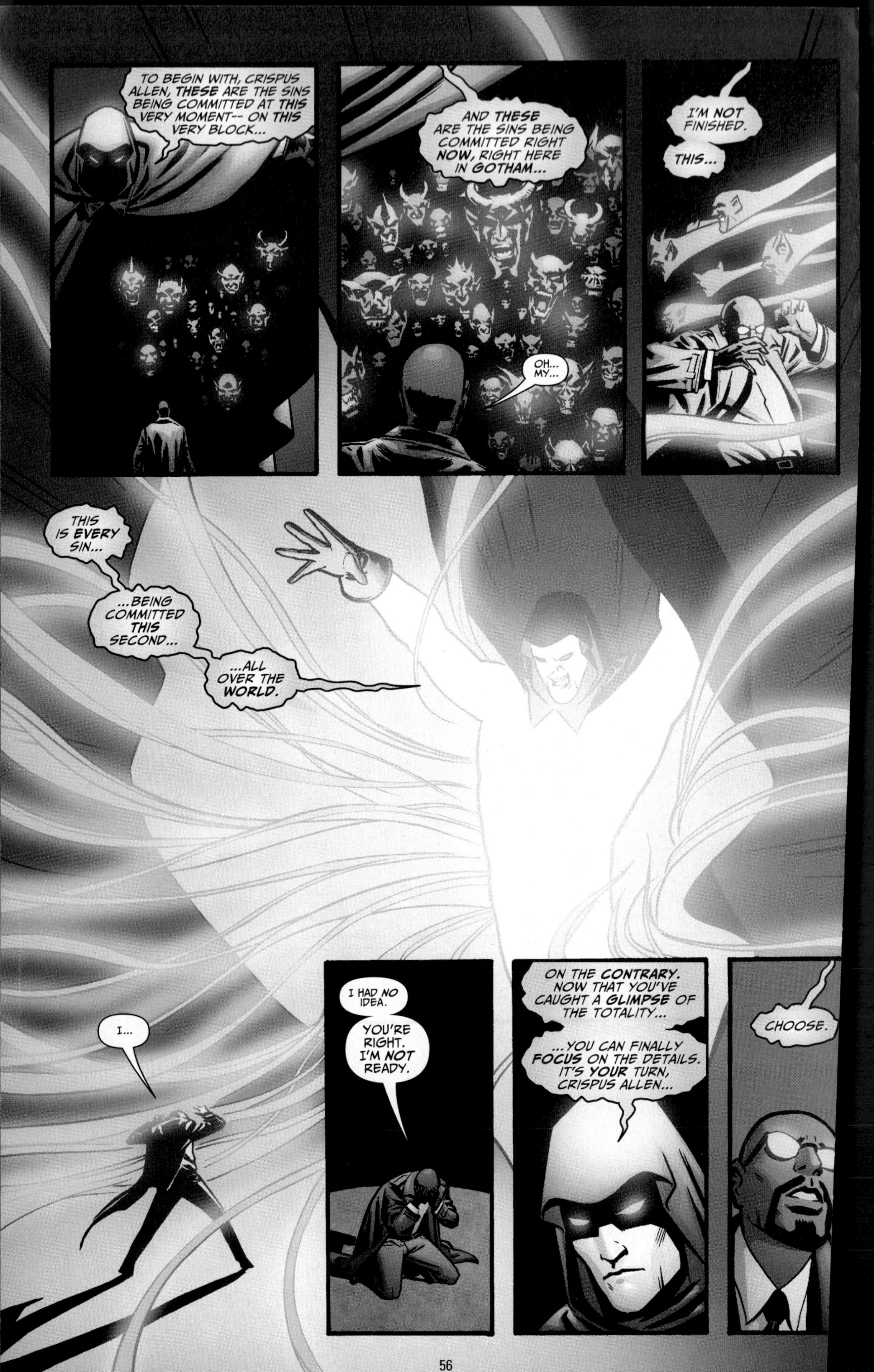
TO BEGIN WITH, CRISPUS ALLEN, THESE ARE THE SINS BEING COMMITTED AT THIS VERY MOMENT-- ON THIS VERY BLOCK...
AND THESE ARE THE SINS BEING COMMITTED RIGHT NOW, RIGHT HERE IN GOTHAM...
OH... MY...
I'M NOT FINISHED.
THIS...
THIS IS EVERY SIN...
...BEING COMMITTED THIS SECOND...
...ALL OVER THE WORLD.
I...
I HAD NO IDEA.
YOU'RE RIGHT. I'M NOT READY.
ON THE CONTRARY. NOW THAT YOU'VE CAUGHT A GLIMPSE OF THE TOTALITY...
...YOU CAN FINALLY FOCUS ON THE DETAILS. IT'S YOUR TURN, CRISPUS ALLEN...
CHOOSE.

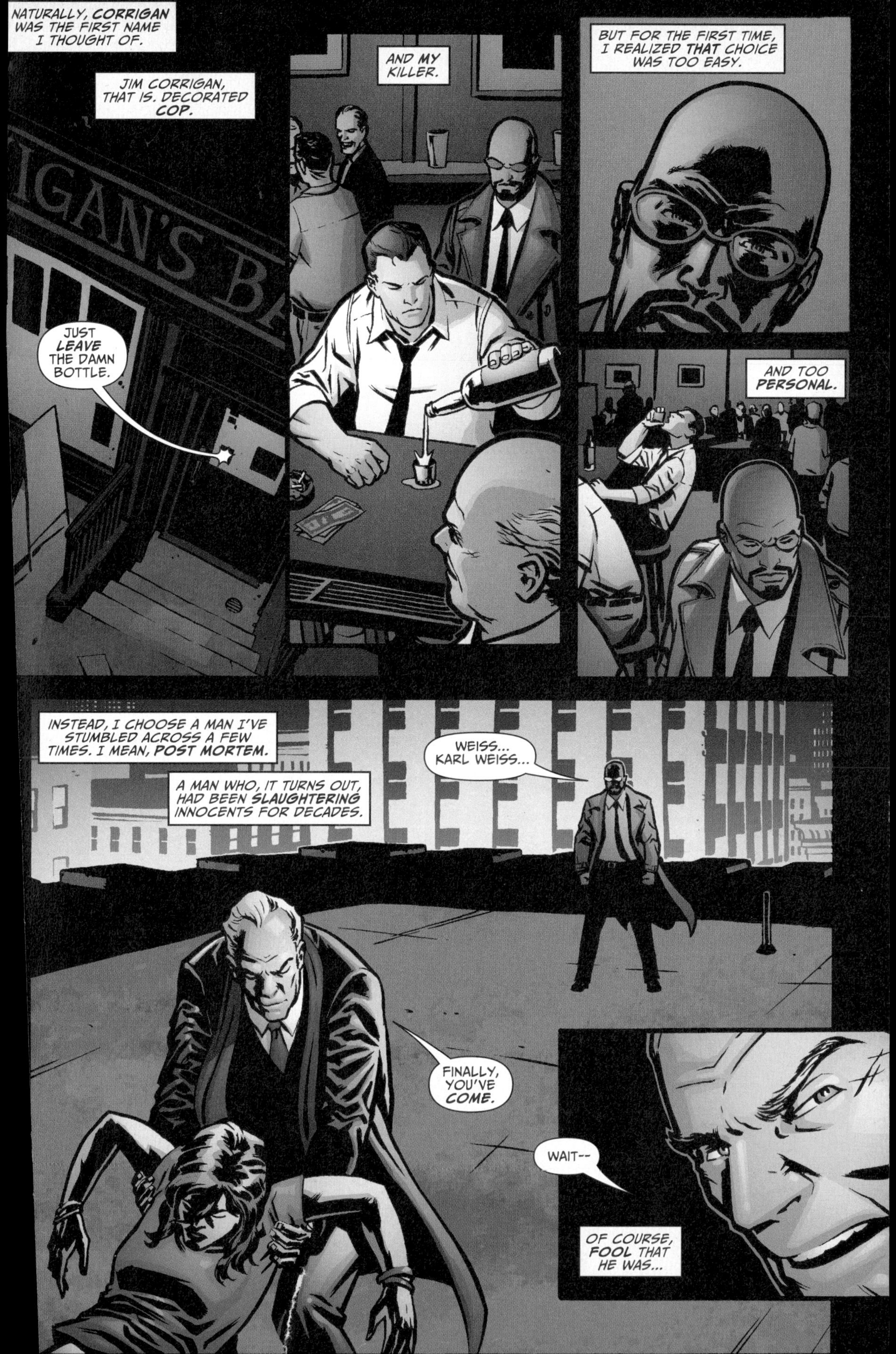

NATURALLY, CORRIGAN WAS THE FIRST NAME I THOUGHT OF.
JIM CORRIGAN, THAT IS. DECORATED COP.
IGAN'S BA
JUST LEAVE THE DAMN BOTTLE.
AND MY KILLER.
BUT FOR THE FIRST TIME, I REALIZED THAT CHOICE WAS TOO EASY.
AND TOO PERSONAL.
INSTEAD, I CHOOSE A MAN I'VE STUMBLED ACROSS A FEW TIMES. I MEAN, POST MORTEM.
A MAN WHO, IT TURNS OUT, HAD BEEN SLAUGHTERING INNOCENTS FOR DECADES.
WEISS... KARL WEISS...
FINALLY, YOU'VE COME.
WAIT--
OF COURSE, FOOL THAT HE WAS...

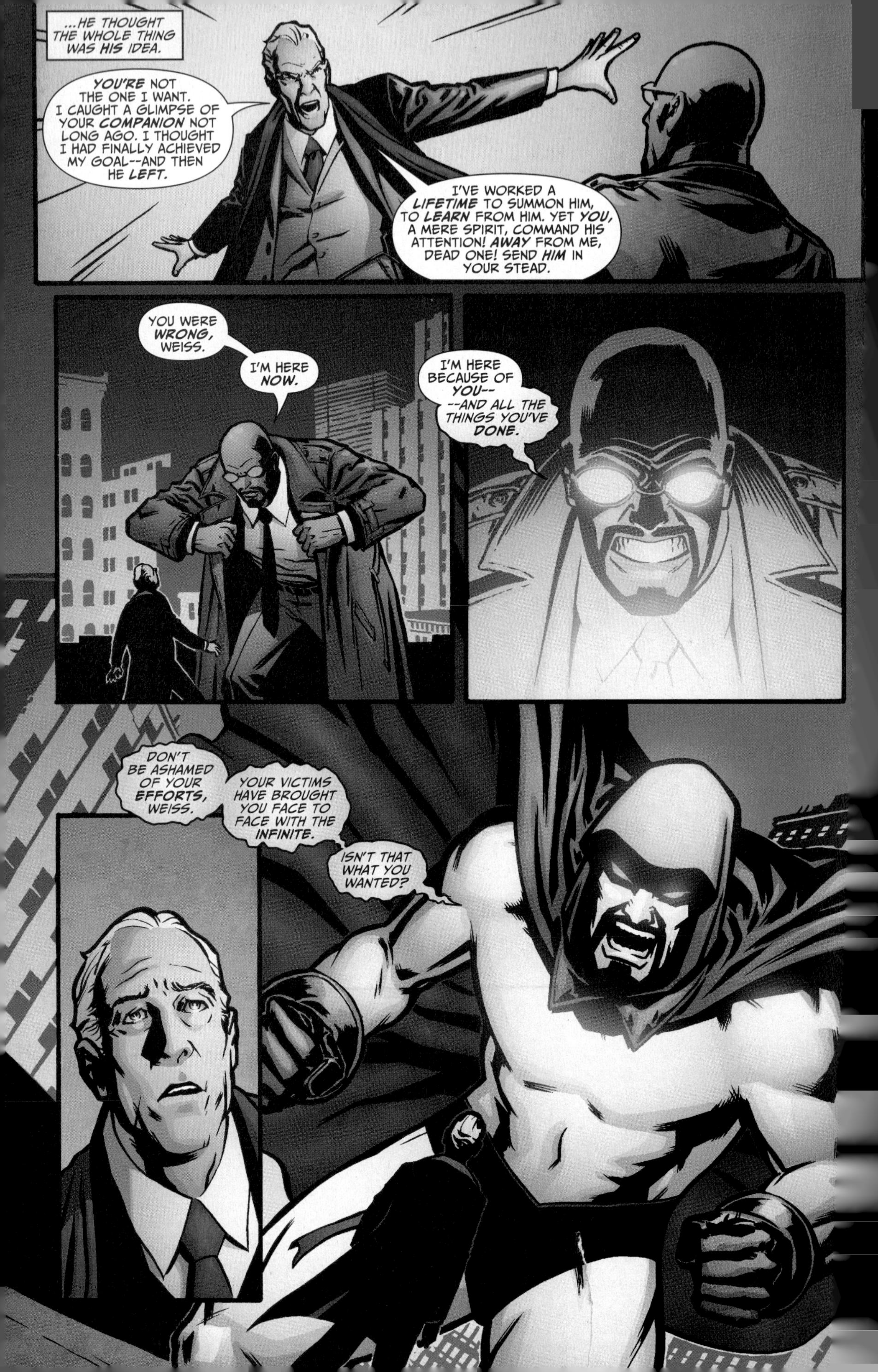
...HE THOUGHT THE WHOLE THING WAS HIS IDEA.
YOU'RE NOT THE ONE I WANT. I CAUGHT A GLIMPSE OF YOUR COMPANION NOT LONG AGO. I THOUGHT I HAD FINALLY ACHIEVED MY GOAL--AND THEN HE LEFT.
I'VE WORKED A LIFETIME TO SUMMON HIM, TO LEARN FROM HIM. YET YOU, A MERE SPIRIT, COMMAND HIS ATTENTION! AWAY FROM ME, DEAD ONE! SEND HIM IN YOUR STEAD.
YOU WERE WRONG, WEISS.
I'M HERE NOW.
I'M HERE BECAUSE OF YOU--
--AND ALL THE THINGS YOU'VE DONE.
DON'T BE ASHAMED OF YOUR EFFORTS, WEISS.
YOUR VICTIMS HAVE BROUGHT YOU FACE TO FACE WITH THE INFINITE.
ISN'T THAT WHAT YOU WANTED?

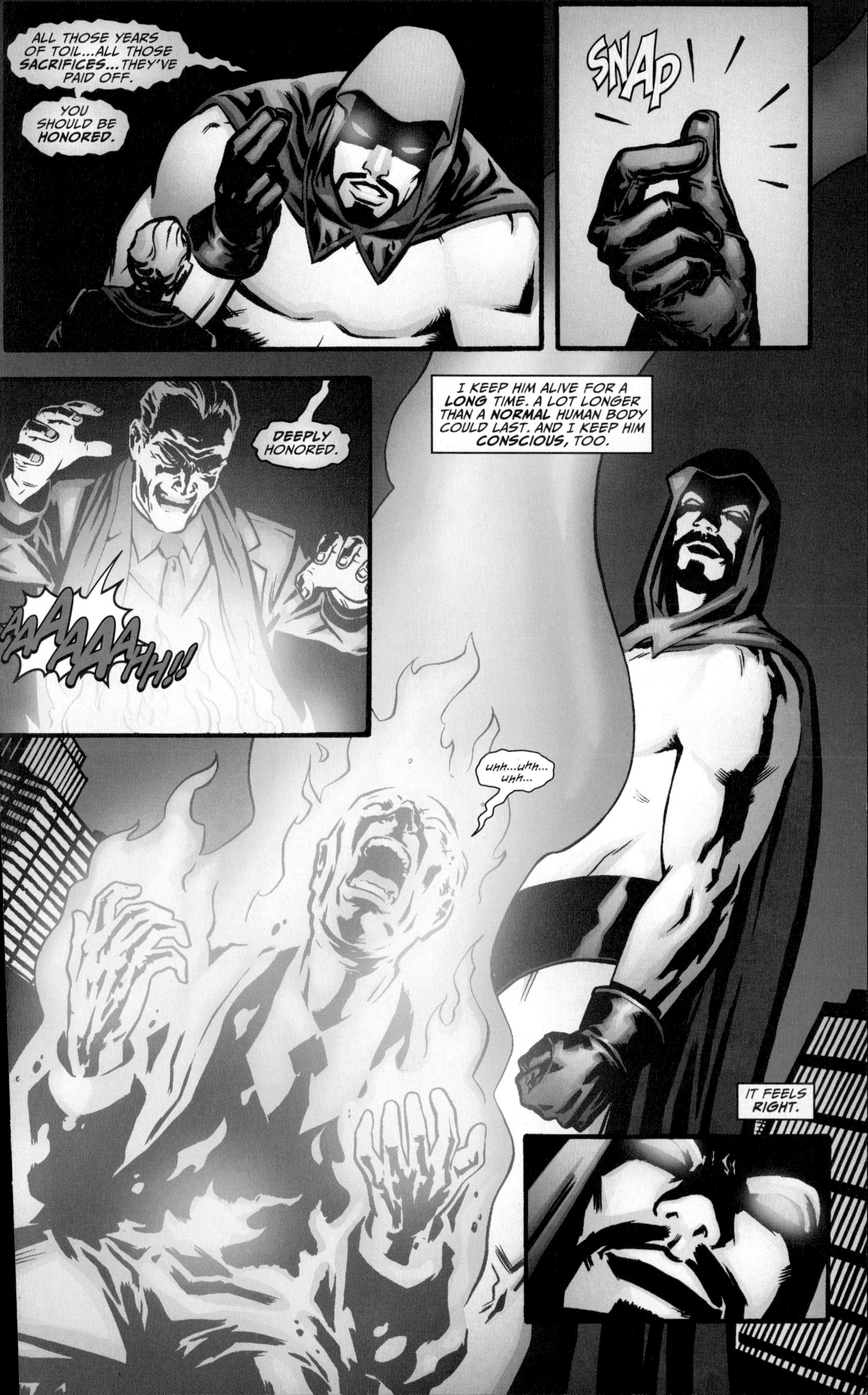
ALL THOSE YEARS OF TOIL...ALL THOSE SACRIFICES...THEY'VE PAID OFF.
YOU SHOULD BE HONORED.
SNAP
DEEPLY HONORED.
AAAAAAAHH!!
I KEEP HIM ALIVE FOR A LONG TIME. A LOT LONGER THAN A NORMAL HUMAN BODY COULD LAST. AND I KEEP HIM CONSCIOUS, TOO.
uhh...uhh... uhh...
IT FEELS RIGHT.

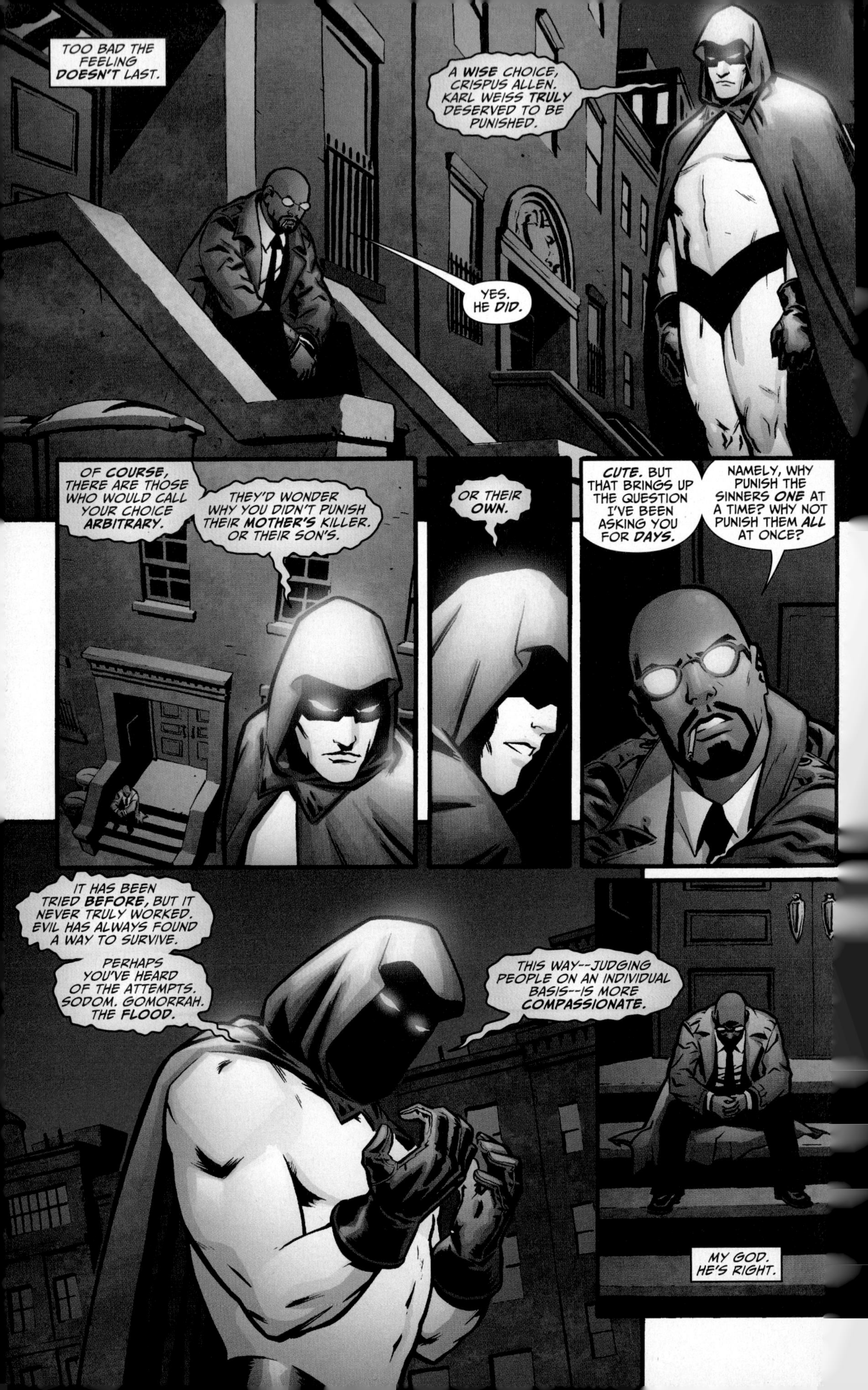
TOO BAD THE FEELING DOESN'T LAST.
A WISE CHOICE, CRISPUS ALLEN. KARL WEISS TRULY DESERVED TO BE PUNISHED.
YES. HE DID.
OF COURSE, THERE ARE THOSE WHO WOULD CALL YOUR CHOICE ARBITRARY.
THEY'D WONDER WHY YOU DIDN'T PUNISH THEIR MOTHER'S KILLER. OR THEIR SON'S.
OR THEIR OWN.
CUTE. BUT THAT BRINGS UP THE QUESTION I'VE BEEN ASKING YOU FOR DAYS.
NAMELY, WHY PUNISH THE SINNERS ONE AT A TIME? WHY NOT PUNISH THEM ALL AT ONCE?
IT HAS BEEN TRIED BEFORE, BUT IT NEVER TRULY WORKED. EVIL HAS ALWAYS FOUND A WAY TO SURVIVE.
PERHAPS YOU'VE HEARD OF THE ATTEMPTS. SODOM. GOMORRAH. THE FLOOD.
THIS WAY--JUDGING PEOPLE ON AN INDIVIDUAL BASIS--IS MORE COMPASSIONATE.
MY GOD. HE'S RIGHT.

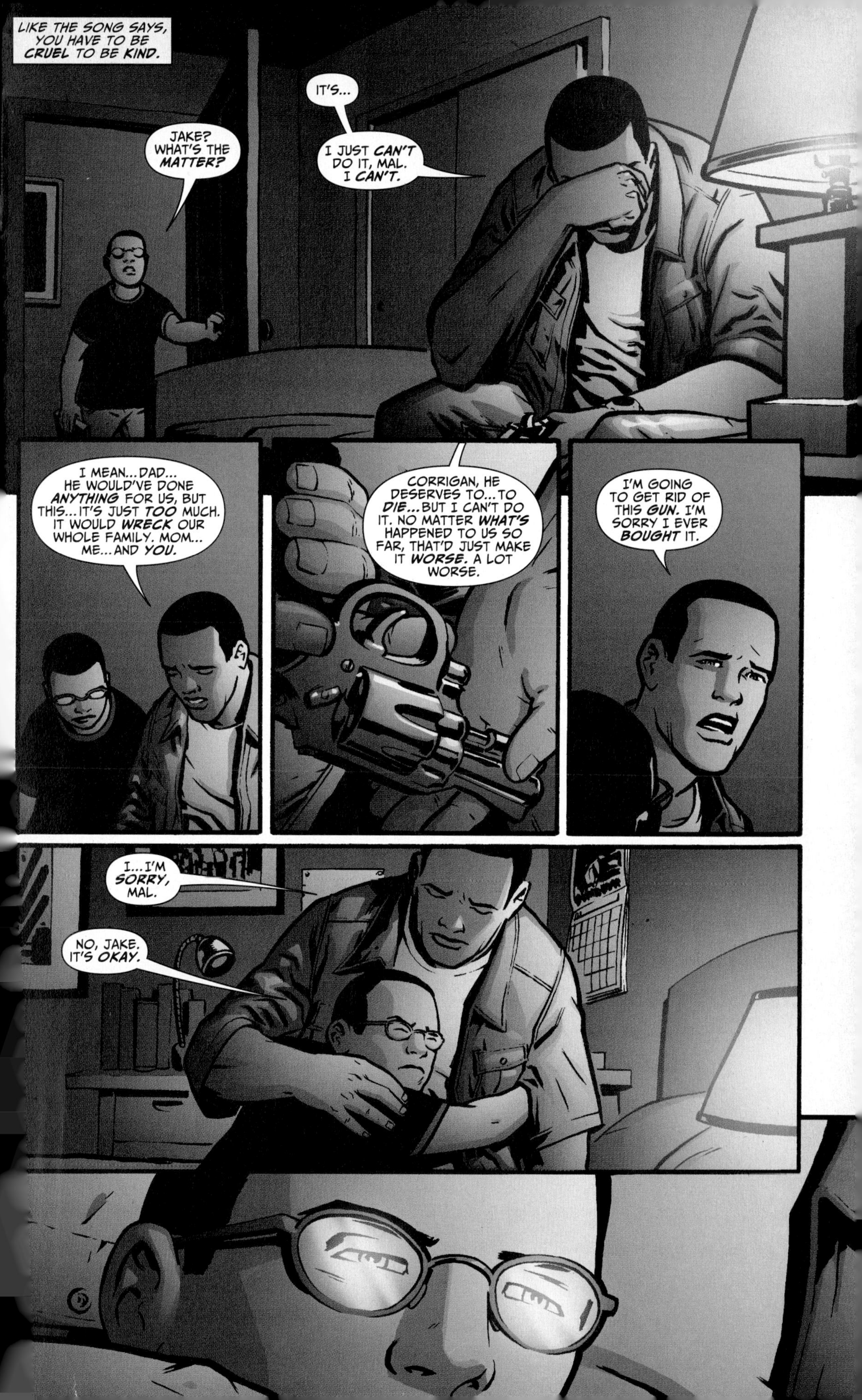
LIKE THE SONG SAYS, YOU HAVE TO BE CRUEL TO BE KIND.
JAKE? WHAT'S THE MATTER?
IT'S...
I JUST CAN'T DO IT, MAL. I CAN'T.
I MEAN...DAD... HE WOULD'VE DONE ANYTHING FOR US, BUT THIS...IT'S JUST TOO MUCH. IT WOULD WRECK OUR WHOLE FAMILY. MOM... ME...AND YOU.
CORRIGAN, HE DESERVES TO...TO DIE...BUT I CAN'T DO IT. NO MATTER WHAT'S HAPPENED TO US SO FAR, THAT'D JUST MAKE IT WORSE. A LOT WORSE.
I'M GOING TO GET RID OF THIS GUN. I'M SORRY I EVER BOUGHT IT.
I...I'M SORRY, MAL.
NO, JAKE. IT'S OKAY.

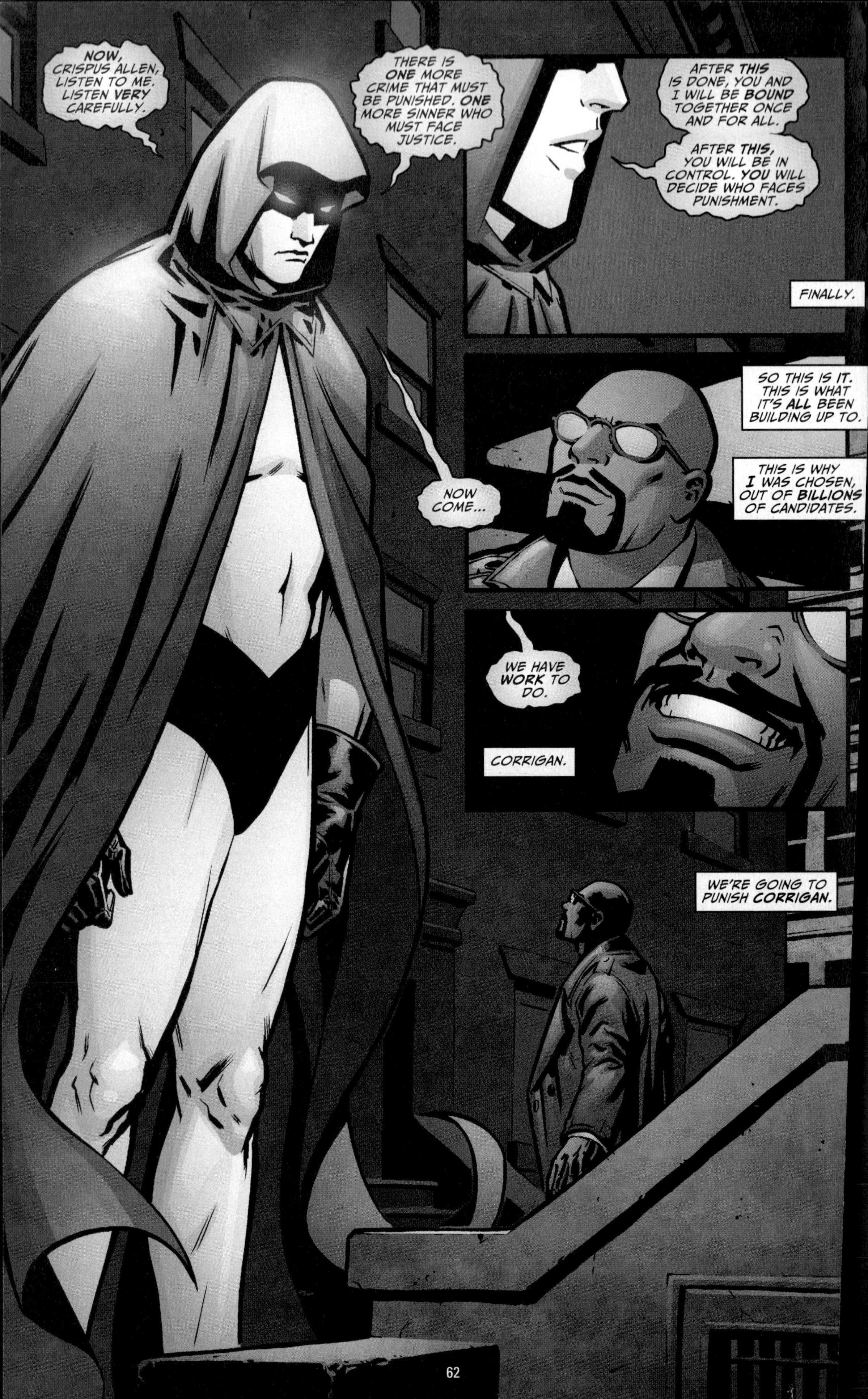
NOW, CRISPUS ALLEN, LISTEN TO ME. LISTEN VERY CAREFULLY.
THERE IS ONE MORE CRIME THAT MUST BE PUNISHED. ONE MORE SINNER WHO MUST FACE JUSTICE.
AFTER THIS IS DONE, YOU AND I WILL BE BOUND TOGETHER ONCE AND FOR ALL.
AFTER THIS, YOU WILL BE IN CONTROL. YOU WILL DECIDE WHO FACES PUNISHMENT.
FINALLY.
SO THIS IS IT. THIS IS WHAT IT'S ALL BEEN BUILDING UP TO.
THIS IS WHY I WAS CHOSEN, OUT OF BILLIONS OF CANDIDATES.
NOW COME...
WE HAVE WORK TO DO.
CORRIGAN.
WE'RE GOING TO PUNISH CORRIGAN.

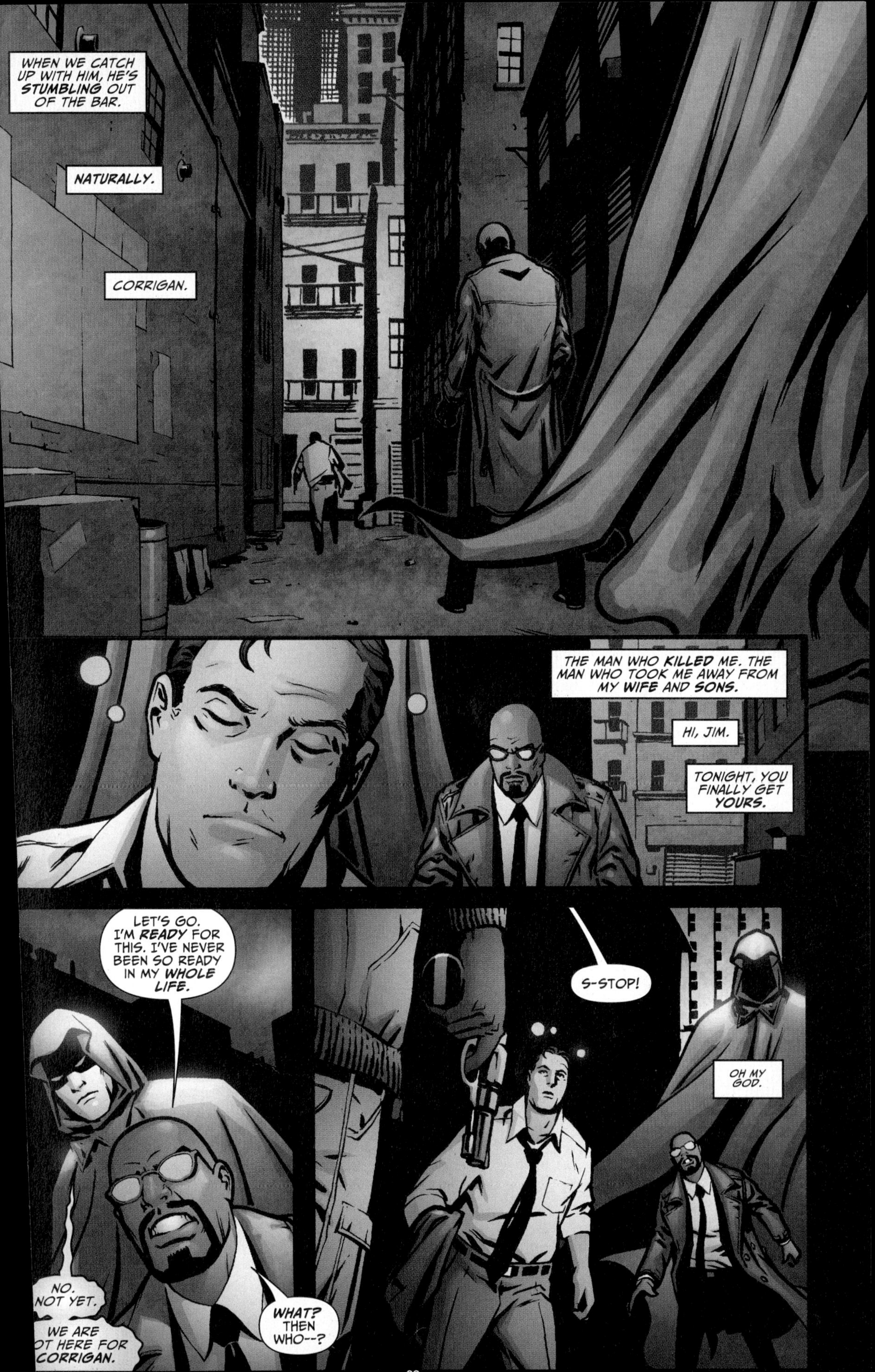
WHEN WE CATCH UP WITH HIM, HE'S STUMBLING OUT OF THE BAR.
NATURALLY.
CORRIGAN.
THE MAN WHO KILLED ME. THE MAN WHO TOOK ME AWAY FROM MY WIFE AND SONS.
HI, JIM.
TONIGHT, YOU FINALLY GET YOURS.
LET'S GO. I'M READY FOR THIS. I'VE NEVER BEEN SO READY IN MY WHOLE LIFE.
NO. NOT YET.
WE ARE OT HERE FOR CORRIGAN.
WHAT? THEN WHO--?
S-STOP!
OH MY GOD.

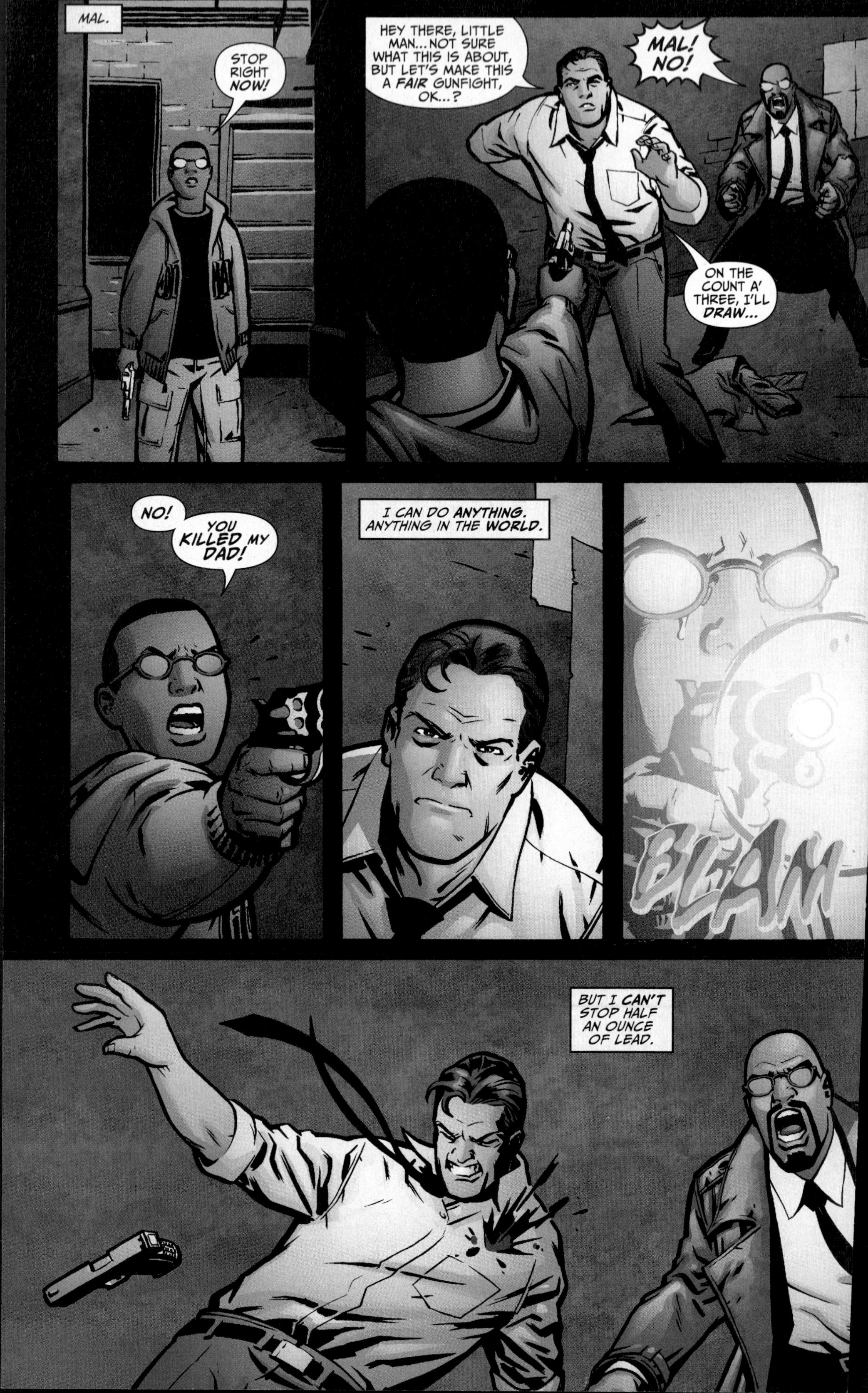
MAL.
STOP RIGHT NOW!
HEY THERE, LITTLE MAN... NOT SURE WHAT THIS IS ABOUT, BUT LET'S MAKE THIS A FAIR GUNFIGHT, OK...?
MAL! NO!
ON THE COUNT A' THREE, I'LL DRAW...
NO!
YOU KILLED MY DAD!
I CAN DO ANYTHING. ANYTHING IN THE WORLD.
BLAM
BUT I CAN'T STOP HALF AN OUNCE OF LEAD.

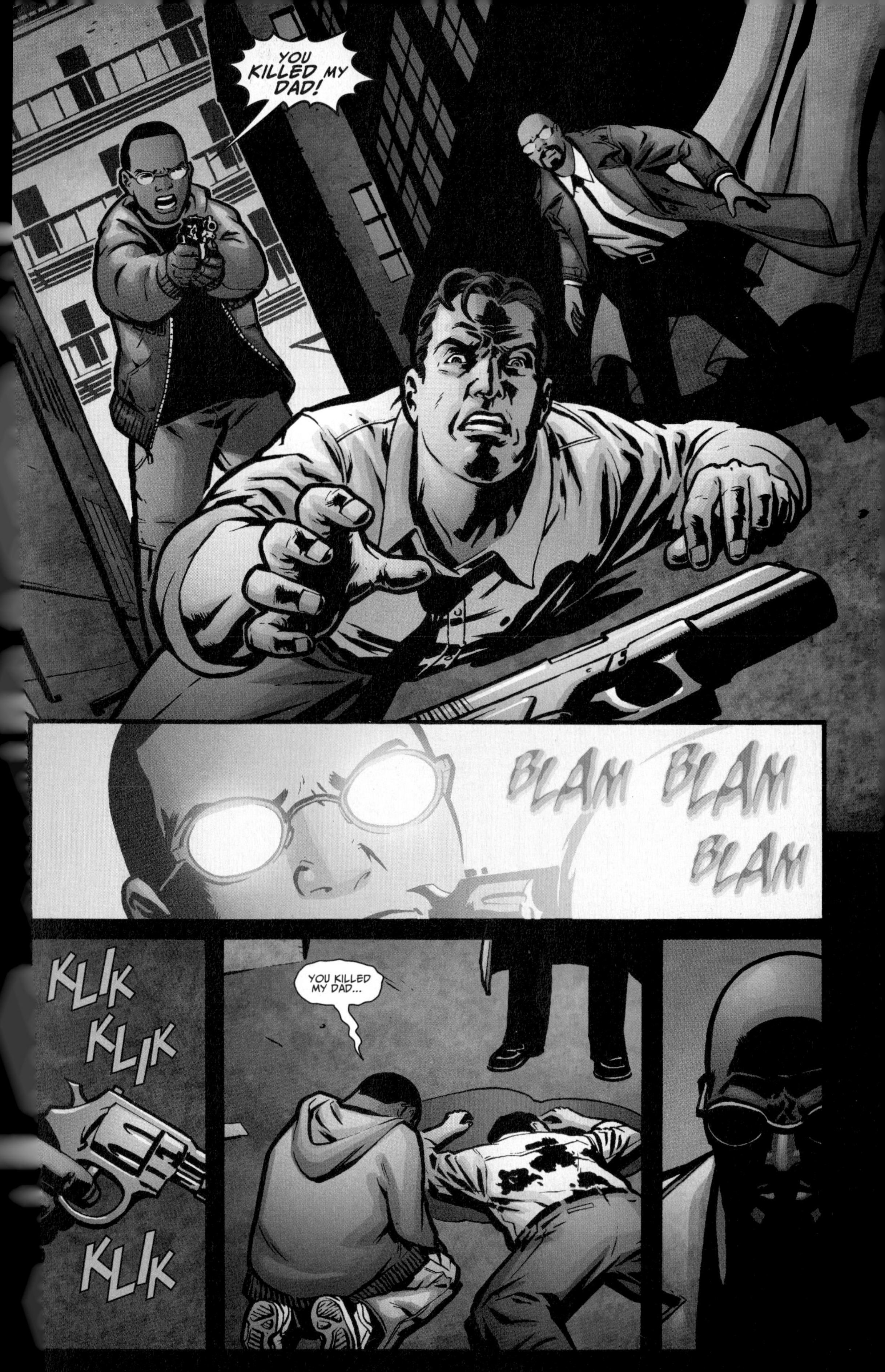
YOU KILLED MY DAD!
BLAM BLAM BLAM
KLIK KLIK
KLIK
YOU KILLED MY DAD...

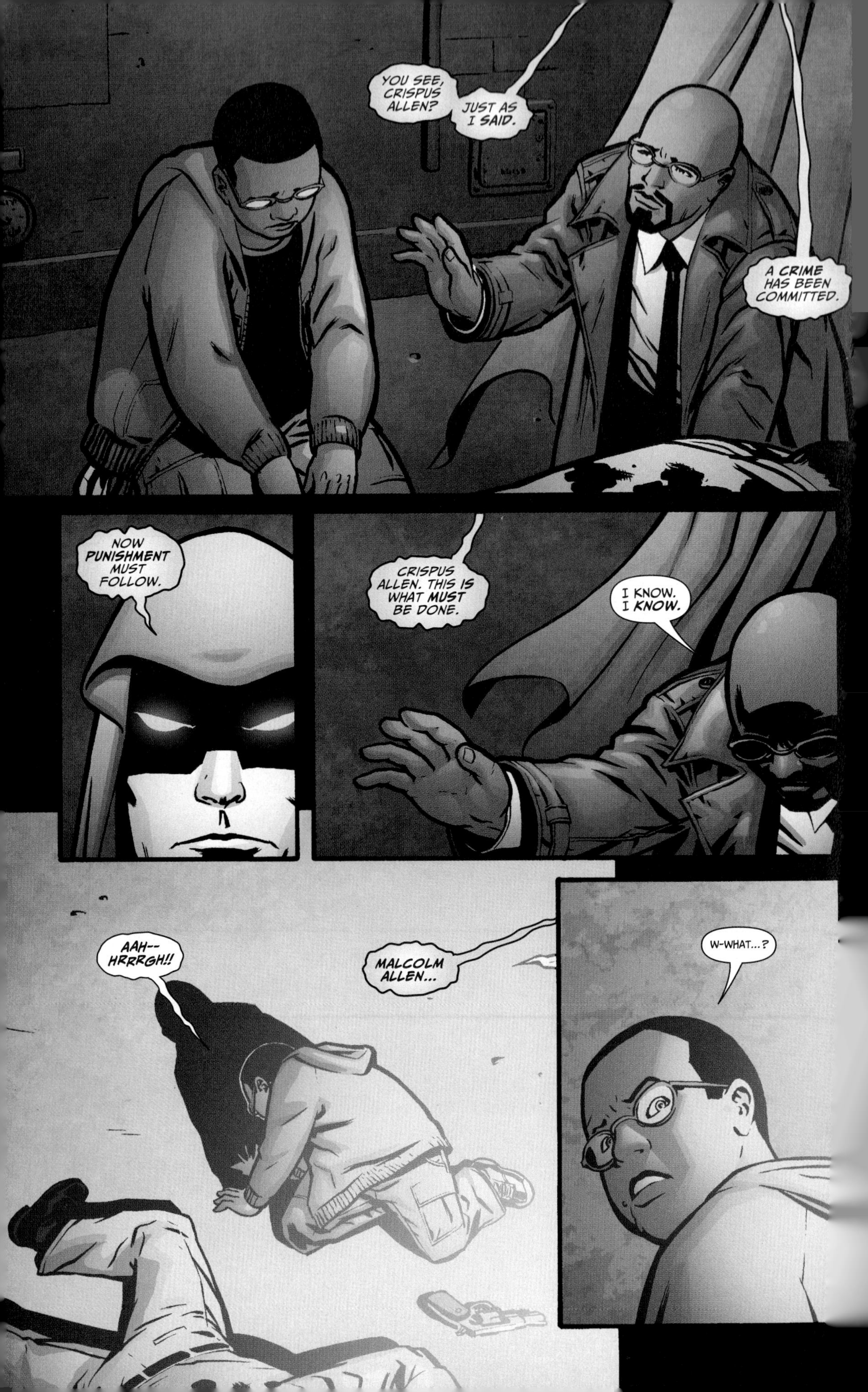
YOU SEE, CRISPUS ALLEN?
JUST AS I SAID.
A CRIME HAS BEEN COMMITTED.
NOW PUNISHMENT MUST FOLLOW.
CRISPUS ALLEN. THIS IS WHAT MUST BE DONE.
I KNOW. I KNOW.
AAH--HRRRGH!!
MALCOLM ALLEN...
W-WHAT...?

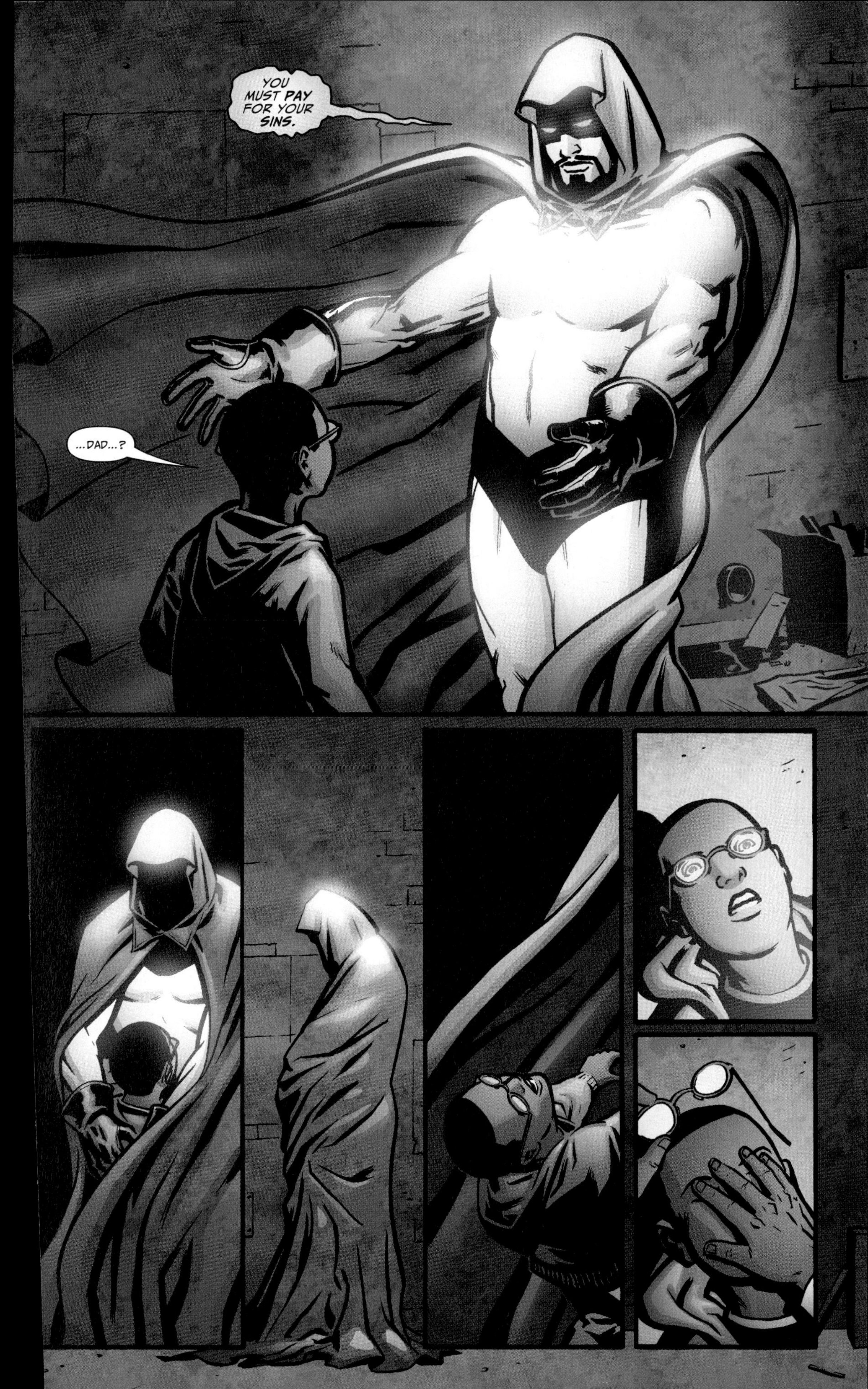
YOU MUST PAY FOR YOUR SINS.
...DAD...?

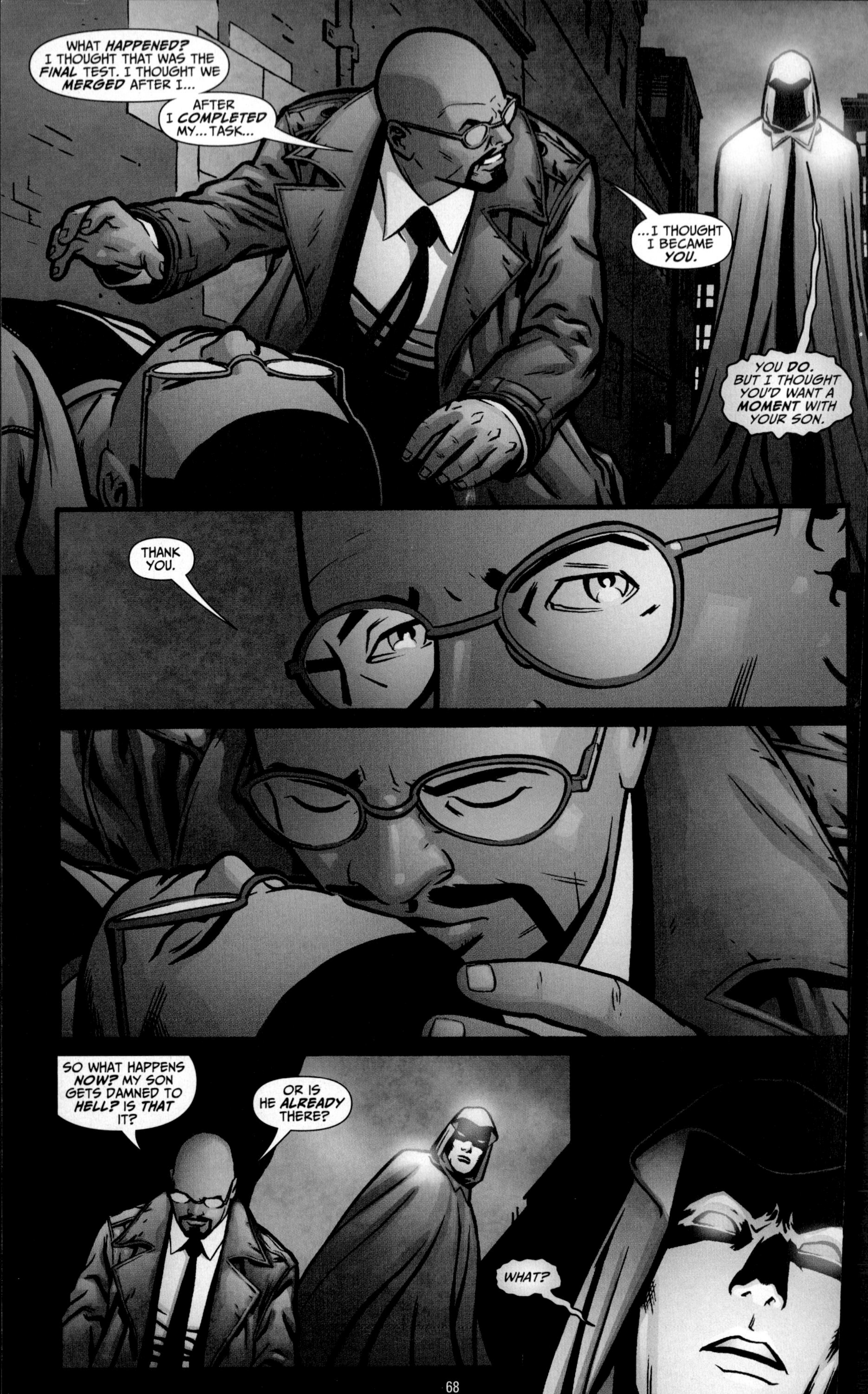
WHAT HAPPENED? I THOUGHT THAT WAS THE FINAL TEST. I THOUGHT WE MERGED AFTER I...
AFTER I COMPLETED MY... TASK...
...I THOUGHT I BECAME YOU.
YOU DO. BUT I THOUGHT YOU'D WANT A MOMENT WITH YOUR SON.
THANK YOU.
SO WHAT HAPPENS NOW? MY SON GETS DAMNED TO HELL? IS THAT IT?
OR IS HE ALREADY THERE?
WHAT?

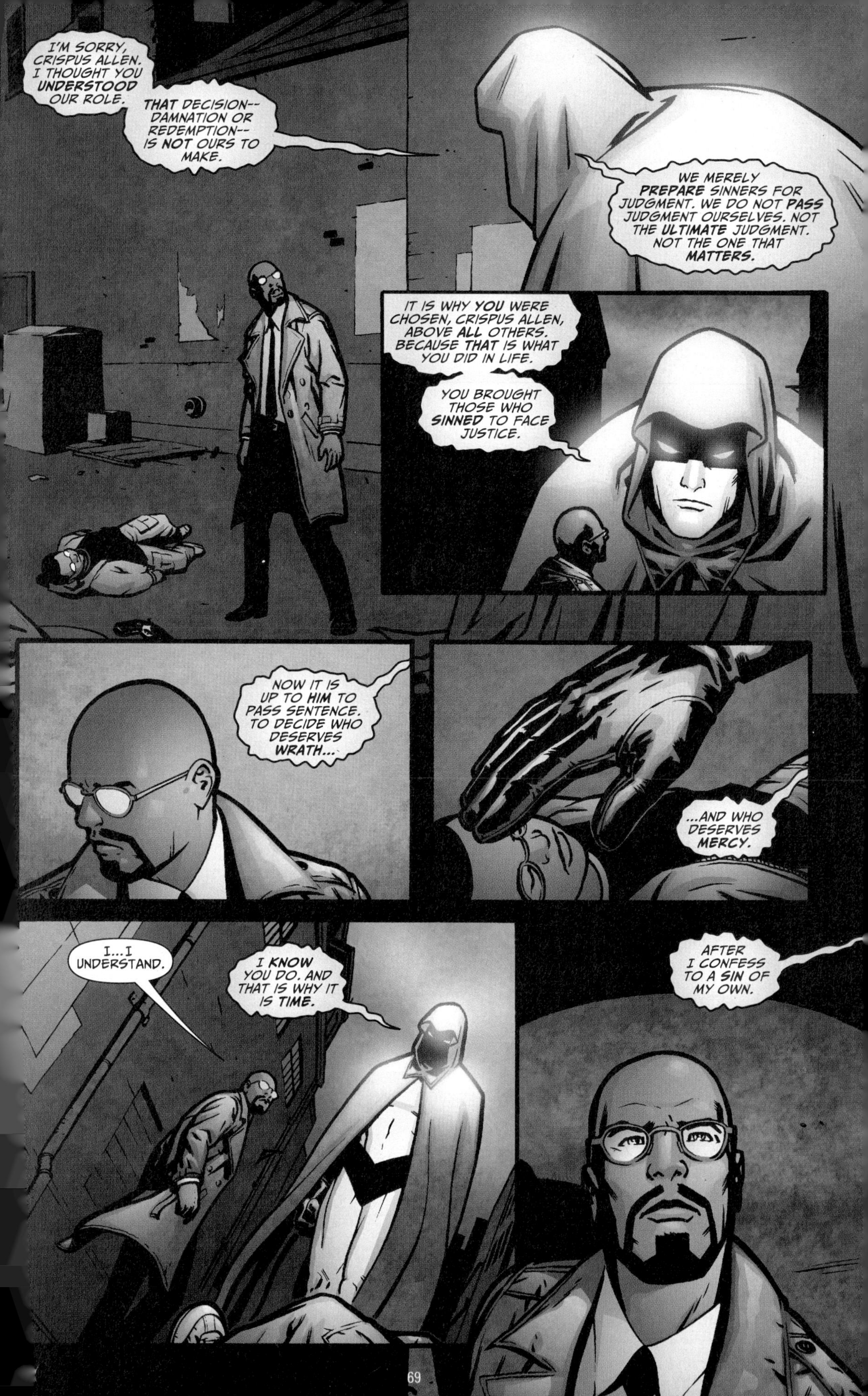
I'M SORRY, CRISPUS ALLEN. I THOUGHT YOU UNDERSTOOD OUR ROLE.
THAT DECISION-- DAMNATION OR REDEMPTION-- IS NOT OURS TO MAKE.
WE MERELY PREPARE SINNERS FOR JUDGMENT. WE DO NOT PASS JUDGMENT OURSELVES. NOT THE ULTIMATE JUDGMENT. NOT THE ONE THAT MATTERS.
IT IS WHY YOU WERE CHOSEN, CRISPUS ALLEN, ABOVE ALL OTHERS. BECAUSE THAT IS WHAT YOU DID IN LIFE.
YOU BROUGHT THOSE WHO SINNED TO FACE JUSTICE.
NOW IT IS UP TO HIM TO PASS SENTENCE. TO DECIDE WHO DESERVES WRATH...
...AND WHO DESERVES MERCY.
I...I UNDERSTAND.
I KNOW YOU DO. AND THAT IS WHY IT IS TIME.
AFTER I CONFESS TO A SIN OF MY OWN.

THOUGH WE ARE ABOUT TO BOND *PERMANENTLY,* THOUGH YOU ARE ABOUT TO BECOME *ME,* AND I, *YOU...* THIS IS *NOT* THE FIRST TIME WE HAVE DONE SO.

I KNOW. WE'VE BEEN JOINING FORCES FOR *DAYS* NOW.

NO. THAT IS *NOT* WHAT I MEAN.

WHEN I FIRST *OFFERED* YOU THIS OPPORTUNITY, YOU *CHOSE* NOT TO ACCEPT IT.

I DID NOT *RESPECT* THAT CHOICE.

"I NEEDED SOME CONNECTION TO HUMANITY, NO MATTER HOW TENUOUS. YOU DO NOT REMEMBER, BUT I *USED* YOU TO ENSURE THE FIGHT FOR JUSTICE *CONTINUED.*"

"I HAD *NO* CHOICE."

BUT YOU DO, CRISPUS ALLEN. DO YOU STILL WISH TO TAKE UP THIS *HOLY* MISSION?

WHO AM *I* TO STAND IN THE WAY OF *JUSTICE?*

YES.

I *SHOULD* BE FURIOUS. AND BEFORE, I PROBABLY *WOULD* HAVE BEEN.

BUT *NOT* NOW. NOT AFTER WHAT I'VE SEEN. HE DID WHAT *HAD* TO BE DONE. HOW CAN I ARGUE WITH *THAT?*

AND SO, AS T... SPECTRE W... REBORN...

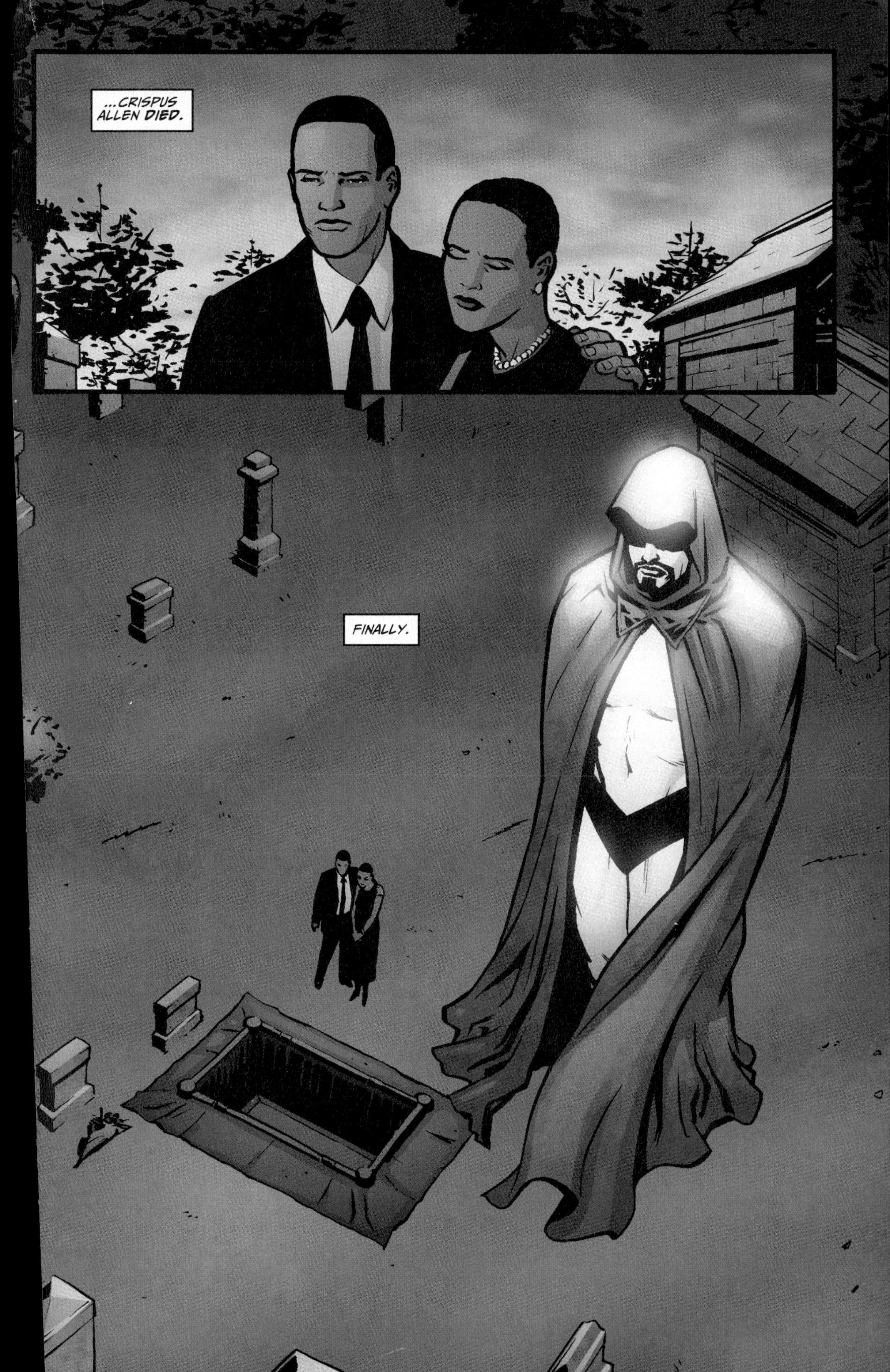
...CRISPUS ALLEN DIED.
FINALLY.

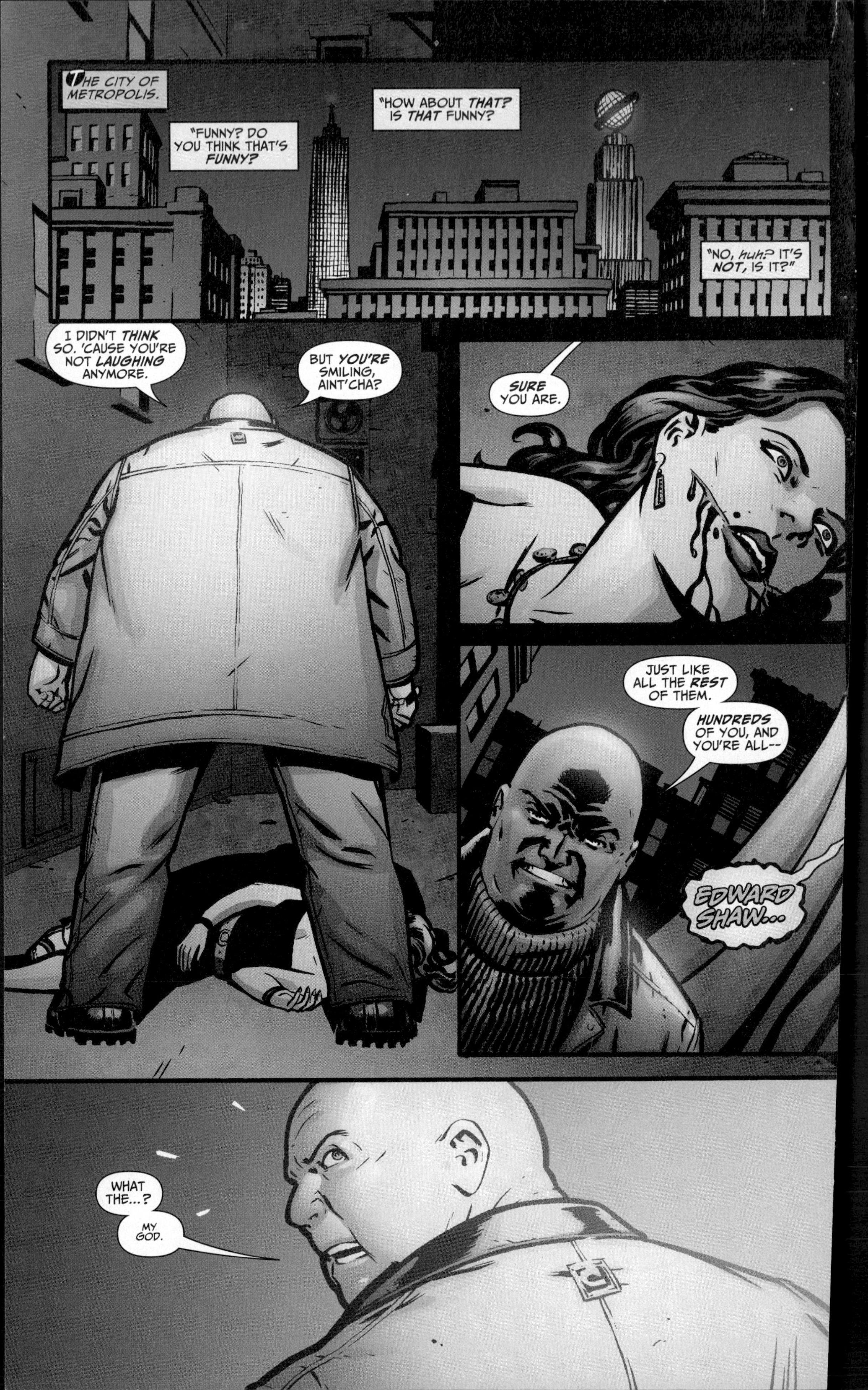
THE CITY OF METROPOLIS.
"FUNNY? DO YOU THINK THAT'S FUNNY?
"HOW ABOUT THAT? IS THAT FUNNY?
"NO, huh? IT'S NOT, IS IT?"
I DIDN'T THINK SO. 'CAUSE YOU'RE NOT LAUGHING ANYMORE.
BUT YOU'RE SMILING, AINT'CHA?
SURE YOU ARE.
JUST LIKE ALL THE REST OF THEM.
HUNDREDS OF YOU, AND YOU'RE ALL--
EDWARD SHAW...
WHAT THE...?
MY GOD.

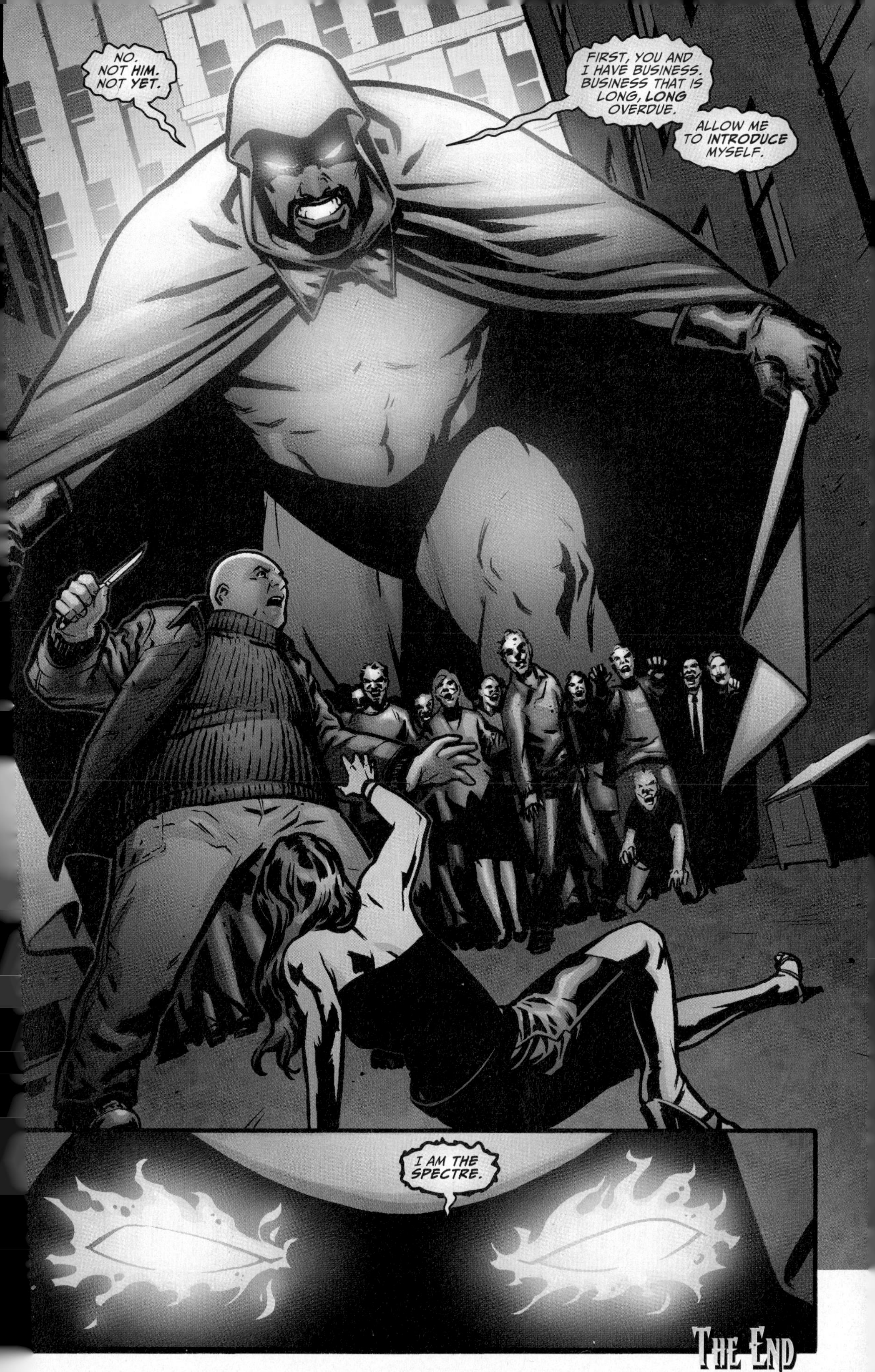
NO. NOT HIM. NOT YET.
FIRST, YOU AND I HAVE BUSINESS. BUSINESS THAT IS LONG, LONG OVERDUE.
ALLOW ME TO INTRODUCE MYSELF.
I AM THE SPECTRE.
THE END

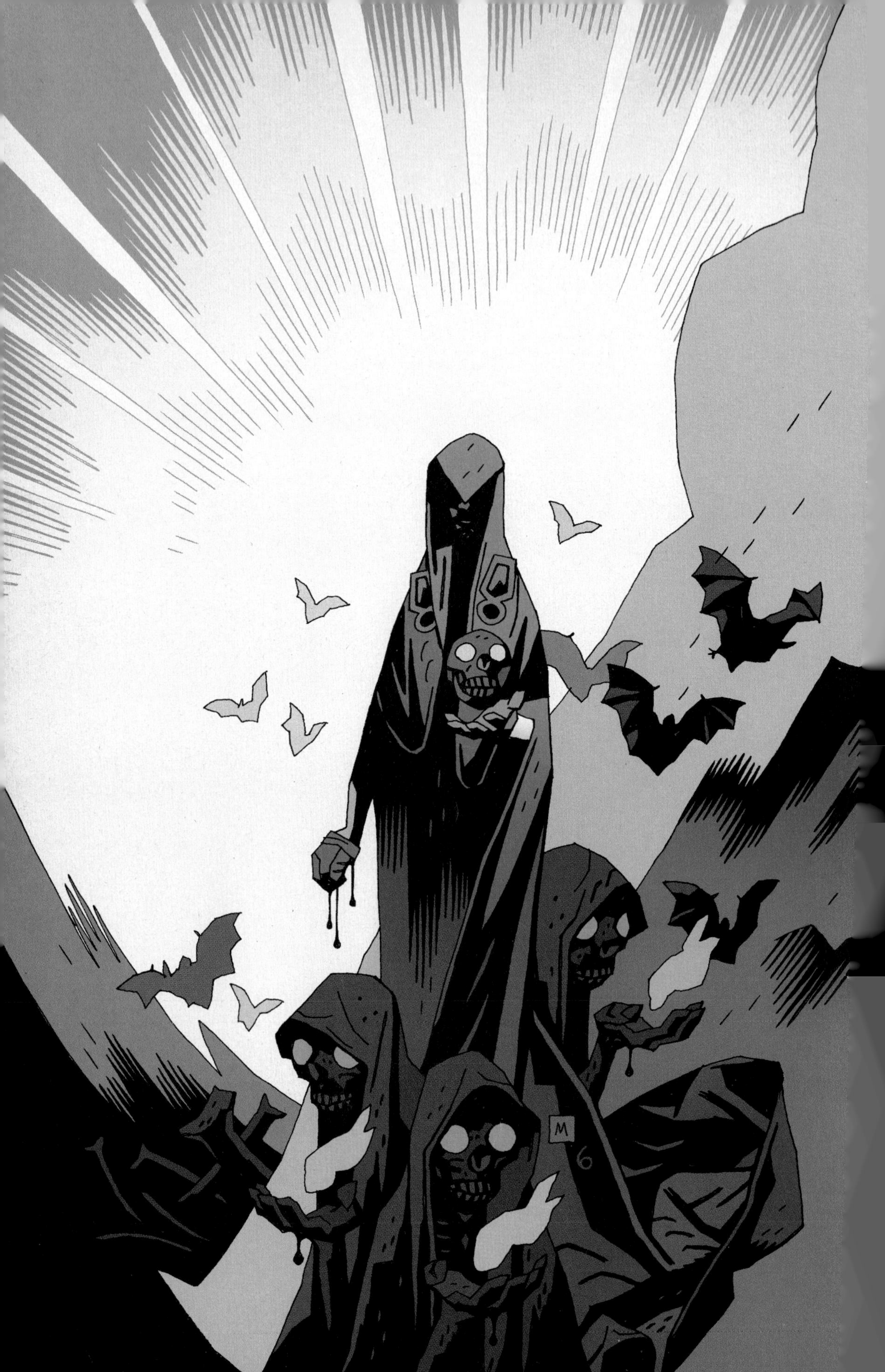
M
6
art by Mike Mignola & Dave Stewart

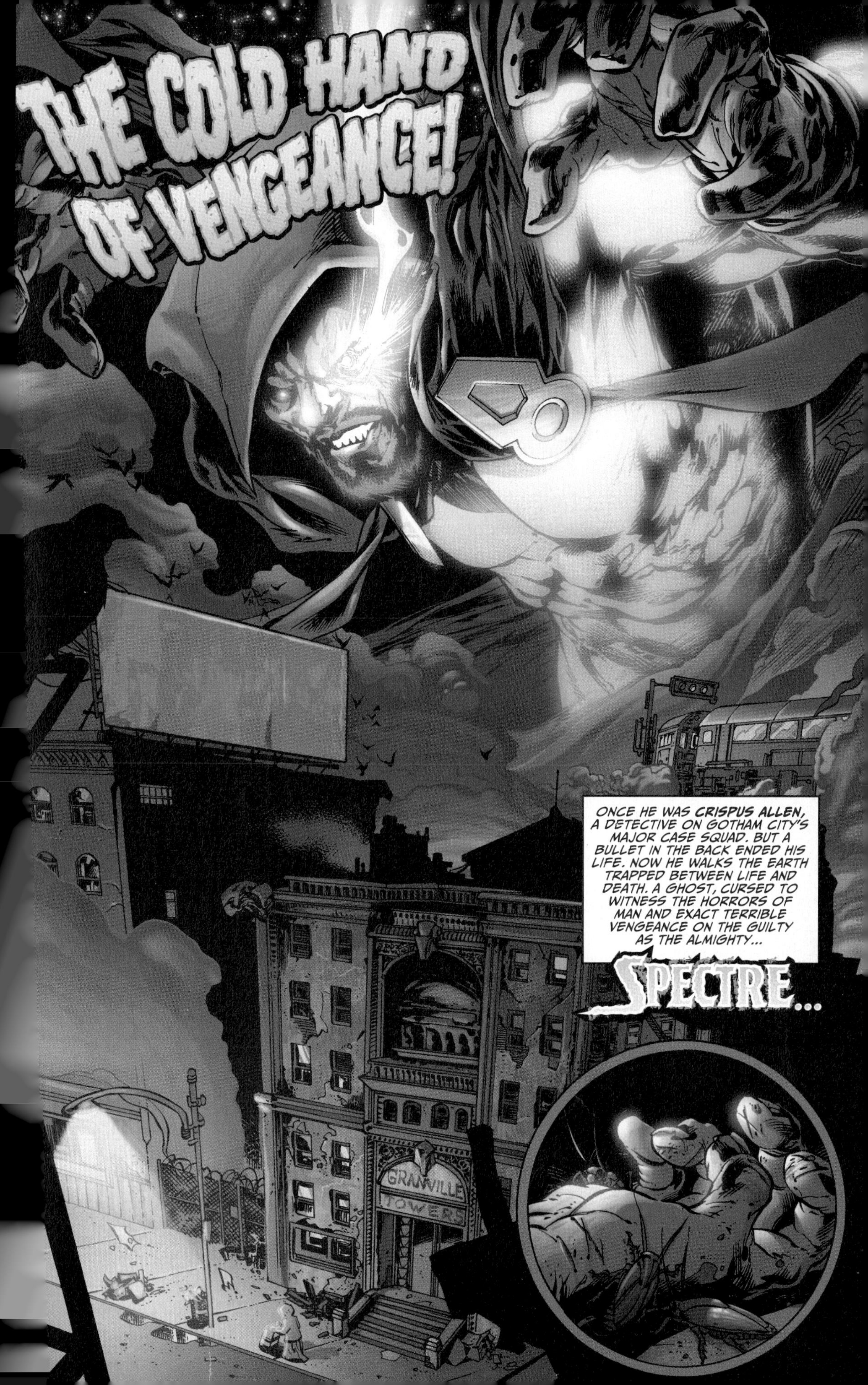
THE COLD HAND OF VENGEANCE!
ONCE HE WAS CRISPUS ALLEN, A DETECTIVE ON GOTHAM CITY'S MAJOR CASE SQUAD. BUT A BULLET IN THE BACK ENDED HIS LIFE. NOW HE WALKS THE EARTH TRAPPED BETWEEN LIFE AND DEATH. A GHOST, CURSED TO WITNESS THE HORRORS OF MAN AND EXACT TERRIBLE VENGEANCE ON THE GUILTY AS THE ALMIGHTY...
SPECTRE...
GRANVILLE TOWERS

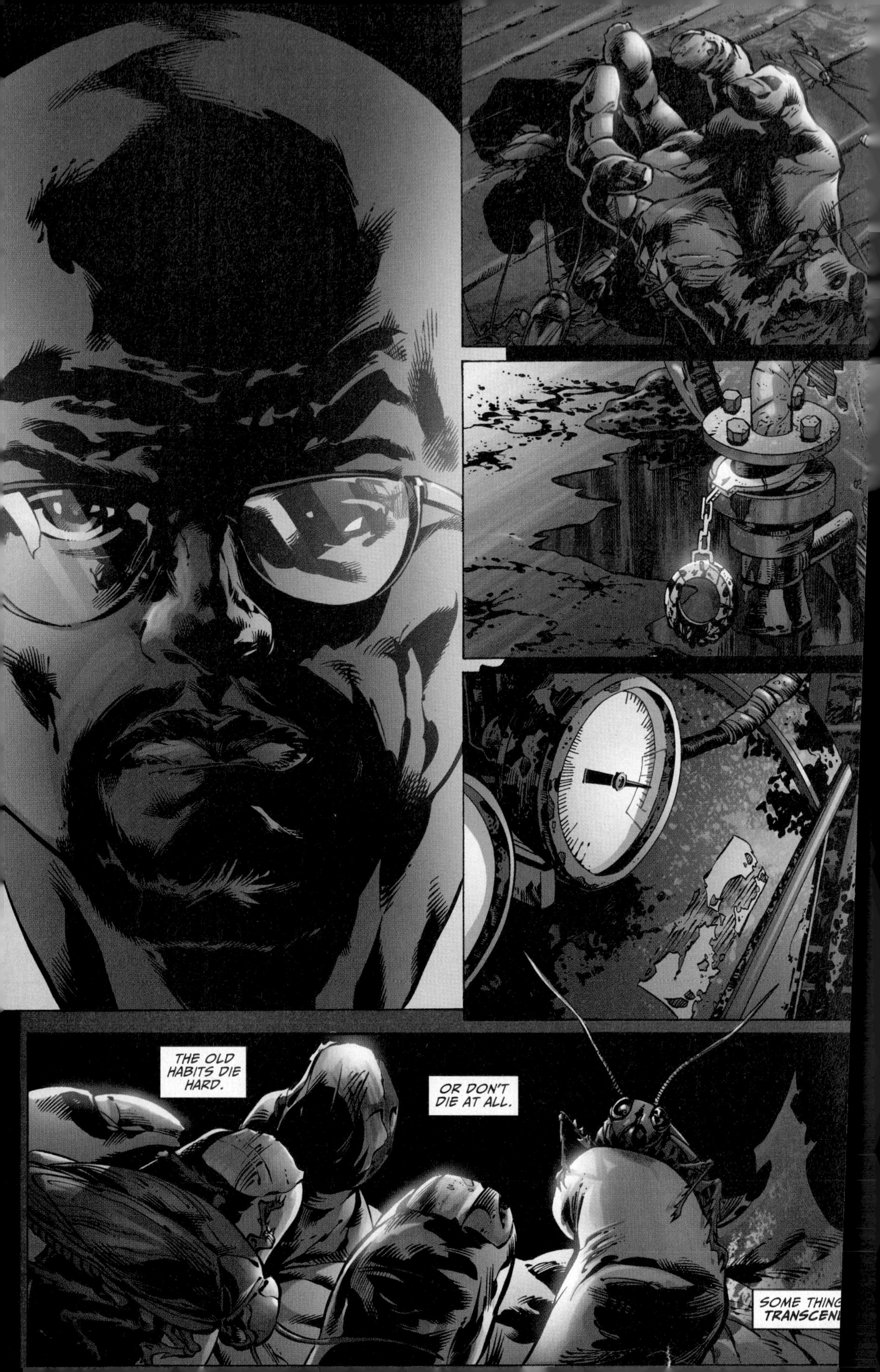
THE OLD HABITS DIE HARD.
OR DON'T DIE AT ALL.
SOME THING
TRANSCEN

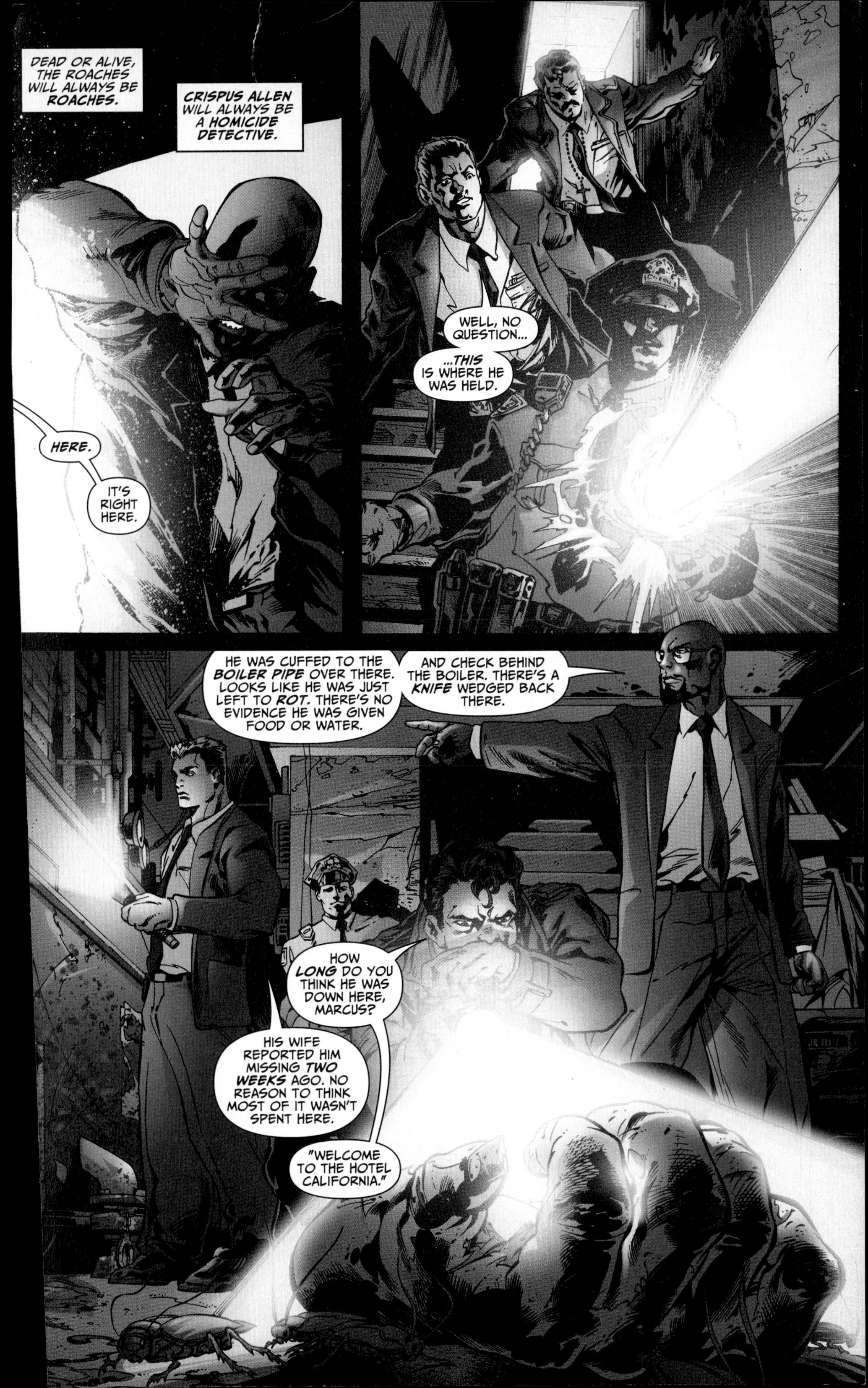
DEAD OR ALIVE, THE ROACHES WILL ALWAYS BE ROACHES.
CRISPUS ALLEN WILL ALWAYS BE A HOMICIDE DETECTIVE.
HERE.
IT'S RIGHT HERE.
WELL, NO QUESTION...
...THIS IS WHERE HE WAS HELD.
HE WAS CUFFED TO THE BOILER PIPE OVER THERE. LOOKS LIKE HE WAS JUST LEFT TO ROT. THERE'S NO EVIDENCE HE WAS GIVEN FOOD OR WATER.
AND CHECK BEHIND THE BOILER. THERE'S A KNIFE WEDGED BACK THERE.
HOW LONG DO YOU THINK HE WAS DOWN HERE, MARCUS?
HIS WIFE REPORTED HIM MISSING TWO WEEKS AGO. NO REASON TO THINK MOST OF IT WASN'T SPENT HERE.
"WELCOME TO THE HOTEL CALIFORNIA."

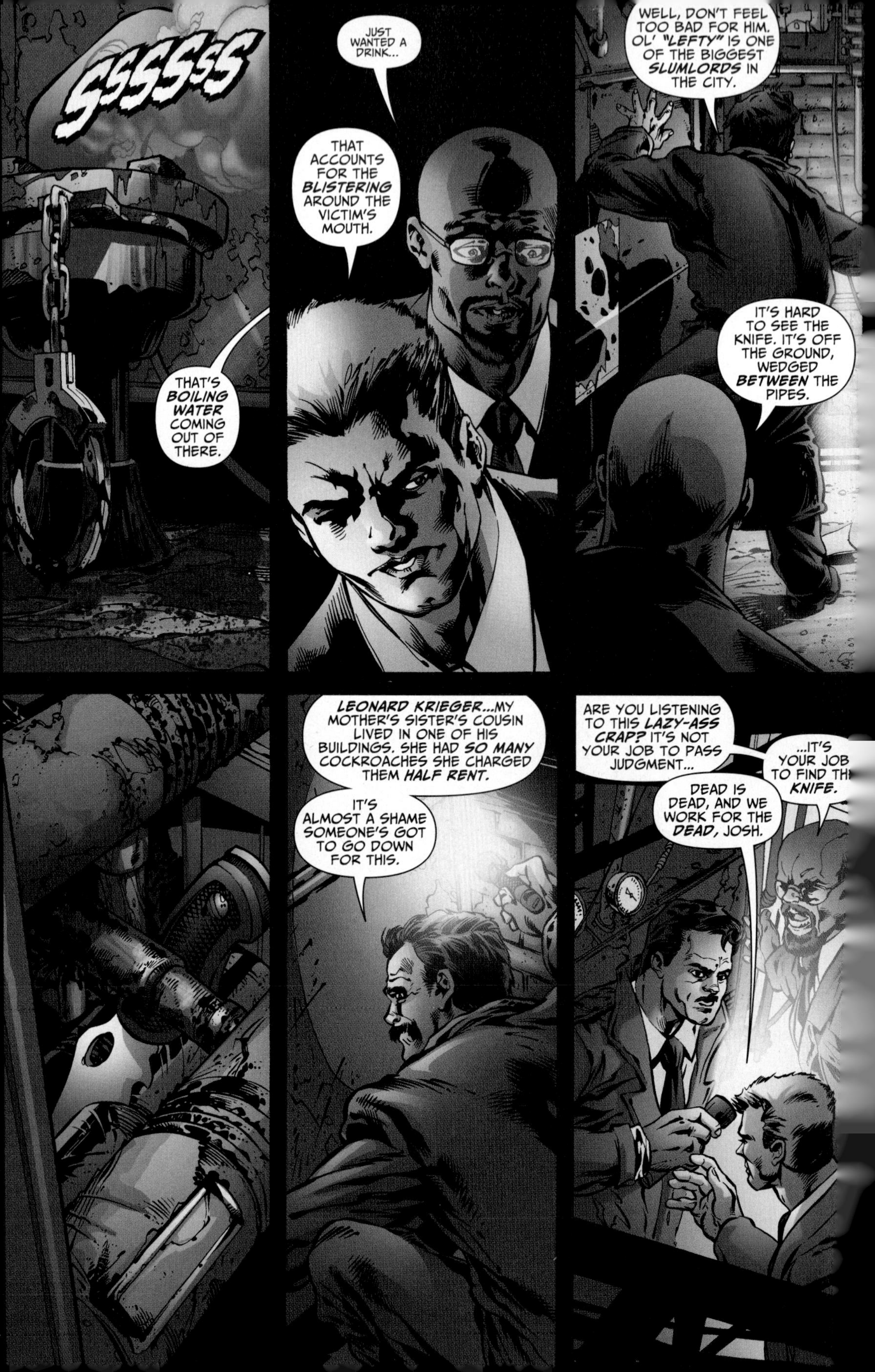
SSSSSS
THAT'S BOILING WATER COMING OUT OF THERE.
JUST WANTED A DRINK...
THAT ACCOUNTS FOR THE BLISTERING AROUND THE VICTIM'S MOUTH.
WELL, DON'T FEEL TOO BAD FOR HIM. OL' "LEFTY" IS ONE OF THE BIGGEST SLUMLORDS IN THE CITY.
IT'S HARD TO SEE THE KNIFE. IT'S OFF THE GROUND, WEDGED BETWEEN THE PIPES.
LEONARD KRIEGER...MY MOTHER'S SISTER'S COUSIN LIVED IN ONE OF HIS BUILDINGS. SHE HAD SO MANY COCKROACHES SHE CHARGED THEM HALF RENT.
IT'S ALMOST A SHAME SOMEONE'S GOT TO GO DOWN FOR THIS.
ARE YOU LISTENING TO THIS LAZY-ASS CRAP? IT'S NOT YOUR JOB TO PASS JUDGMENT...
...IT'S YOUR JOB TO FIND THE KNIFE.
DEAD IS DEAD, AND WE WORK FOR THE DEAD, JOSH.

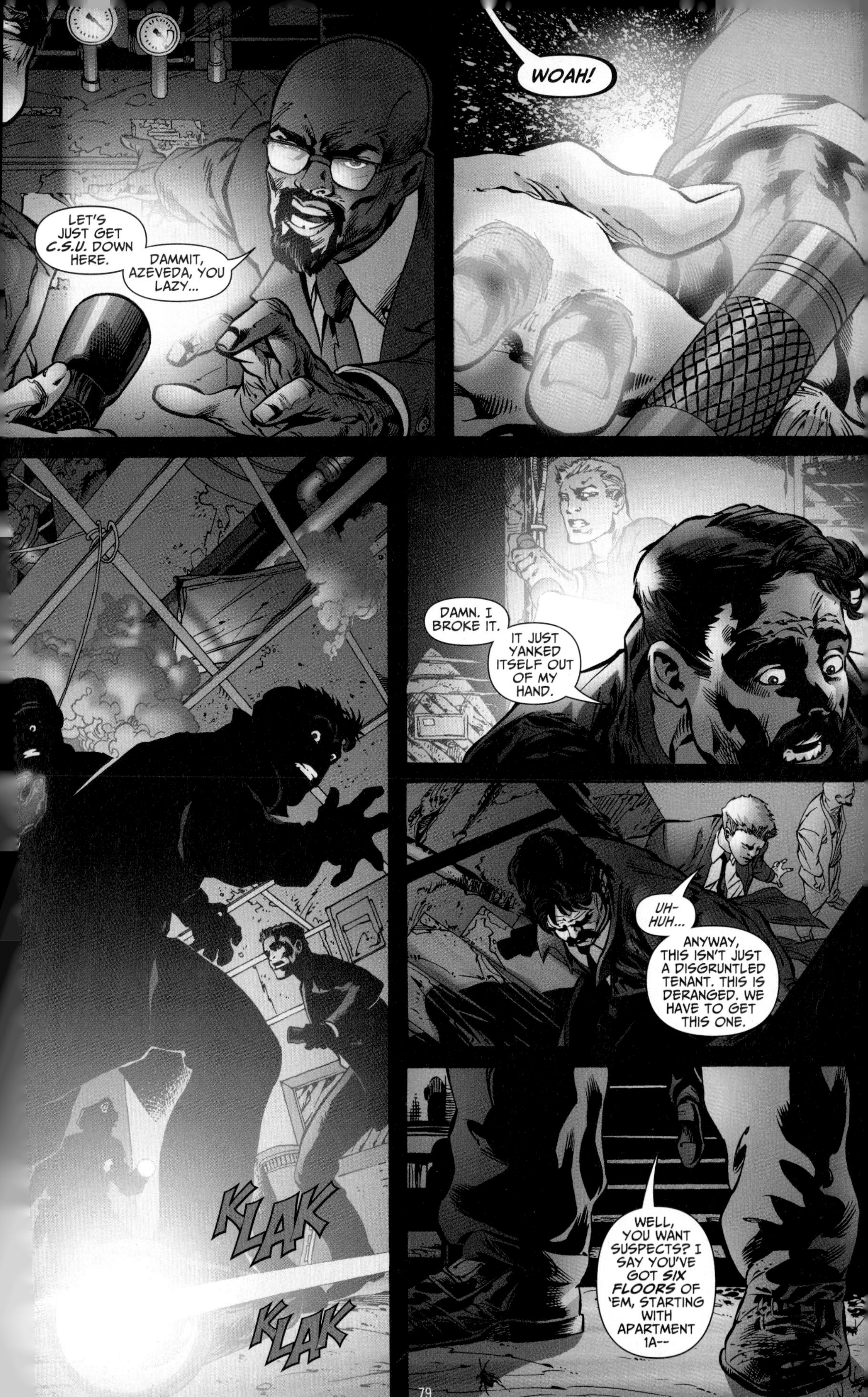

LET'S JUST GET C.S.U. DOWN HERE.
DAMMIT, AZEVEDA, YOU LAZY...
WOAH!
KLAK
KLAK
DAMN. I BROKE IT.
IT JUST YANKED ITSELF OUT OF MY HAND.
UH-HUH...
ANYWAY, THIS ISN'T JUST A DISGRUNTLED TENANT. THIS IS DERANGED. WE HAVE TO GET THIS ONE.
WELL, YOU WANT SUSPECTS? I SAY YOU'VE GOT SIX FLOORS OF 'EM, STARTING WITH APARTMENT 1A--

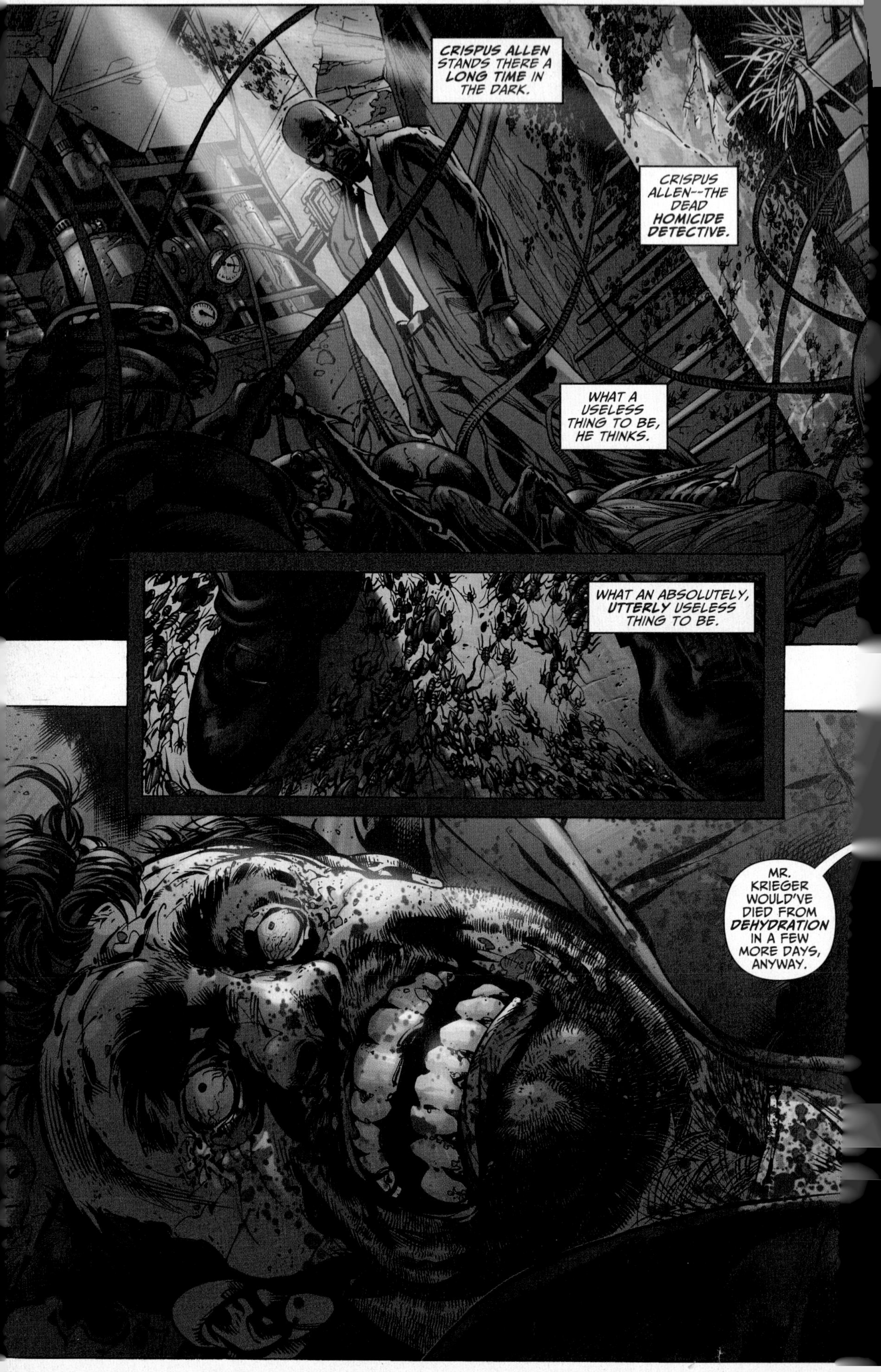
CRISPUS ALLEN STANDS THERE A LONG TIME IN THE DARK.
CRISPUS ALLEN--THE DEAD HOMICIDE DETECTIVE.
WHAT A USELESS THING TO BE, HE THINKS.
WHAT AN ABSOLUTELY, UTTERLY USELESS THING TO BE.
MR. KRIEGER WOULD'VE DIED FROM DEHYDRATION IN A FEW MORE DAYS, ANYWAY.

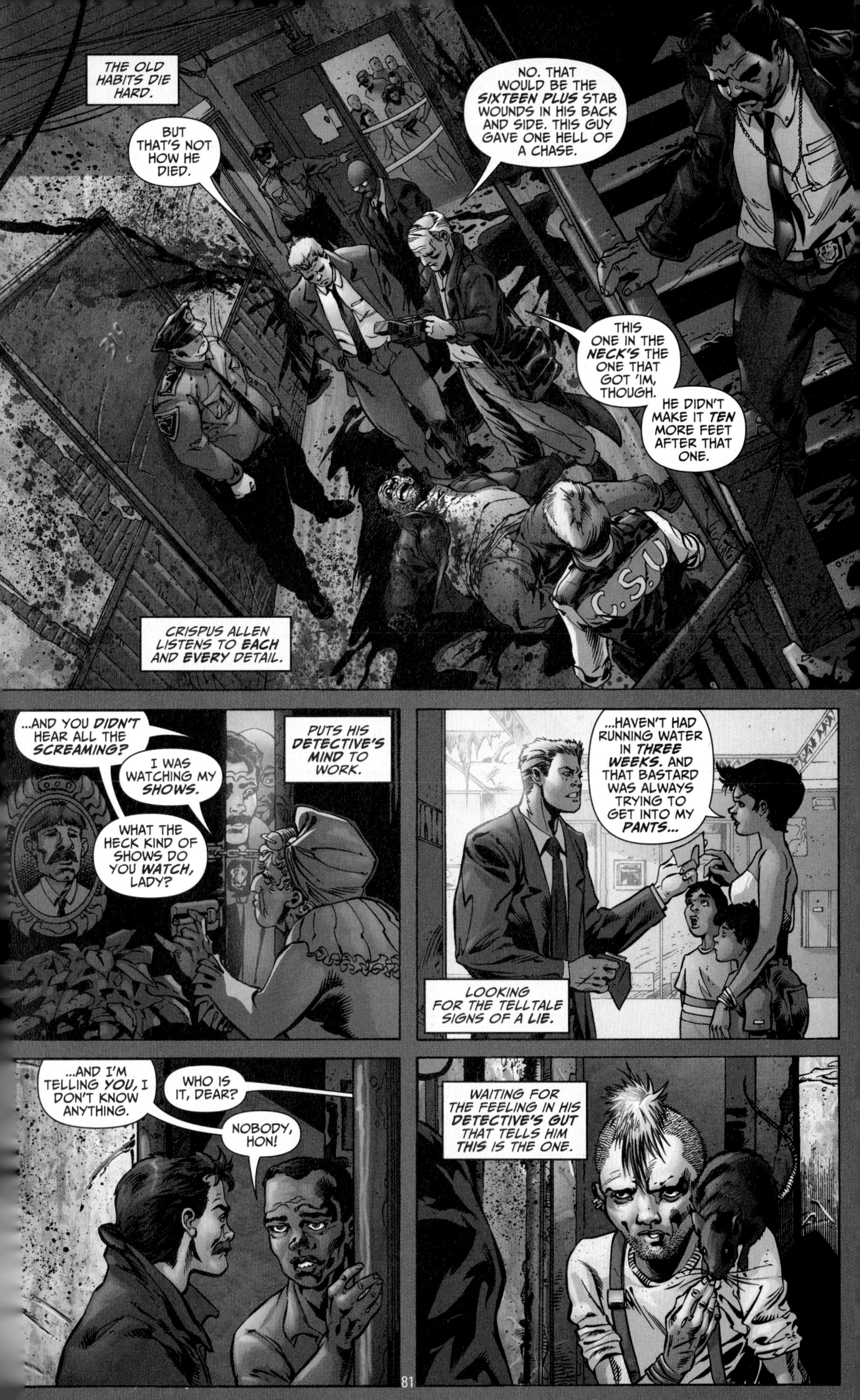
THE OLD HABITS DIE HARD.
BUT THAT'S NOT HOW HE DIED.
NO. THAT WOULD BE THE SIXTEEN PLUS STAB WOUNDS IN HIS BACK AND SIDE. THIS GUY GAVE ONE HELL OF A CHASE.
THIS ONE IN THE NECK'S THE ONE THAT GOT 'IM, THOUGH.
HE DIDN'T MAKE IT TEN MORE FEET AFTER THAT ONE.
C.S.U.
CRISPUS ALLEN LISTENS TO EACH AND EVERY DETAIL.
...AND YOU DIDN'T HEAR ALL THE SCREAMING?
I WAS WATCHING MY SHOWS.
WHAT THE HECK KIND OF SHOWS DO YOU WATCH, LADY?
PUTS HIS DETECTIVE'S MIND TO WORK.
...HAVEN'T HAD RUNNING WATER IN THREE WEEKS. AND THAT BASTARD WAS ALWAYS TRYING TO GET INTO MY PANTS...
LOOKING FOR THE TELLTALE SIGNS OF A LIE.
...AND I'M TELLING YOU, I DON'T KNOW ANYTHING.
WHO IS IT, DEAR?
NOBODY, HON!
WAITING FOR THE FEELING IN HIS DETECTIVE'S GUT THAT TELLS HIM THIS IS THE ONE.

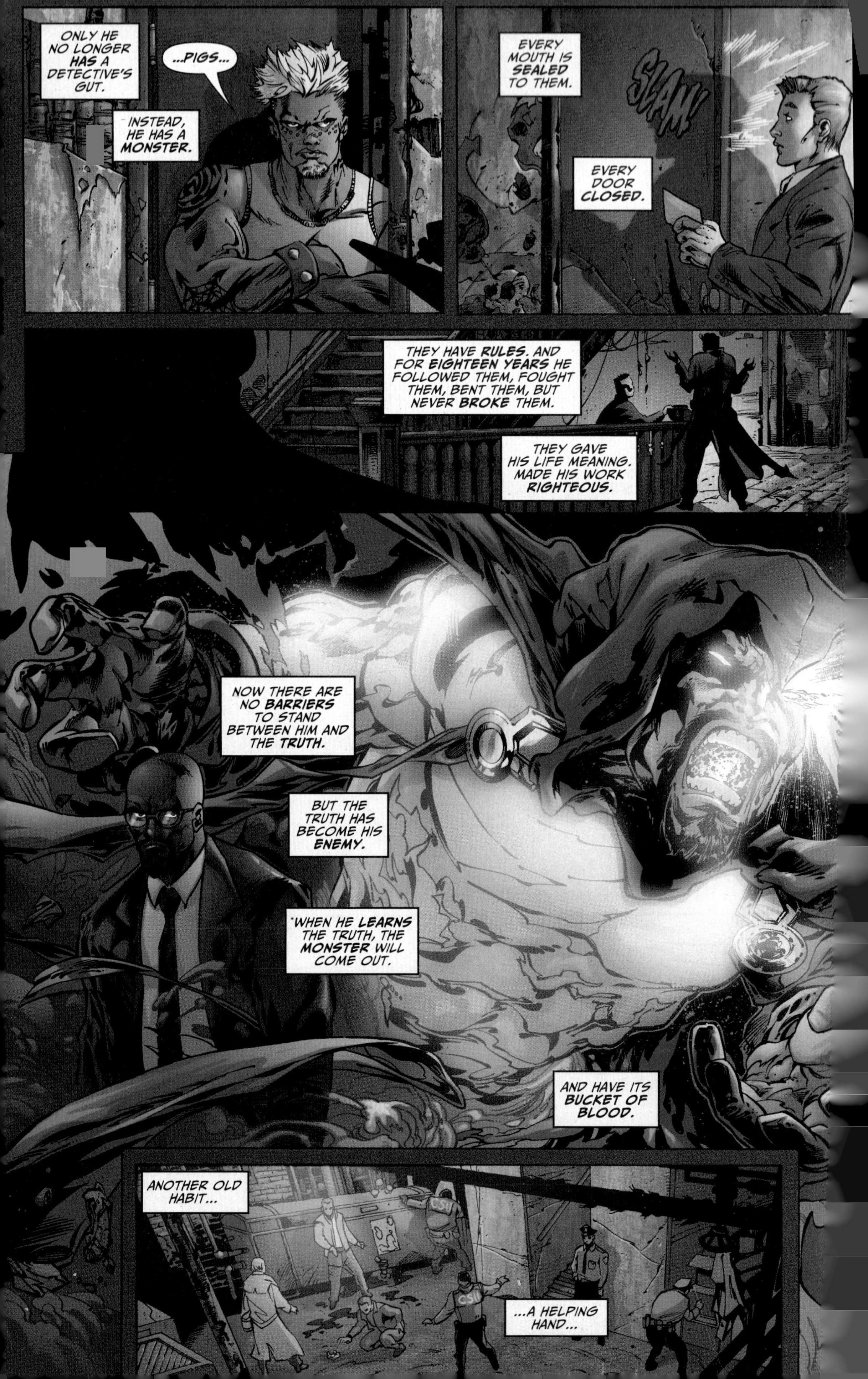
ONLY HE NO LONGER HAS A DETECTIVE'S GUT.
...PIGS...
INSTEAD, HE HAS A MONSTER.
EVERY MOUTH IS SEALED TO THEM.
SLAM!
EVERY DOOR CLOSED.
THEY HAVE RULES. AND FOR EIGHTEEN YEARS HE FOLLOWED THEM, FOUGHT THEM, BENT THEM, BUT NEVER BROKE THEM.
THEY GAVE HIS LIFE MEANING. MADE HIS WORK RIGHTEOUS.
NOW THERE ARE NO BARRIERS TO STAND BETWEEN HIM AND THE TRUTH.
BUT THE TRUTH HAS BECOME HIS ENEMY.
WHEN HE LEARNS THE TRUTH, THE MONSTER WILL COME OUT.
AND HAVE ITS BUCKET OF BLOOD.
ANOTHER OLD HABIT...
...A HELPING HAND...

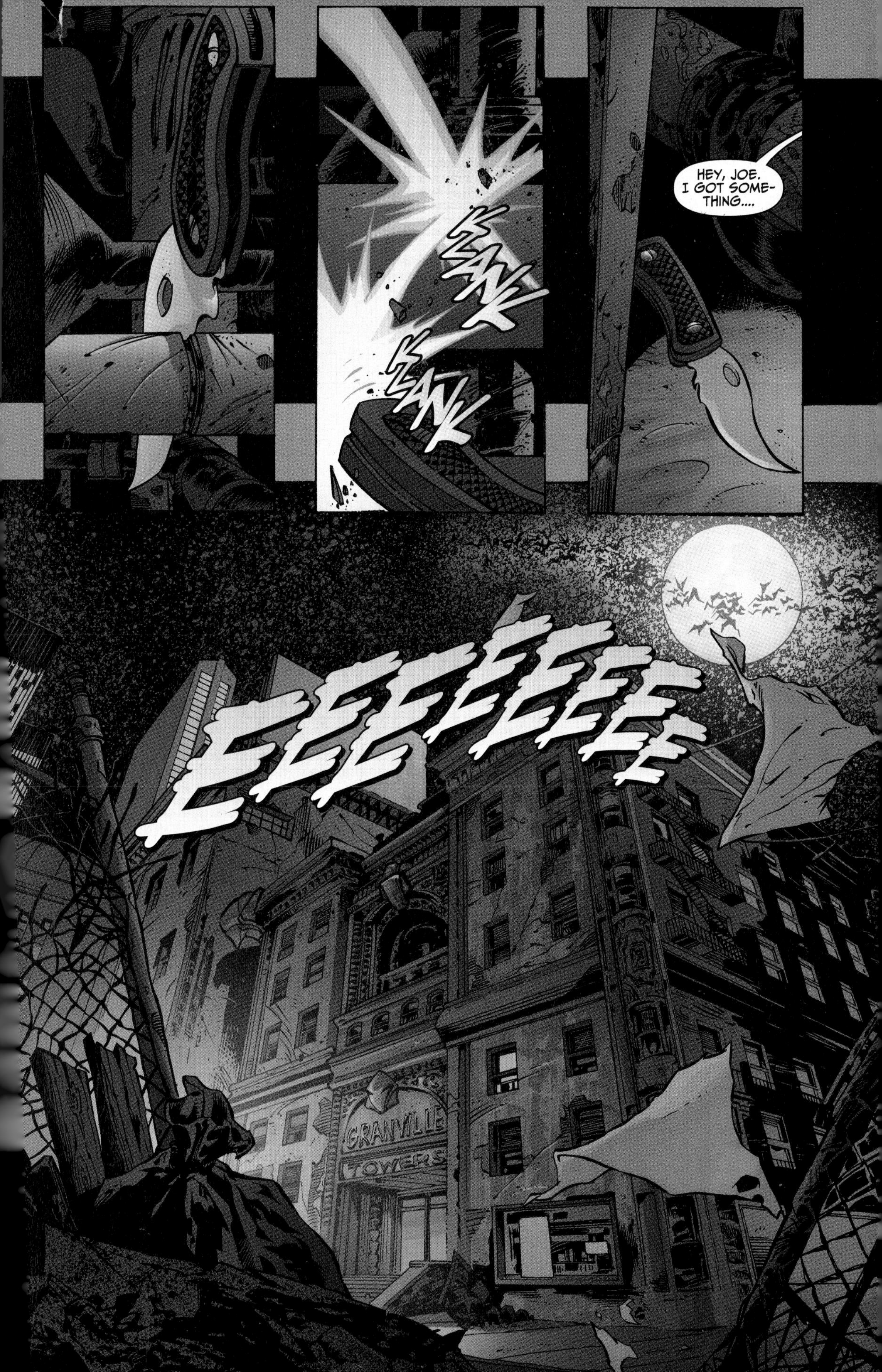
KLANK
KLANK
HEY, JOE. I GOT SOME-THING....
EEEEEEEEEE
GRANVILLE TOWERS

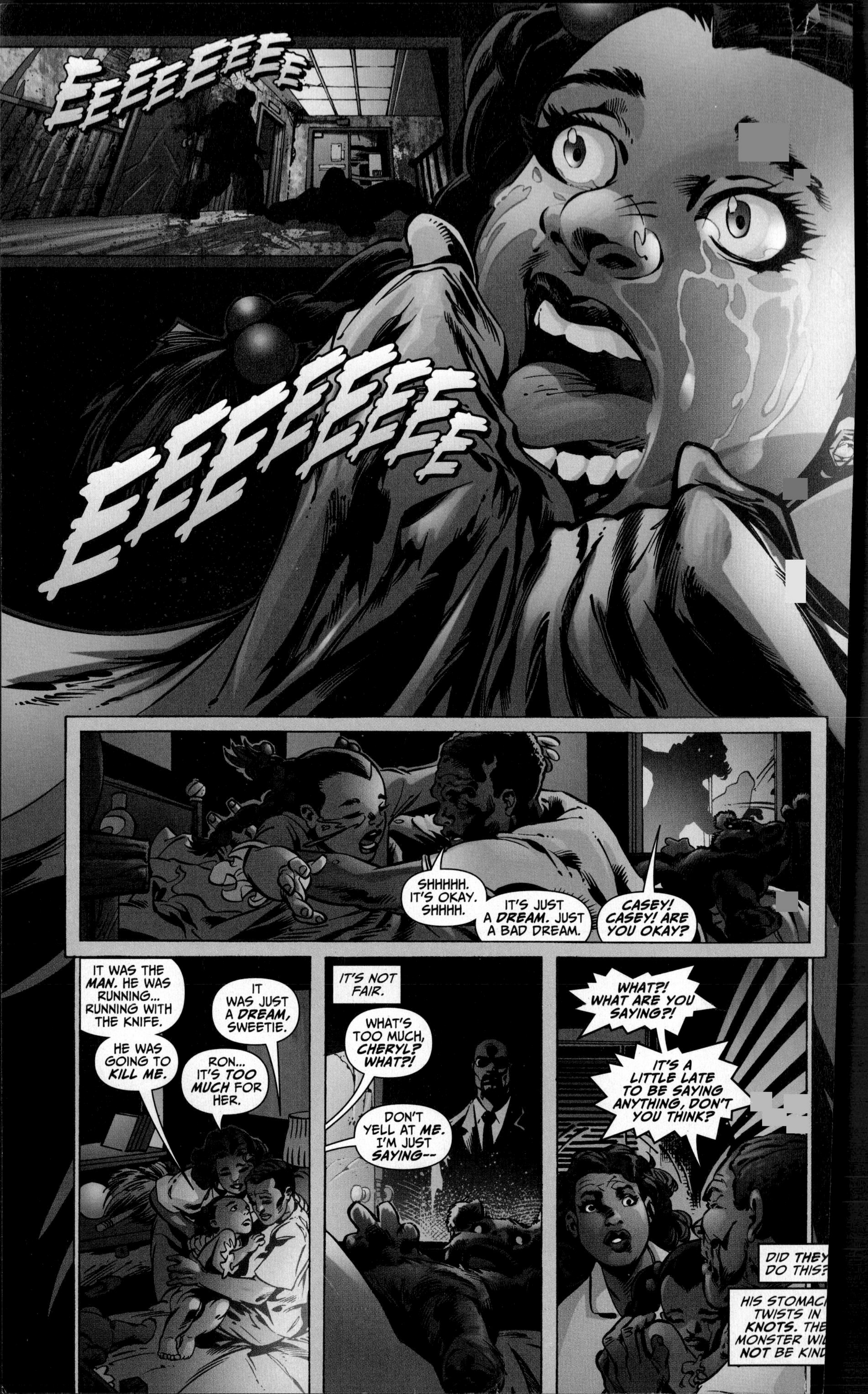
EEEEEEEEE
EEEEEEEEE
SHHHHH. IT'S OKAY. SHHHH.
IT'S JUST A DREAM. JUST A BAD DREAM.
CASEY! CASEY! ARE YOU OKAY?
IT WAS THE MAN. HE WAS RUNNING... RUNNING WITH THE KNIFE.
HE WAS GOING TO KILL ME.
IT WAS JUST A DREAM, SWEETIE.
RON... IT'S TOO MUCH FOR HER.
IT'S NOT FAIR.
WHAT'S TOO MUCH, CHERYL? WHAT?!
DON'T YELL AT ME. I'M JUST SAYING--
WHAT?! WHAT ARE YOU SAYING?!
IT'S A LITTLE LATE TO BE SAYING ANYTHING, DON'T YOU THINK?
DID THEY DO THIS?
HIS STOMACH TWISTS IN KNOTS. THE MONSTER WILL NOT BE KIND

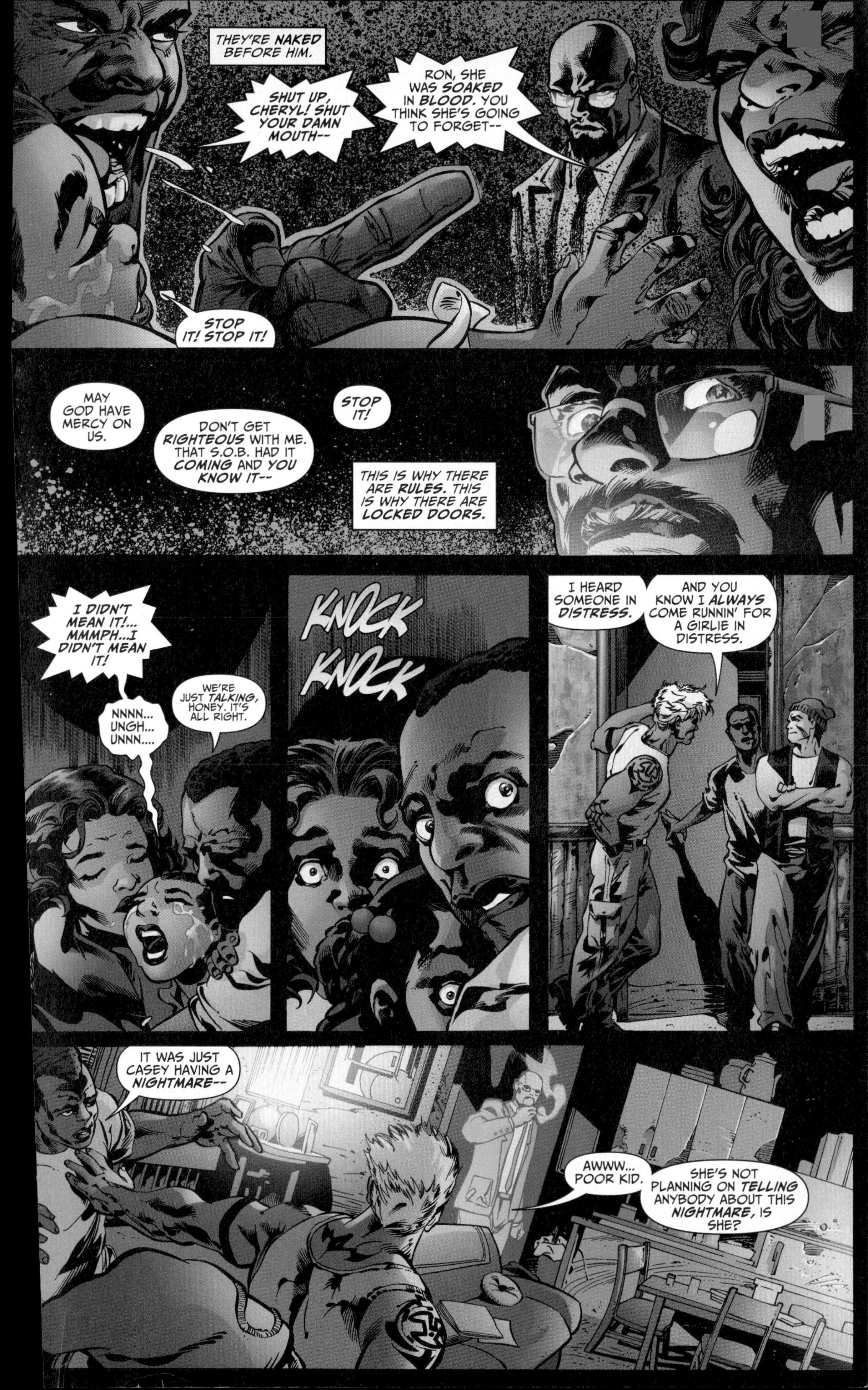
THEY'RE NAKED BEFORE HIM.
SHUT UP, CHERYL! SHUT YOUR DAMN MOUTH--
RON, SHE WAS SOAKED IN BLOOD. YOU THINK SHE'S GOING TO FORGET--
STOP IT! STOP IT!
MAY GOD HAVE MERCY ON US.
DON'T GET RIGHTEOUS WITH ME. THAT S.O.B. HAD IT COMING AND YOU KNOW IT--
STOP IT!
THIS IS WHY THERE ARE RULES. THIS IS WHY THERE ARE LOCKED DOORS.
I DIDN'T MEAN IT!... MMMPH...I DIDN'T MEAN IT!
NNNN... UNGH... UNNN....
WE'RE JUST TALKING, HONEY. IT'S ALL RIGHT.
KNOCK
KNOCK
I HEARD SOMEONE IN DISTRESS.
AND YOU KNOW I ALWAYS COME RUNNIN' FOR A GIRLIE IN DISTRESS.
IT WAS JUST CASEY HAVING A NIGHTMARE--
AWWW... POOR KID.
SHE'S NOT PLANNING ON TELLING ANYBODY ABOUT THIS NIGHTMARE, IS SHE?

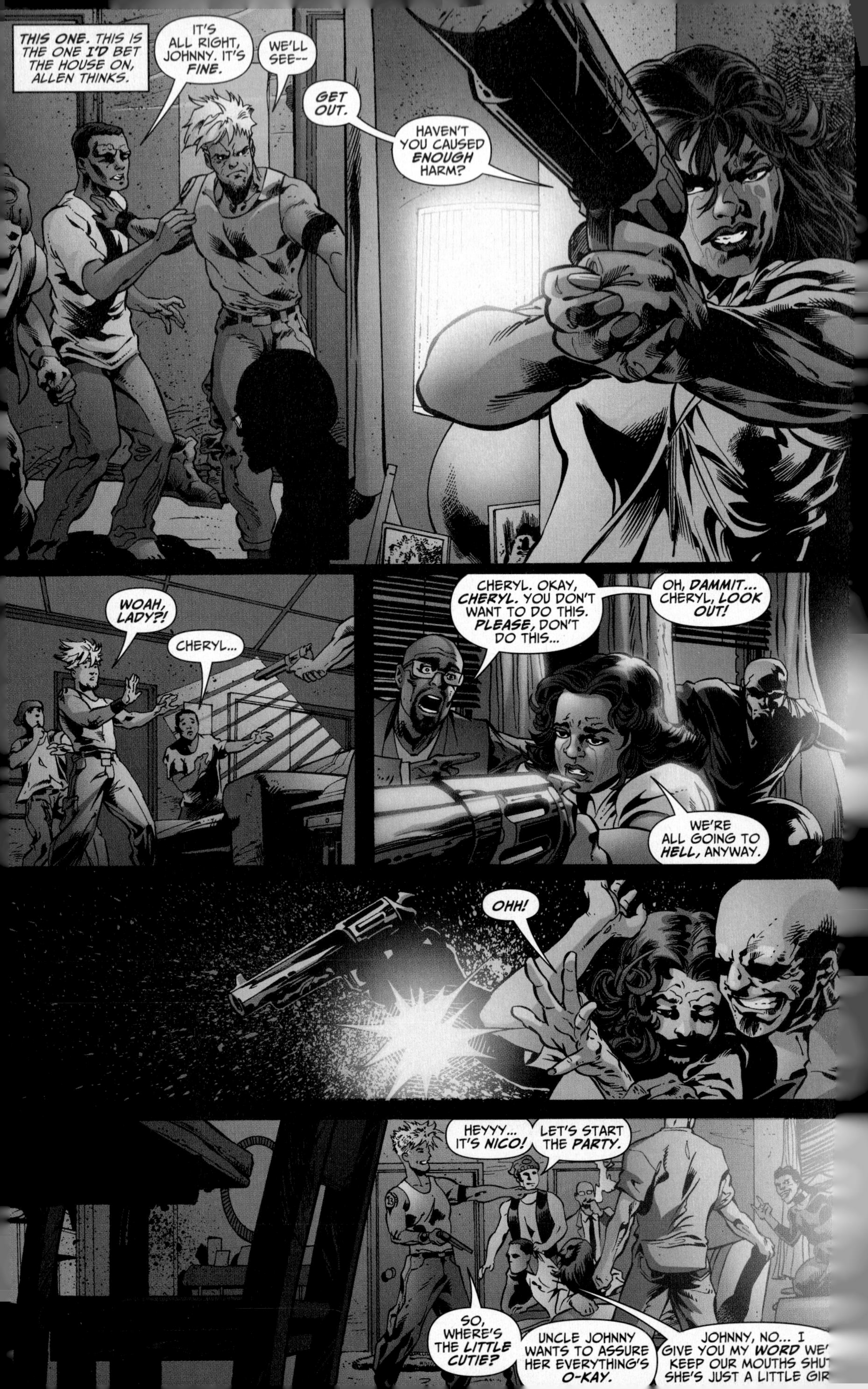
THIS ONE. THIS IS THE ONE I'D BET THE HOUSE ON, ALLEN THINKS.
IT'S ALL RIGHT, JOHNNY. IT'S FINE.
WE'LL SEE--
GET OUT.
HAVEN'T YOU CAUSED ENOUGH HARM?
WOAH, LADY?!
CHERYL...
CHERYL. OKAY, CHERYL. YOU DON'T WANT TO DO THIS. PLEASE, DON'T DO THIS...
OH, DAMMIT... CHERYL, LOOK OUT!
WE'RE ALL GOING TO HELL, ANYWAY.
OHH!
HEYYY... IT'S NICO!
LET'S START THE PARTY.
SO, WHERE'S THE LITTLE CUTIE?
UNCLE JOHNNY WANTS TO ASSURE HER EVERYTHING'S O-KAY.
JOHNNY, NO... I GIVE YOU MY WORD WE' KEEP OUR MOUTHS SHUT SHE'S JUST A LITTLE GIR

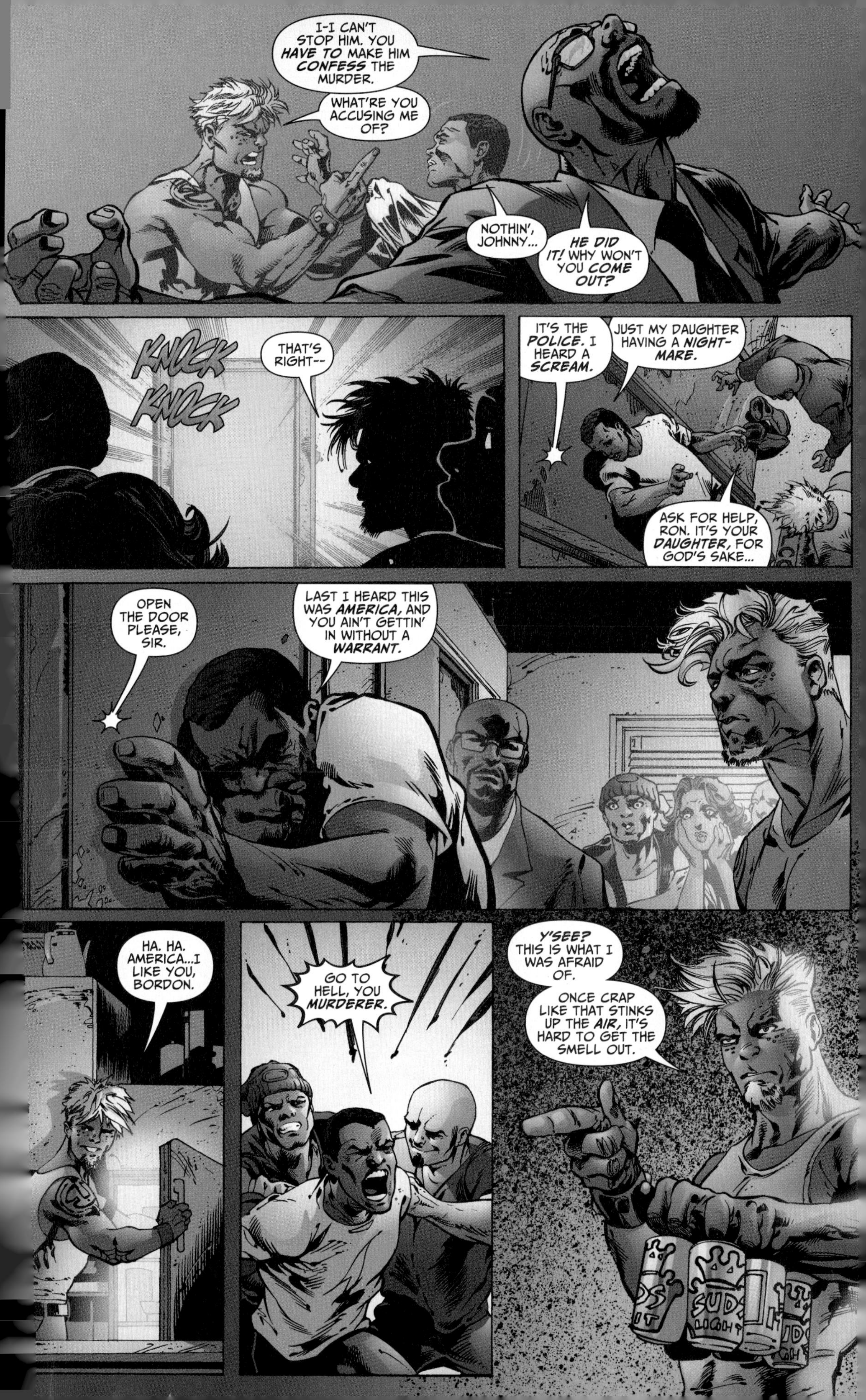
I-I CAN'T STOP HIM. YOU HAVE TO MAKE HIM CONFESS THE MURDER.
WHAT'RE YOU ACCUSING ME OF?
NOTHIN', JOHNNY...
HE DID IT! WHY WON'T YOU COME OUT?
KNOCK KNOCK
THAT'S RIGHT--
IT'S THE POLICE. I HEARD A SCREAM.
JUST MY DAUGHTER HAVING A NIGHT-MARE.
ASK FOR HELP, RON. IT'S YOUR DAUGHTER, FOR GOD'S SAKE...
OPEN THE DOOR PLEASE, SIR.
LAST I HEARD THIS WAS AMERICA, AND YOU AIN'T GETTIN' IN WITHOUT A WARRANT.
HA. HA. AMERICA...I LIKE YOU, BORDON.
GO TO HELL, YOU MURDERER.
Y'SEE? THIS IS WHAT I WAS AFRAID OF.
ONCE CRAP LIKE THAT STINKS UP THE AIR, IT'S HARD TO GET THE SMELL OUT.

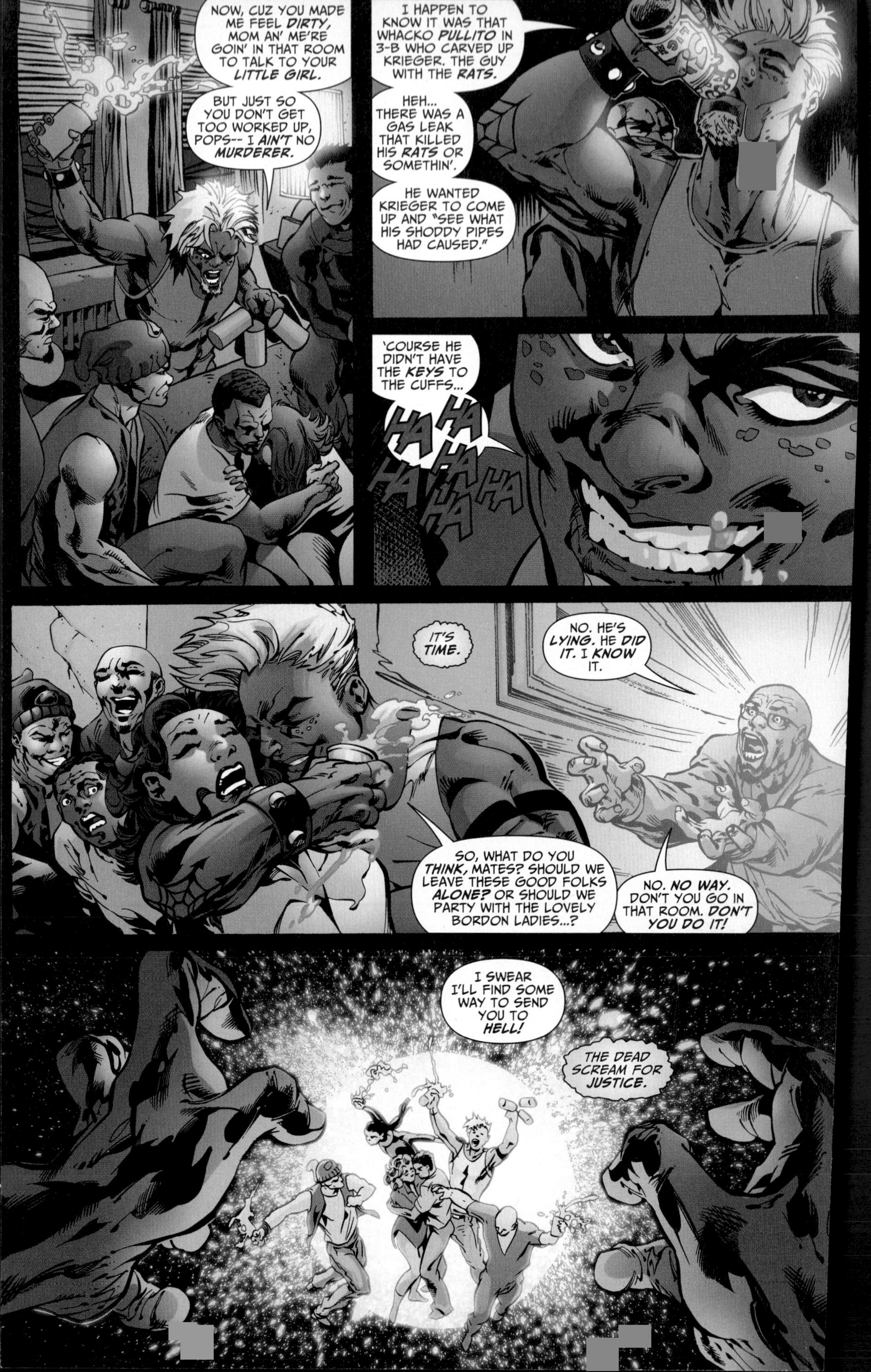

NOW, CUZ YOU MADE ME FEEL DIRTY, MOM AN' ME'RE GOIN' IN THAT ROOM TO TALK TO YOUR LITTLE GIRL.
BUT JUST SO YOU DON'T GET TOO WORKED UP, POPS-- I AIN'T NO MURDERER.
I HAPPEN TO KNOW IT WAS THAT WHACKO PULLITO IN 3-B WHO CARVED UP KRIEGER. THE GUY WITH THE RATS.
HEH... THERE WAS A GAS LEAK THAT KILLED HIS RATS OR SOMETHIN'.
HE WANTED KRIEGER TO COME UP AND "SEE WHAT HIS SHODDY PIPES HAD CAUSED."
'COURSE HE DIDN'T HAVE THE KEYS TO THE CUFFS...
HA HA HA HA HA HA HA
IT'S TIME.
NO. HE'S LYING. HE DID IT. I KNOW IT.
SO, WHAT DO YOU THINK, MATES? SHOULD WE LEAVE THESE GOOD FOLKS ALONE? OR SHOULD WE PARTY WITH THE LOVELY BORDON LADIES...?
NO. NO WAY. DON'T YOU GO IN THAT ROOM. DON'T YOU DO IT!
I SWEAR I'LL FIND SOME WAY TO SEND YOU TO HELL!
THE DEAD SCREAM FOR JUSTICE.

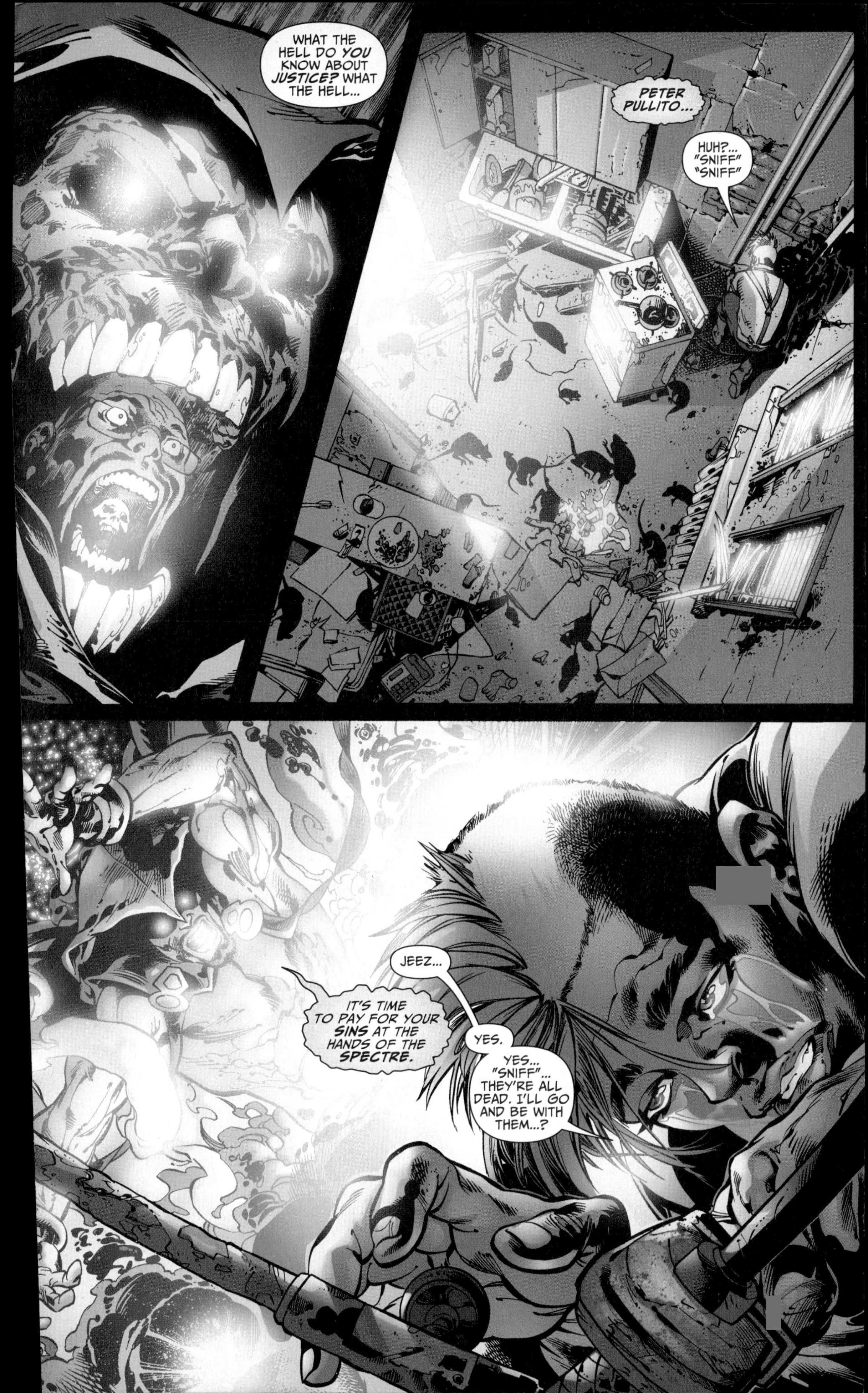
WHAT THE HELL DO YOU KNOW ABOUT JUSTICE? WHAT THE HELL...
PETER PULLITO...
HUH?... "SNIFF" "SNIFF"
JEEZ...
IT'S TIME TO PAY FOR YOUR SINS AT THE HANDS OF THE SPECTRE.
YES.
YES... "SNIFF"... THEY'RE ALL DEAD. I'LL GO AND BE WITH THEM...?

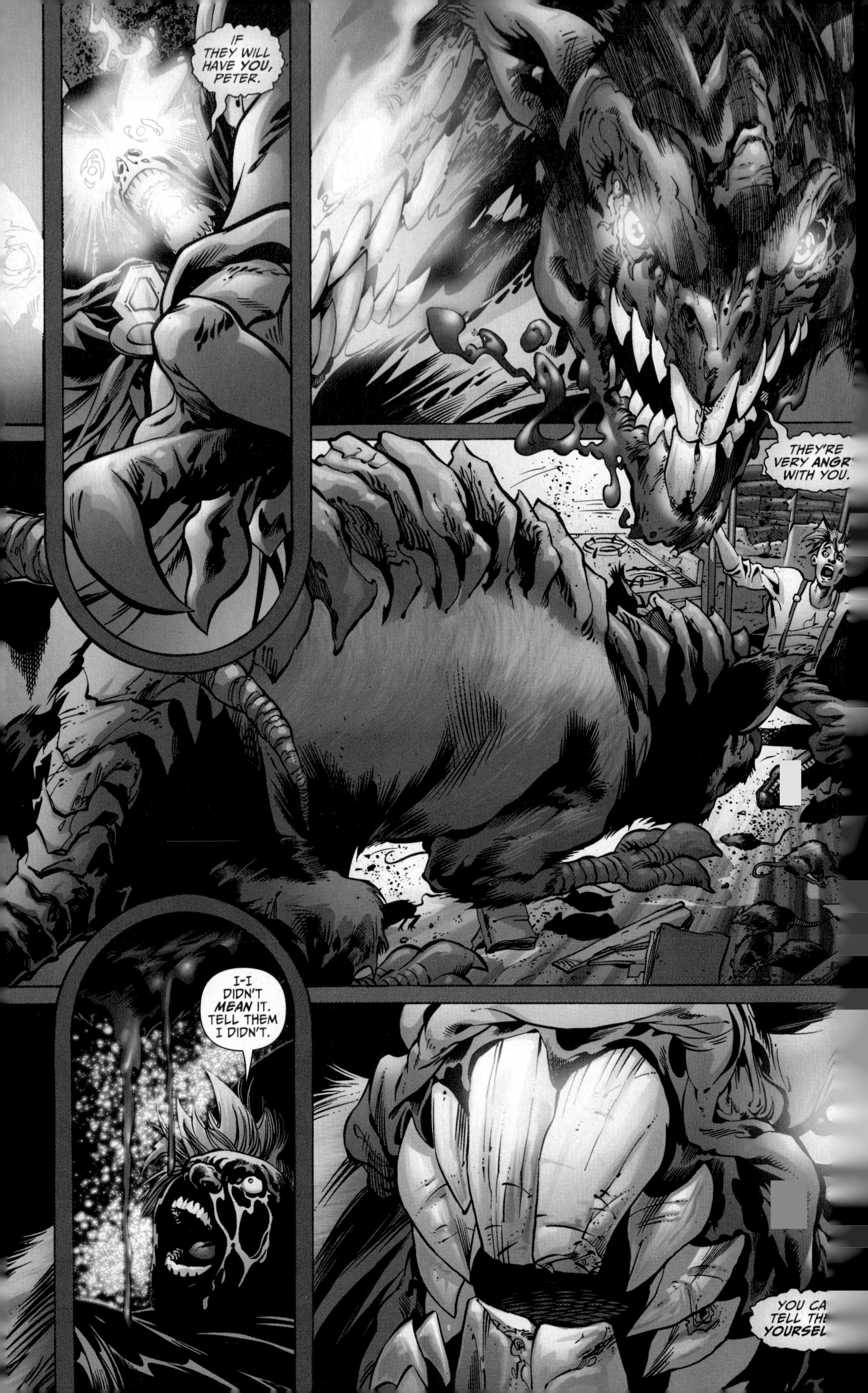
IF THEY WILL HAVE YOU, PETER.
THEY'RE VERY ANGR WITH YOU.
I-I DIDN'T MEAN IT. TELL THEM I DIDN'T.
YOU CA TELL THE YOURSEL

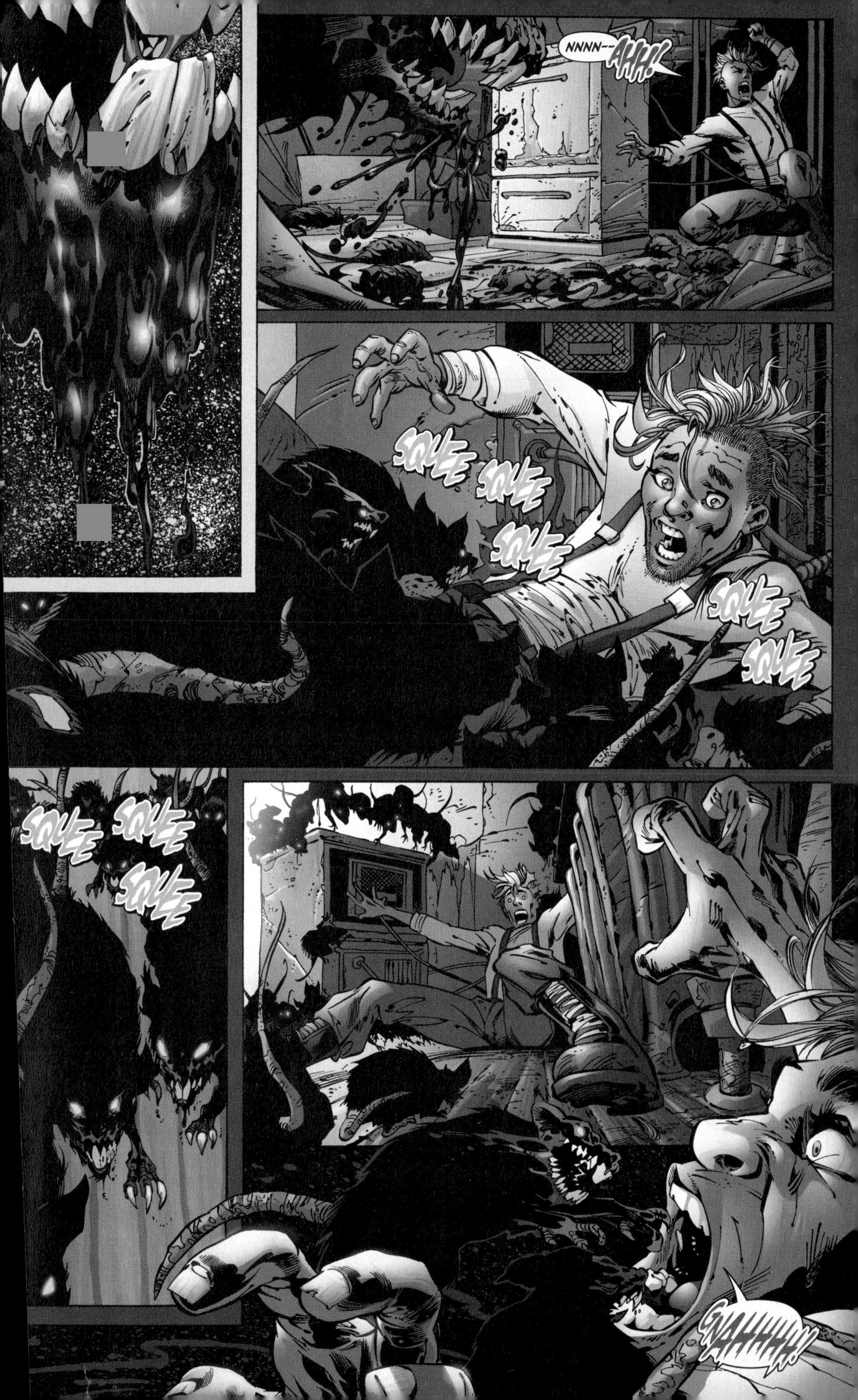
NNNN--AHH!
SQUEE
SQUEE
SQUEE
SQUEE
SQUEE
SQUEE
SQUEE
SQUEE
GNAHHHH!

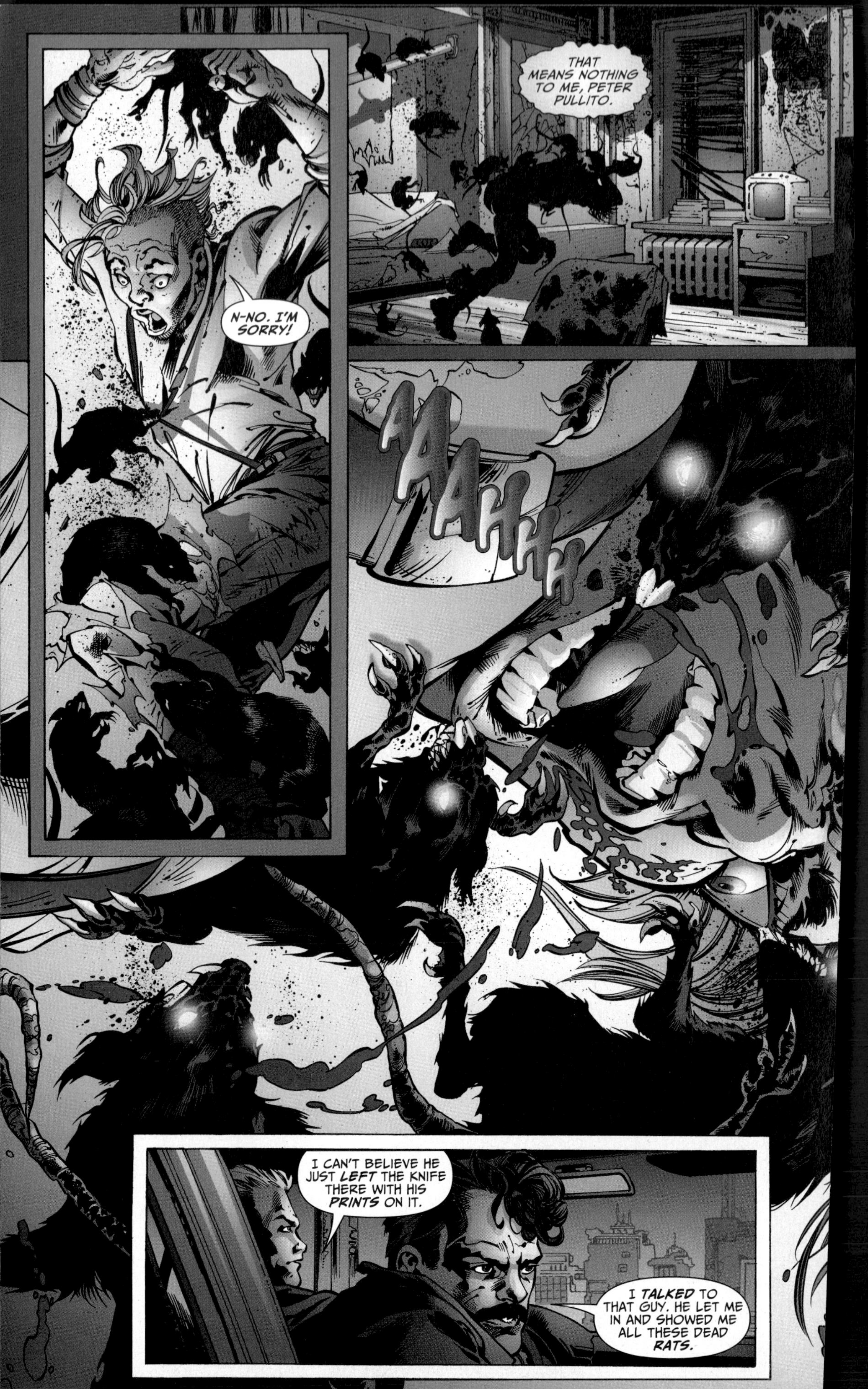
N-NO. I'M SORRY!
THAT MEANS NOTHING TO ME, PETER PULLITO.
AAAHHHH
I CAN'T BELIEVE HE JUST LEFT THE KNIFE THERE WITH HIS PRINTS ON IT.
I TALKED TO THAT GUY. HE LET ME IN AND SHOWED ME ALL THESE DEAD RATS.

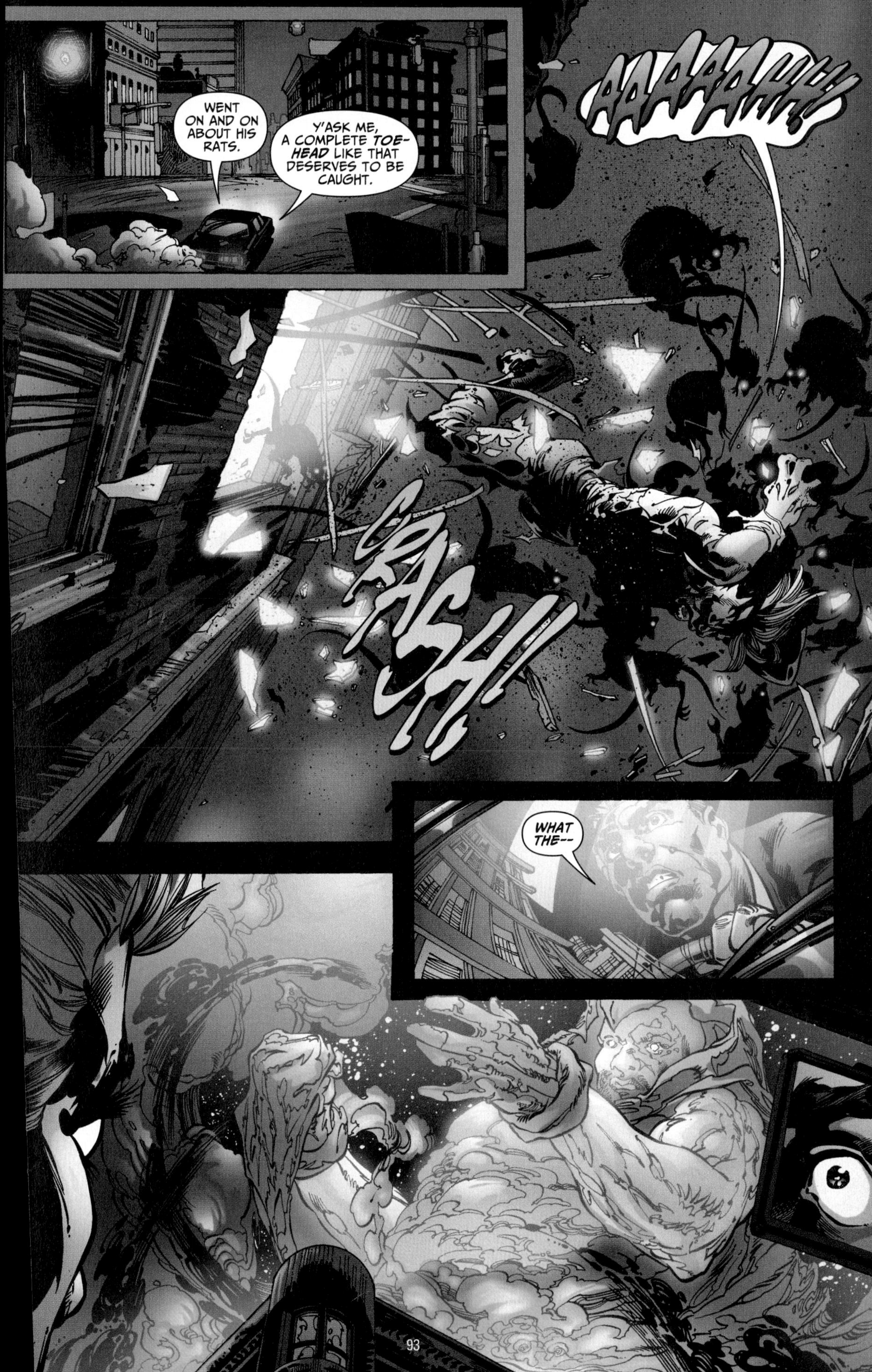
WENT ON AND ON ABOUT HIS RATS.
Y'ASK ME, A COMPLETE TOE-HEAD LIKE THAT DESERVES TO BE CAUGHT.
AAAAAHH!
CRASH!
WHAT THE--

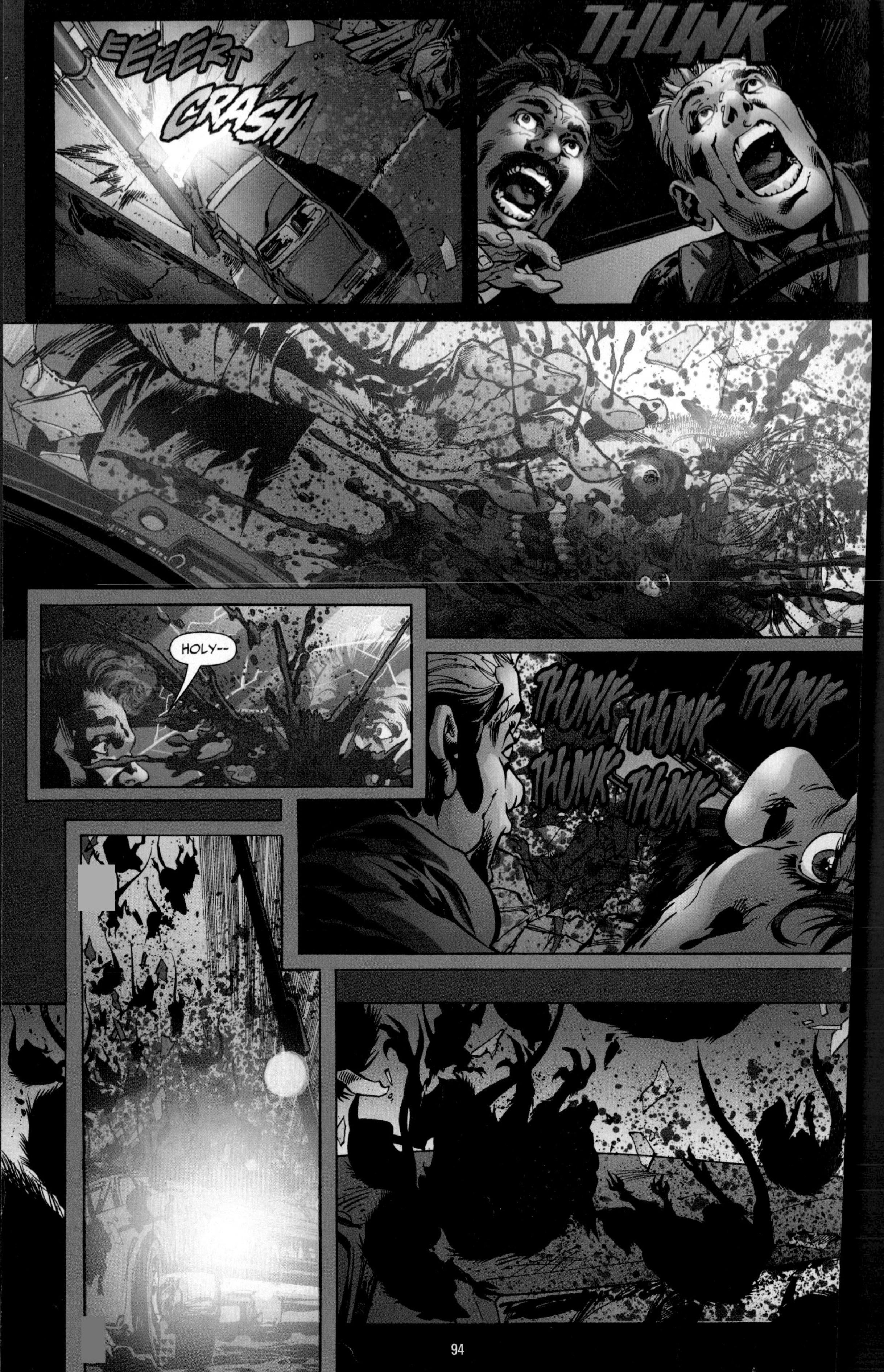
EEEEERT
CRASH
THUNK
HOLY--
THUNK
THUNK
THUNK
THUNK
THUNK

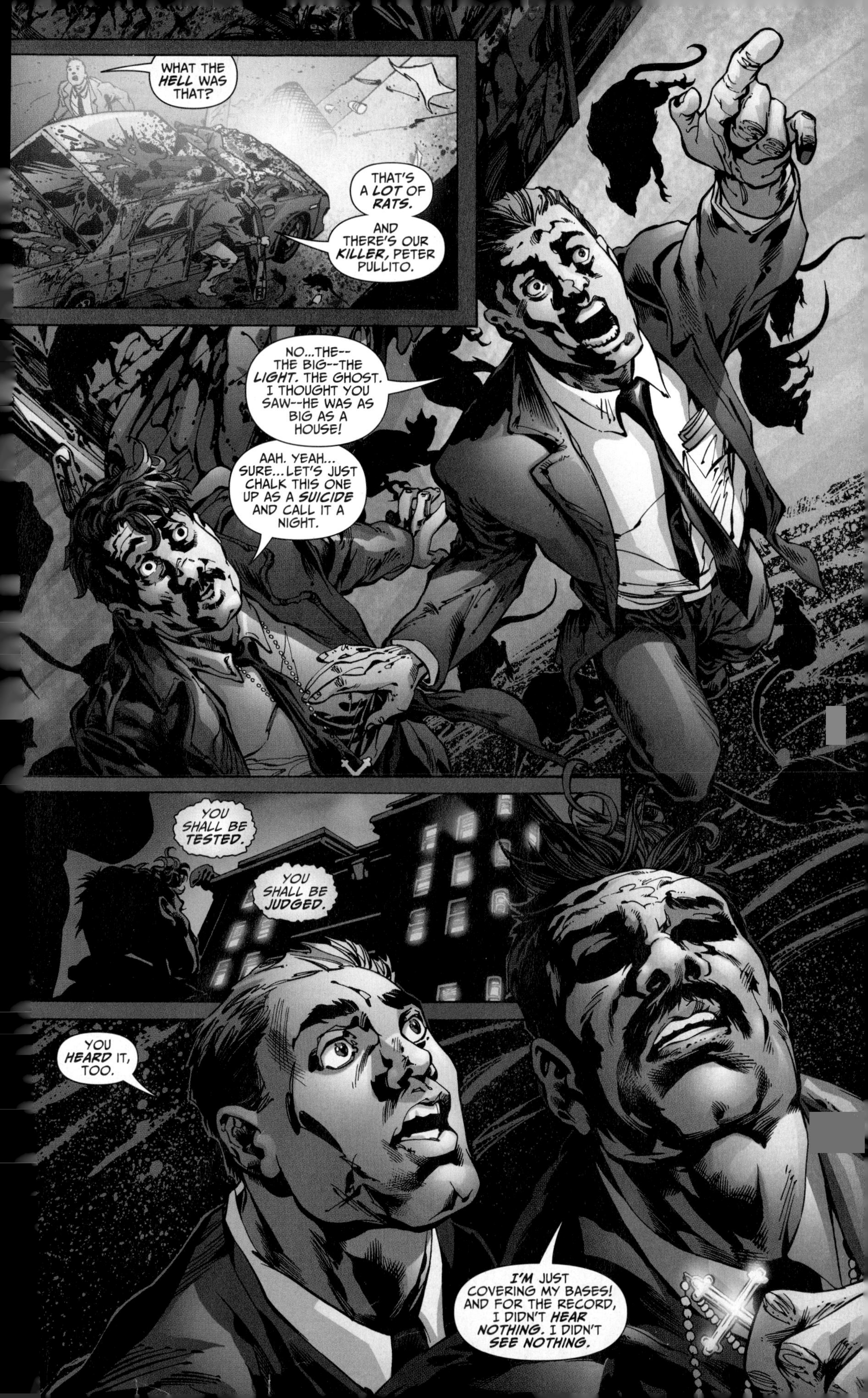
WHAT THE HELL WAS THAT?
THAT'S A LOT OF RATS.
AND THERE'S OUR KILLER, PETER PULLITO.
NO...THE-- THE BIG--THE LIGHT. THE GHOST. I THOUGHT YOU SAW--HE WAS AS BIG AS A HOUSE!
AAH. YEAH... SURE...LET'S JUST CHALK THIS ONE UP AS A SUICIDE AND CALL IT A NIGHT.
YOU SHALL BE TESTED.
YOU SHALL BE JUDGED.
YOU HEARD IT, TOO.
I'M JUST COVERING MY BASES! AND FOR THE RECORD, I DIDN'T HEAR NOTHING. I DIDN'T SEE NOTHING.

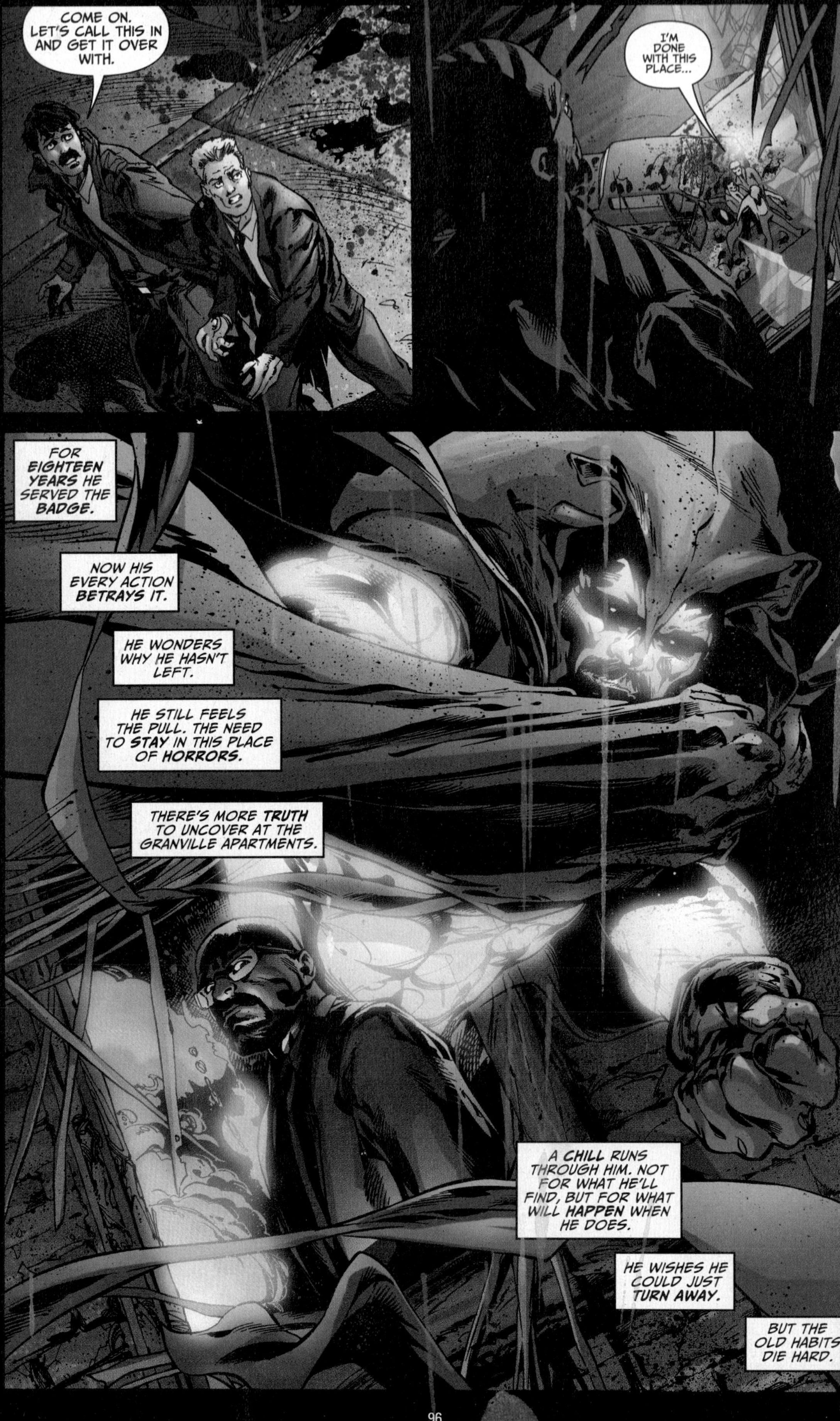
COME ON. LET'S CALL THIS IN AND GET IT OVER WITH.
I'M DONE WITH THIS PLACE...
FOR EIGHTEEN YEARS HE SERVED THE BADGE.
NOW HIS EVERY ACTION BETRAYS IT.
HE WONDERS WHY HE HASN'T LEFT.
HE STILL FEELS THE PULL. THE NEED TO STAY IN THIS PLACE OF HORRORS.
THERE'S MORE TRUTH TO UNCOVER AT THE GRANVILLE APARTMENTS.
A CHILL RUNS THROUGH HIM. NOT FOR WHAT HE'LL FIND, BUT FOR WHAT WILL HAPPEN WHEN HE DOES.
HE WISHES HE COULD JUST TURN AWAY.
BUT THE OLD HABITS DIE HARD.

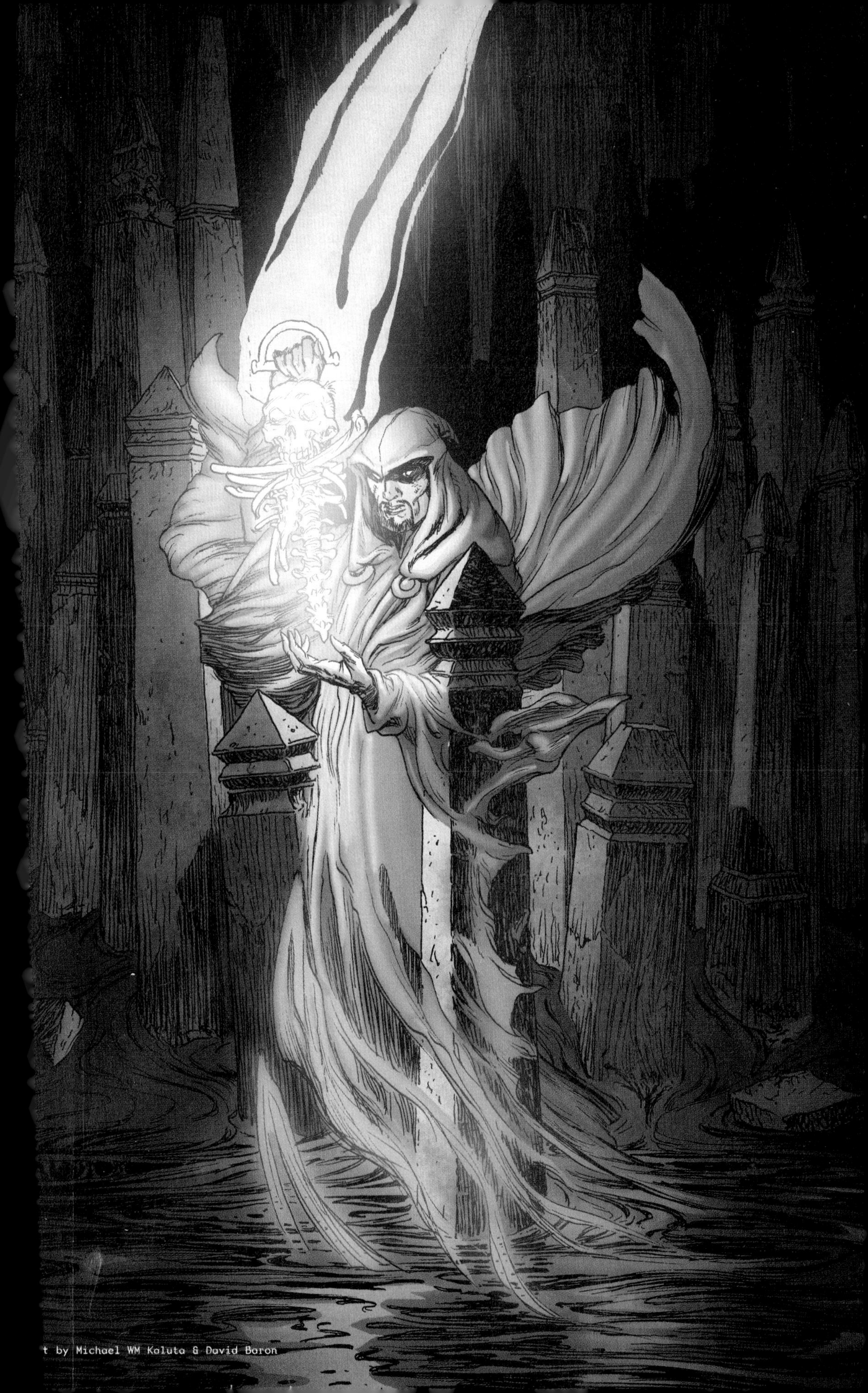
t by Michael WM Kaluta & David Baron

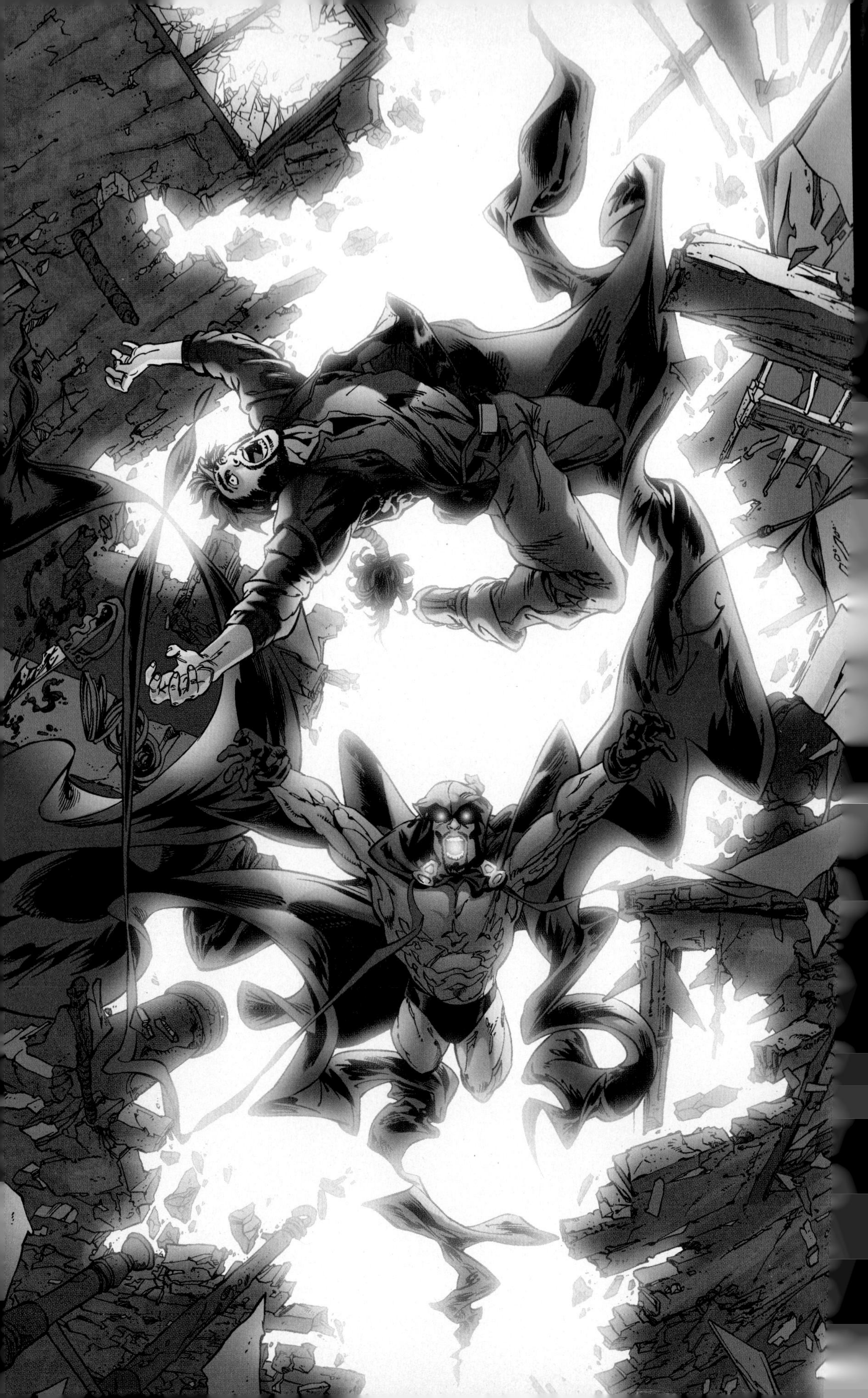

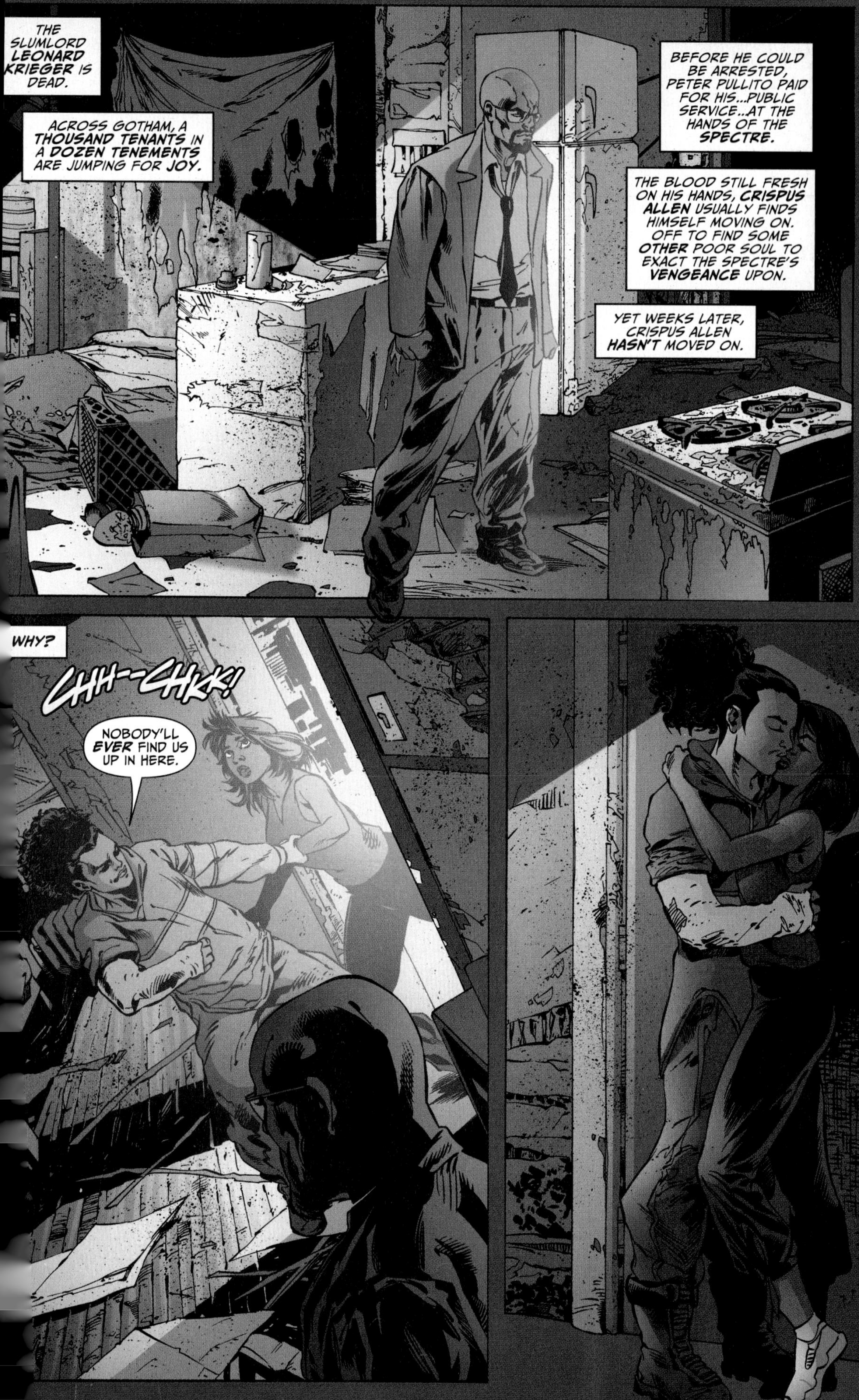
THE SLUMLORD LEONARD KRIEGER IS DEAD.
ACROSS GOTHAM, A THOUSAND TENANTS IN A DOZEN TENEMENTS ARE JUMPING FOR JOY.
BEFORE HE COULD BE ARRESTED, PETER PULLITO PAID FOR HIS...PUBLIC SERVICE...AT THE HANDS OF THE SPECTRE.
THE BLOOD STILL FRESH ON HIS HANDS, CRISPUS ALLEN USUALLY FINDS HIMSELF MOVING ON. OFF TO FIND SOME OTHER POOR SOUL TO EXACT THE SPECTRE'S VENGEANCE UPON.
YET WEEKS LATER, CRISPUS ALLEN HASN'T MOVED ON.
WHY?
CHH--CHKK!
NOBODY'LL EVER FIND US UP IN HERE.

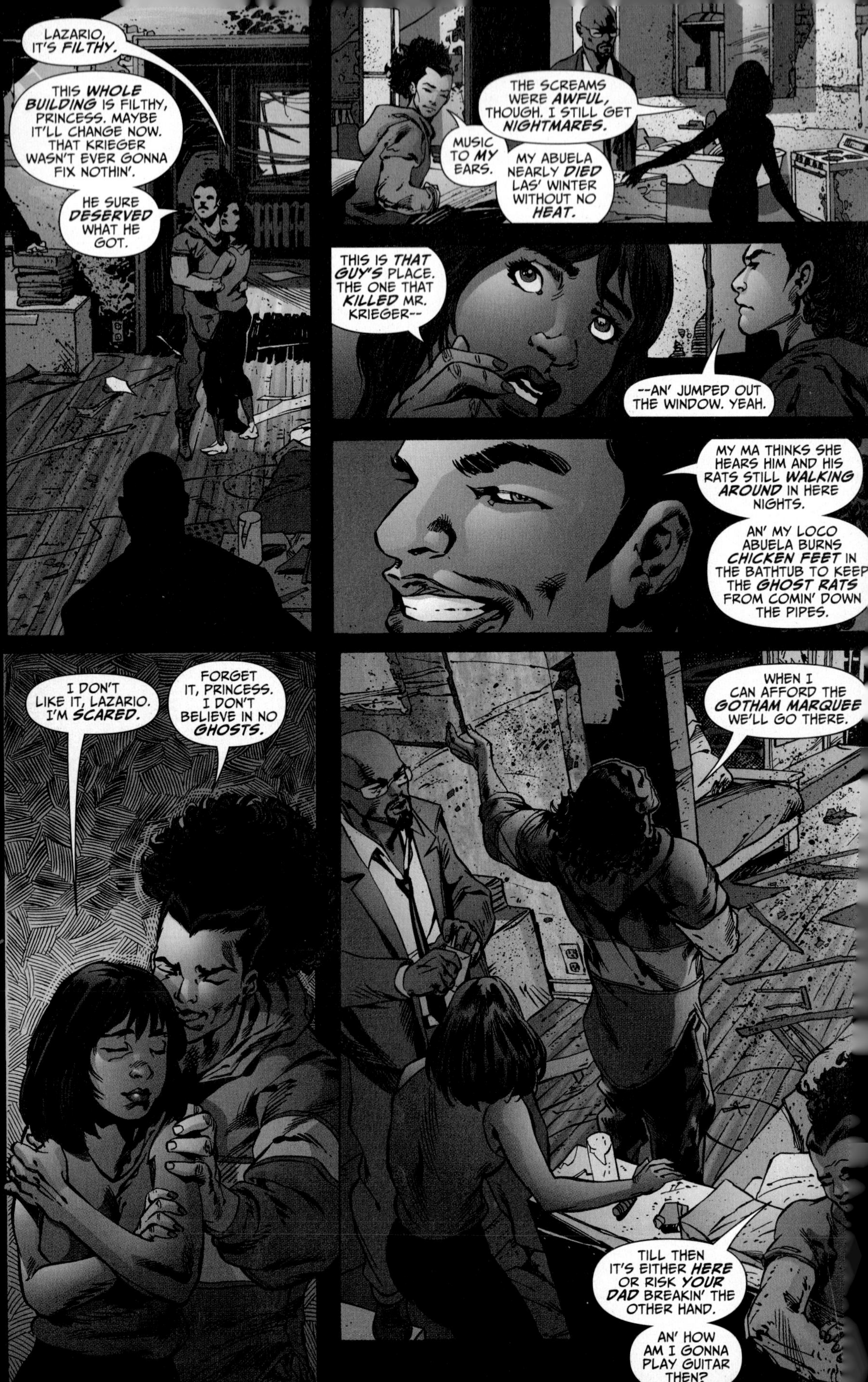
LAZARIO, IT'S FILTHY.
THIS WHOLE BUILDING IS FILTHY, PRINCESS. MAYBE IT'LL CHANGE NOW. THAT KRIEGER WASN'T EVER GONNA FIX NOTHIN'.
HE SURE DESERVED WHAT HE GOT.
THE SCREAMS WERE AWFUL, THOUGH. I STILL GET NIGHTMARES.
MUSIC TO MY EARS.
MY ABUELA NEARLY DIED LAS' WINTER WITHOUT NO HEAT.
THIS IS THAT GUY'S PLACE. THE ONE THAT KILLED MR. KRIEGER--
--AN' JUMPED OUT THE WINDOW. YEAH.
MY MA THINKS SHE HEARS HIM AND HIS RATS STILL WALKING AROUND IN HERE NIGHTS.
AN' MY LOCO ABUELA BURNS CHICKEN FEET IN THE BATHTUB TO KEEP THE GHOST RATS FROM COMIN' DOWN THE PIPES.
I DON'T LIKE IT, LAZARIO. I'M SCARED.
FORGET IT, PRINCESS. I DON'T BELIEVE IN NO GHOSTS.
WHEN I CAN AFFORD THE GOTHAM MARQUEE WE'LL GO THERE.
TILL THEN IT'S EITHER HERE OR RISK YOUR DAD BREAKIN' THE OTHER HAND.
AN' HOW AM I GONNA PLAY GUITAR THEN?

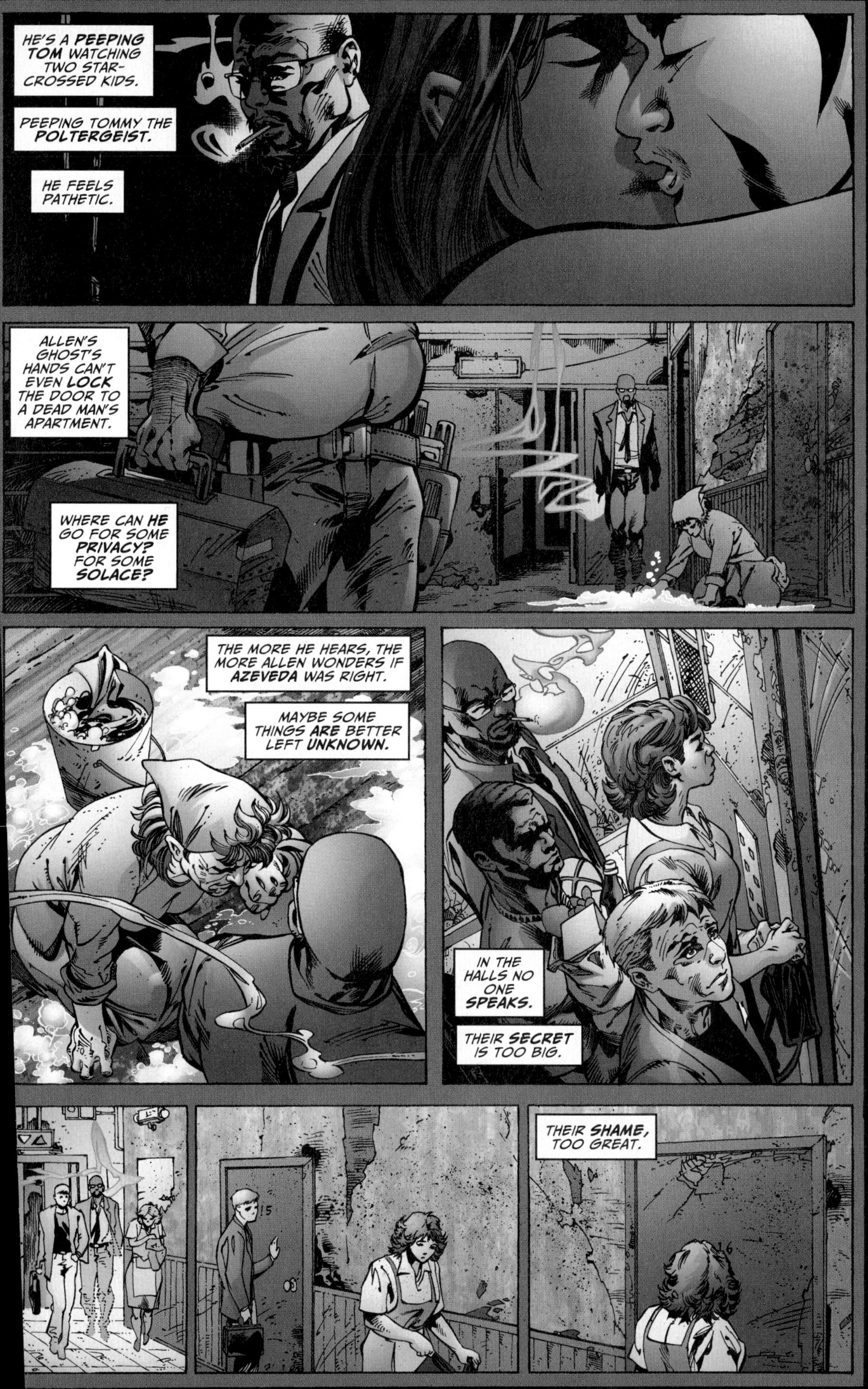
HE'S A PEEPING TOM WATCHING TWO STAR-CROSSED KIDS.
PEEPING TOMMY THE POLTERGEIST.
HE FEELS PATHETIC.
ALLEN'S GHOST'S HANDS CAN'T EVEN LOCK THE DOOR TO A DEAD MAN'S APARTMENT.
WHERE CAN HE GO FOR SOME PRIVACY? FOR SOME SOLACE?
THE MORE HE HEARS, THE MORE ALLEN WONDERS IF AZEVEDA WAS RIGHT.
MAYBE SOME THINGS ARE BETTER LEFT UNKNOWN.
IN THE HALLS NO ONE SPEAKS.
THEIR SECRET IS TOO BIG.
THEIR SHAME, TOO GREAT.

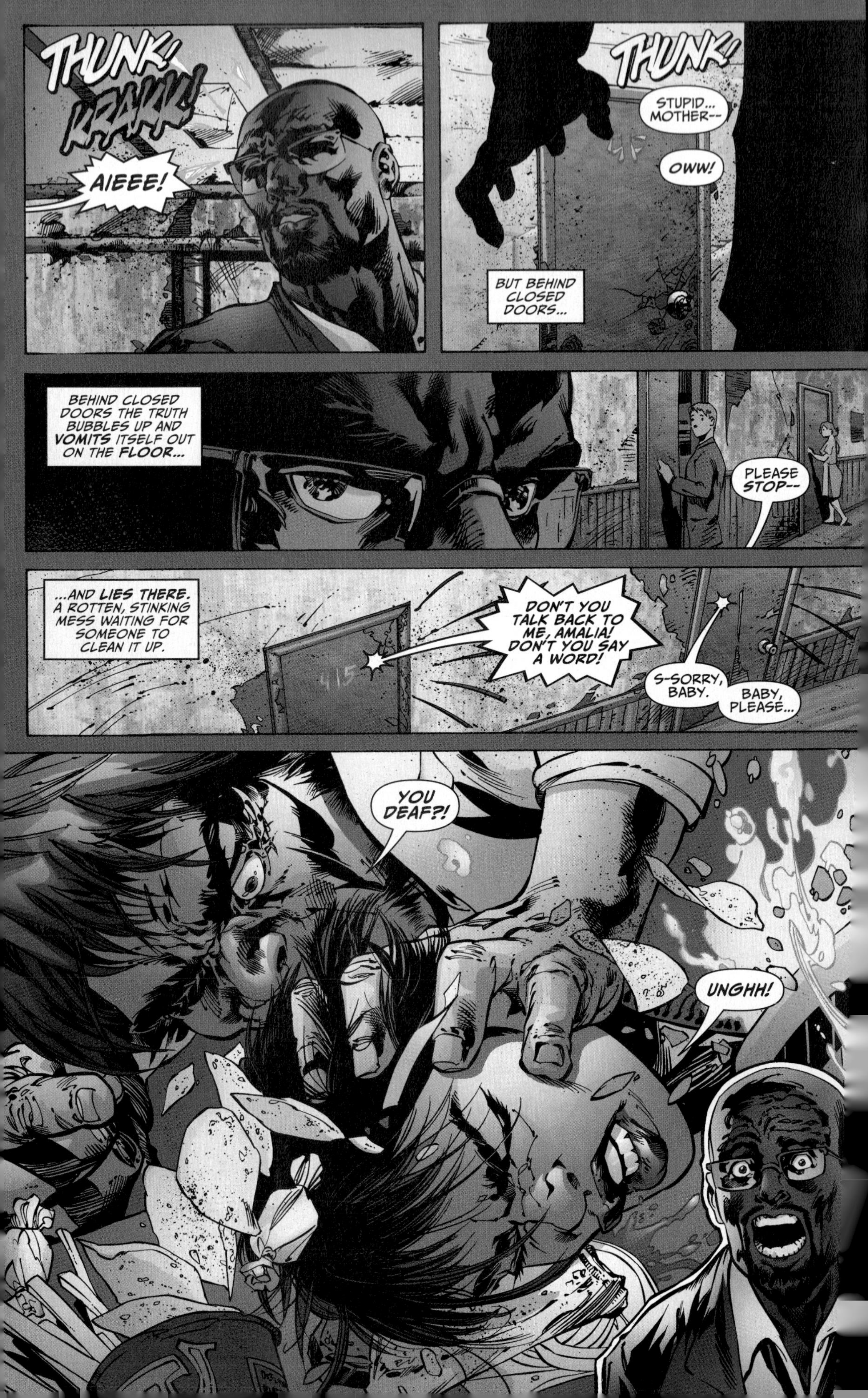
THUNK!
KRAKK!
AIEEE!
THUNK!
STUPID... MOTHER--
OWW!
BUT BEHIND CLOSED DOORS...
BEHIND CLOSED DOORS THE TRUTH BUBBLES UP AND VOMITS ITSELF OUT ON THE FLOOR...
PLEASE STOP--
...AND LIES THERE. A ROTTEN, STINKING MESS WAITING FOR SOMEONE TO CLEAN IT UP.
DON'T YOU TALK BACK TO ME, AMALIA! DON'T YOU SAY A WORD!
S-SORRY, BABY.
BABY, PLEASE...
YOU DEAF?!
UNGHH!

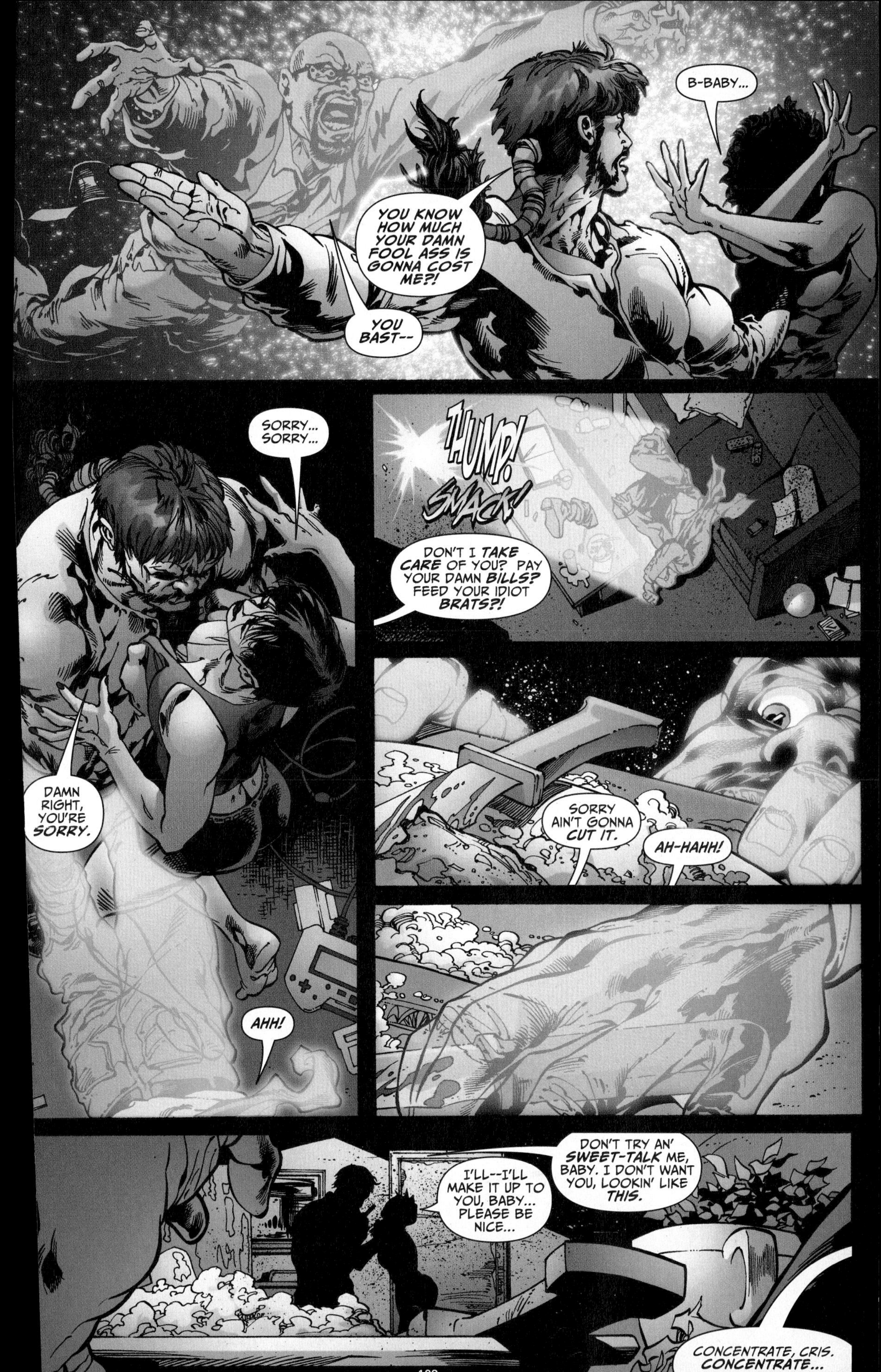
B-BABY...
YOU KNOW HOW MUCH YOUR DAMN FOOL ASS IS GONNA COST ME?!
YOU BAST--
SORRY... SORRY...
DAMN RIGHT, YOU'RE SORRY.
THUMP!
SNACK!
DON'T I TAKE CARE OF YOU? PAY YOUR DAMN BILLS? FEED YOUR IDIOT BRATS?!
AHH!
SORRY AIN'T GONNA CUT IT.
AH-HAHH!
I'LL--I'LL MAKE IT UP TO YOU, BABY... PLEASE BE NICE...
DON'T TRY AN' SWEET-TALK ME, BABY. I DON'T WANT YOU, LOOKIN' LIKE THIS.
CONCENTRATE, CRIS. CONCENTRATE...

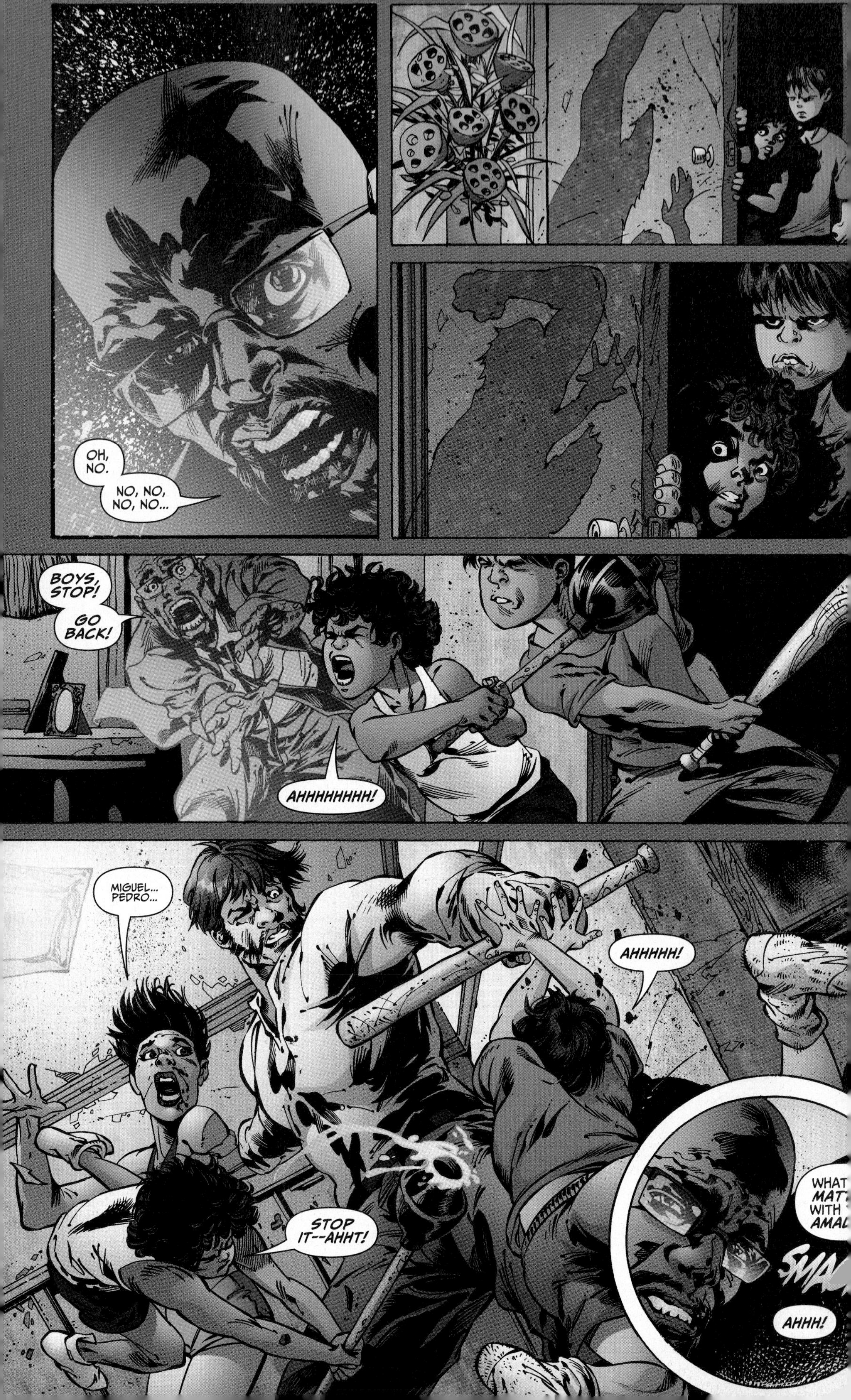
OH, NO.
NO, NO, NO, NO...
BOYS, STOP!
GO BACK!
AHHHHHHHHH!
MIGUEL... PEDRO...
AHHHHH!
STOP IT--AHHT!
WHAT MAT WITH AMAL
AHHH!

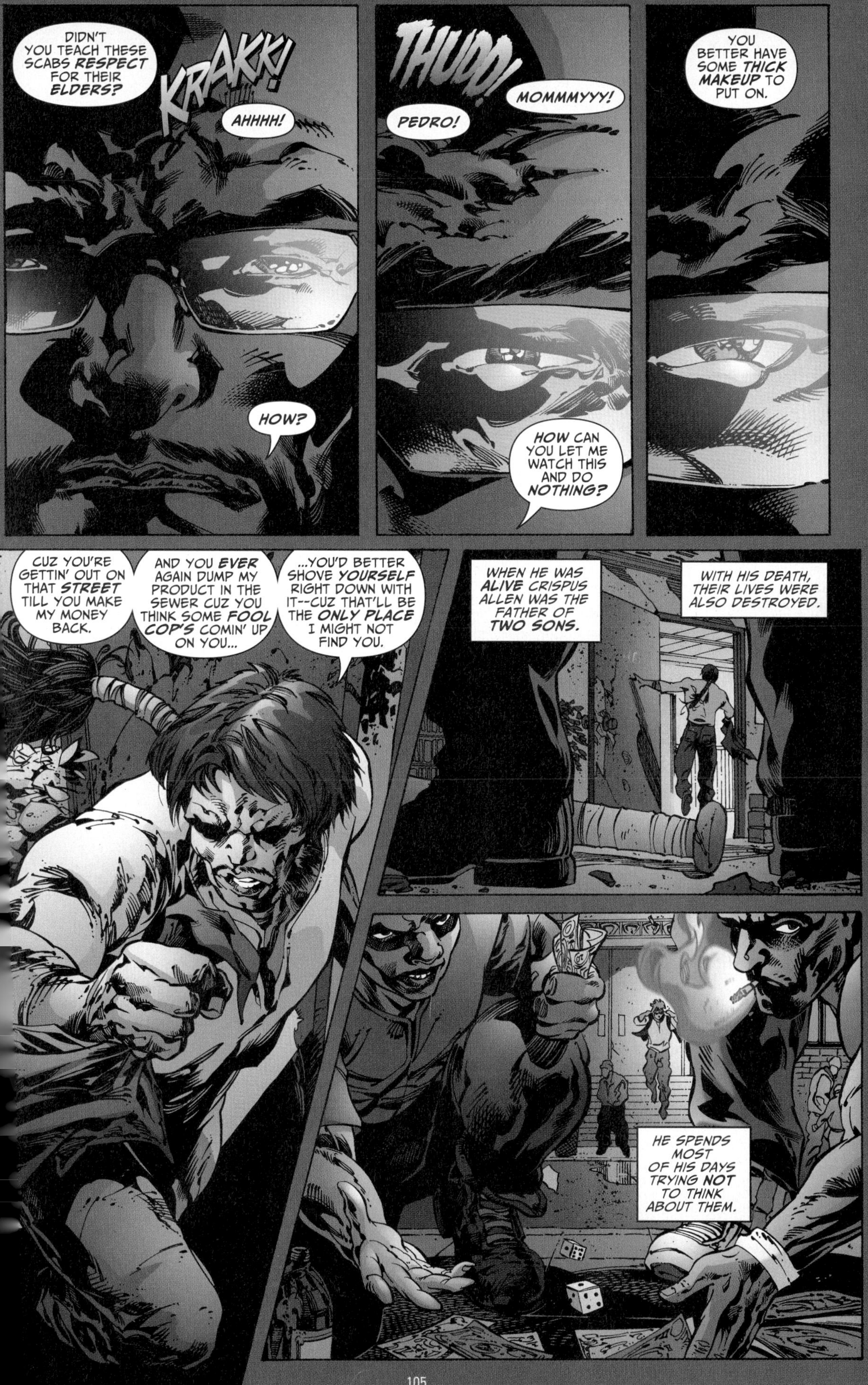
DIDN'T YOU TEACH THESE SCABS RESPECT FOR THEIR ELDERS?
KRAKK!
AHHHH!
HOW?
THUDD!
PEDRO!
MOMMMYYY!
HOW CAN YOU LET ME WATCH THIS AND DO NOTHING?
YOU BETTER HAVE SOME THICK MAKEUP TO PUT ON.
CUZ YOU'RE GETTIN' OUT ON THAT STREET TILL YOU MAKE MY MONEY BACK.
AND YOU EVER AGAIN DUMP MY PRODUCT IN THE SEWER CUZ YOU THINK SOME FOOL COP'S COMIN' UP ON YOU...
...YOU'D BETTER SHOVE YOURSELF RIGHT DOWN WITH IT--CUZ THAT'LL BE THE ONLY PLACE I MIGHT NOT FIND YOU.
WHEN HE WAS ALIVE CRISPUS ALLEN WAS THE FATHER OF TWO SONS.
WITH HIS DEATH, THEIR LIVES WERE ALSO DESTROYED.
HE SPENDS MOST OF HIS DAYS TRYING NOT TO THINK ABOUT THEM.

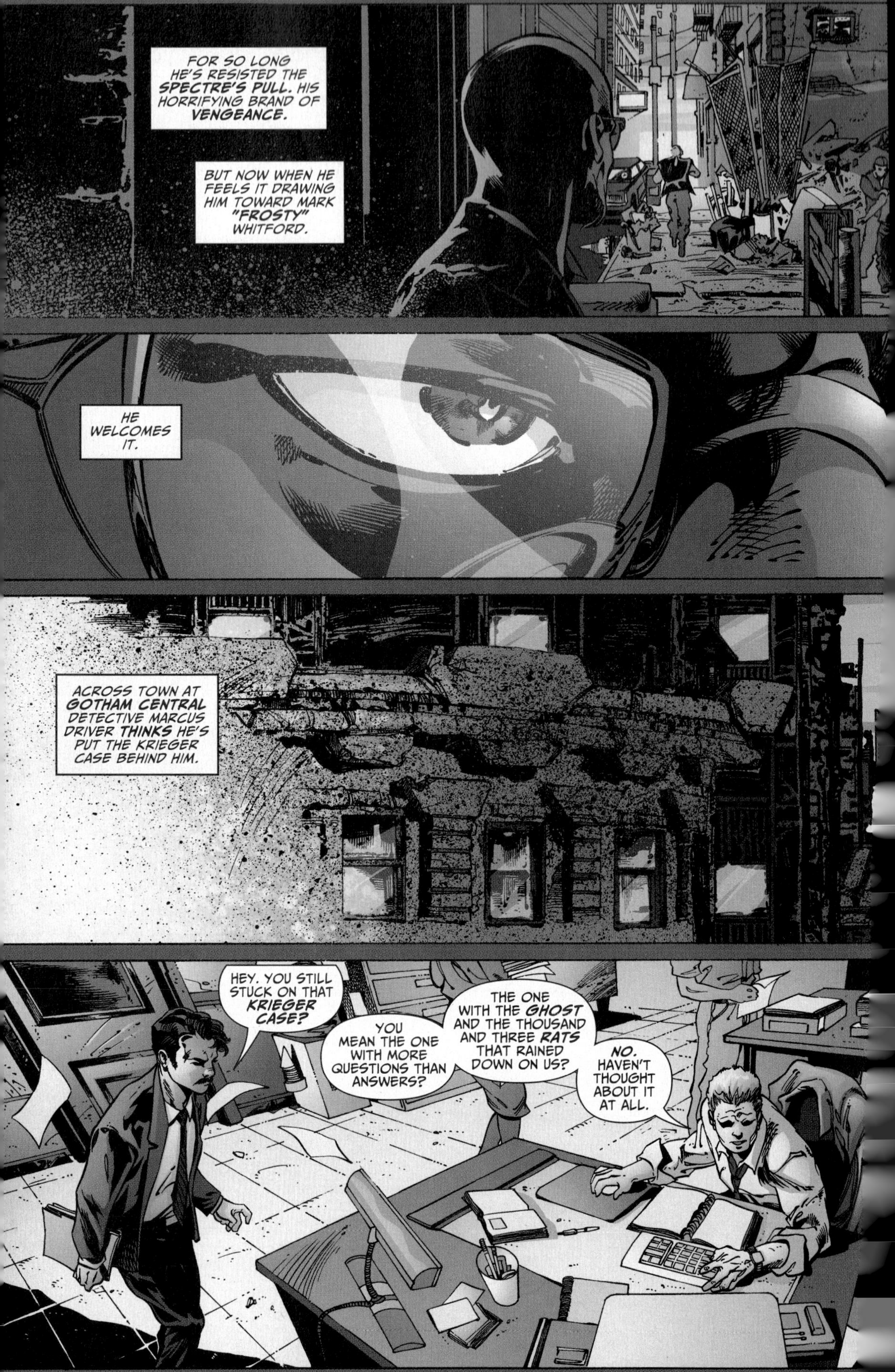
FOR SO LONG HE'S RESISTED THE SPECTRE'S PULL. HIS HORRIFYING BRAND OF VENGEANCE.
BUT NOW WHEN HE FEELS IT DRAWING HIM TOWARD MARK "FROSTY" WHITFORD.
HE WELCOMES IT.
ACROSS TOWN AT GOTHAM CENTRAL DETECTIVE MARCUS DRIVER THINKS HE'S PUT THE KRIEGER CASE BEHIND HIM.
HEY. YOU STILL STUCK ON THAT KRIEGER CASE?
YOU MEAN THE ONE WITH MORE QUESTIONS THAN ANSWERS?
THE ONE WITH THE GHOST AND THE THOUSAND AND THREE RATS THAT RAINED DOWN ON US?
NO. HAVEN'T THOUGHT ABOUT IT AT ALL.

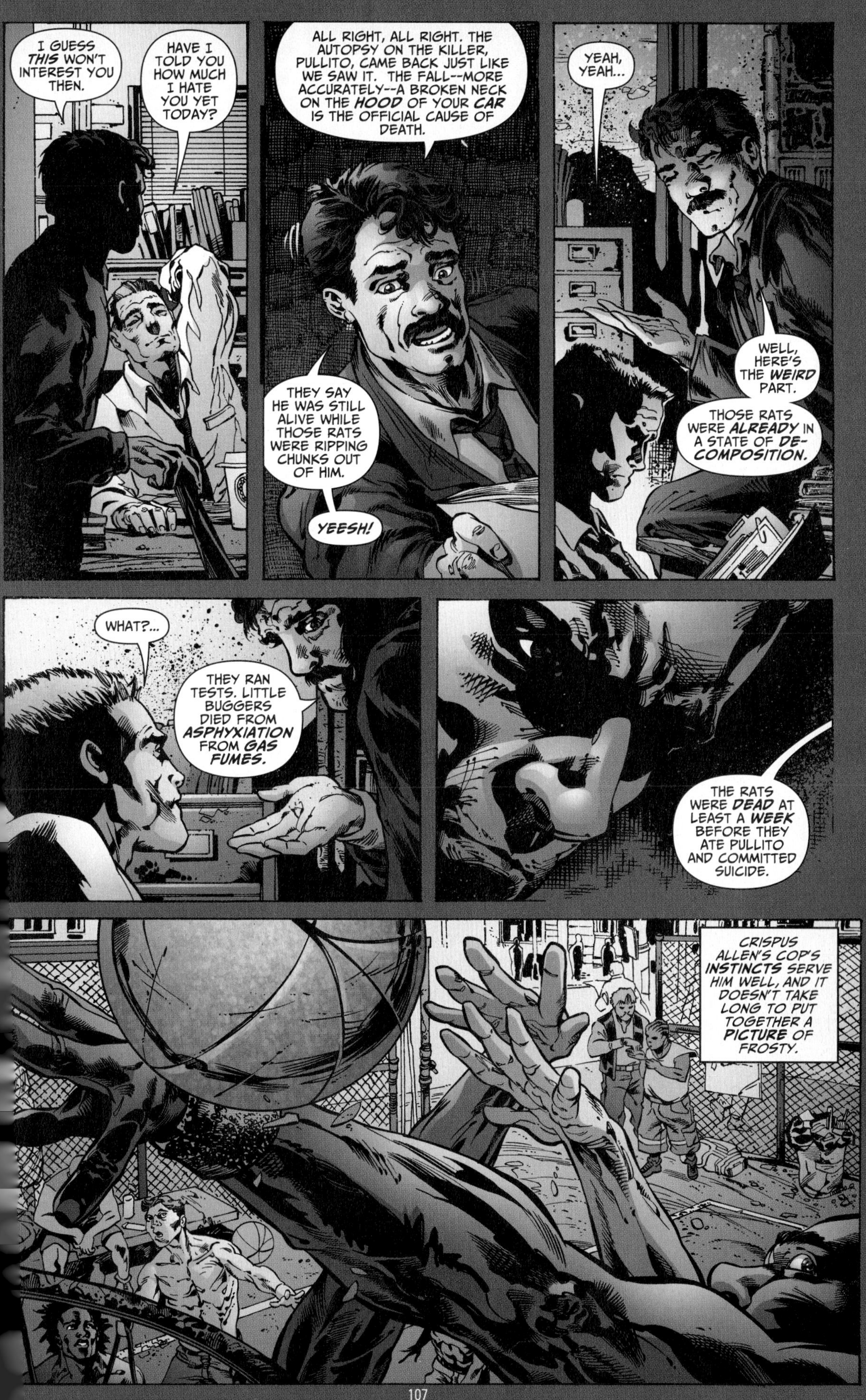
I GUESS THIS WON'T INTEREST YOU THEN.
HAVE I TOLD YOU HOW MUCH I HATE YOU YET TODAY?
ALL RIGHT, ALL RIGHT. THE AUTOPSY ON THE KILLER, PULLITO, CAME BACK JUST LIKE WE SAW IT. THE FALL--MORE ACCURATELY--A BROKEN NECK ON THE HOOD OF YOUR CAR IS THE OFFICIAL CAUSE OF DEATH.
THEY SAY HE WAS STILL ALIVE WHILE THOSE RATS WERE RIPPING CHUNKS OUT OF HIM.
YEESH!
YEAH, YEAH...
WELL, HERE'S THE WEIRD PART.
THOSE RATS WERE ALREADY IN A STATE OF DE-COMPOSITION.
WHAT?...
THEY RAN TESTS. LITTLE BUGGERS DIED FROM ASPHYXIATION FROM GAS FUMES.
THE RATS WERE DEAD AT LEAST A WEEK BEFORE THEY ATE PULLITO AND COMMITTED SUICIDE.
CRISPUS ALLEN'S COP'S INSTINCTS SERVE HIM WELL, AND IT DOESN'T TAKE LONG TO PUT TOGETHER A PICTURE OF FROSTY.

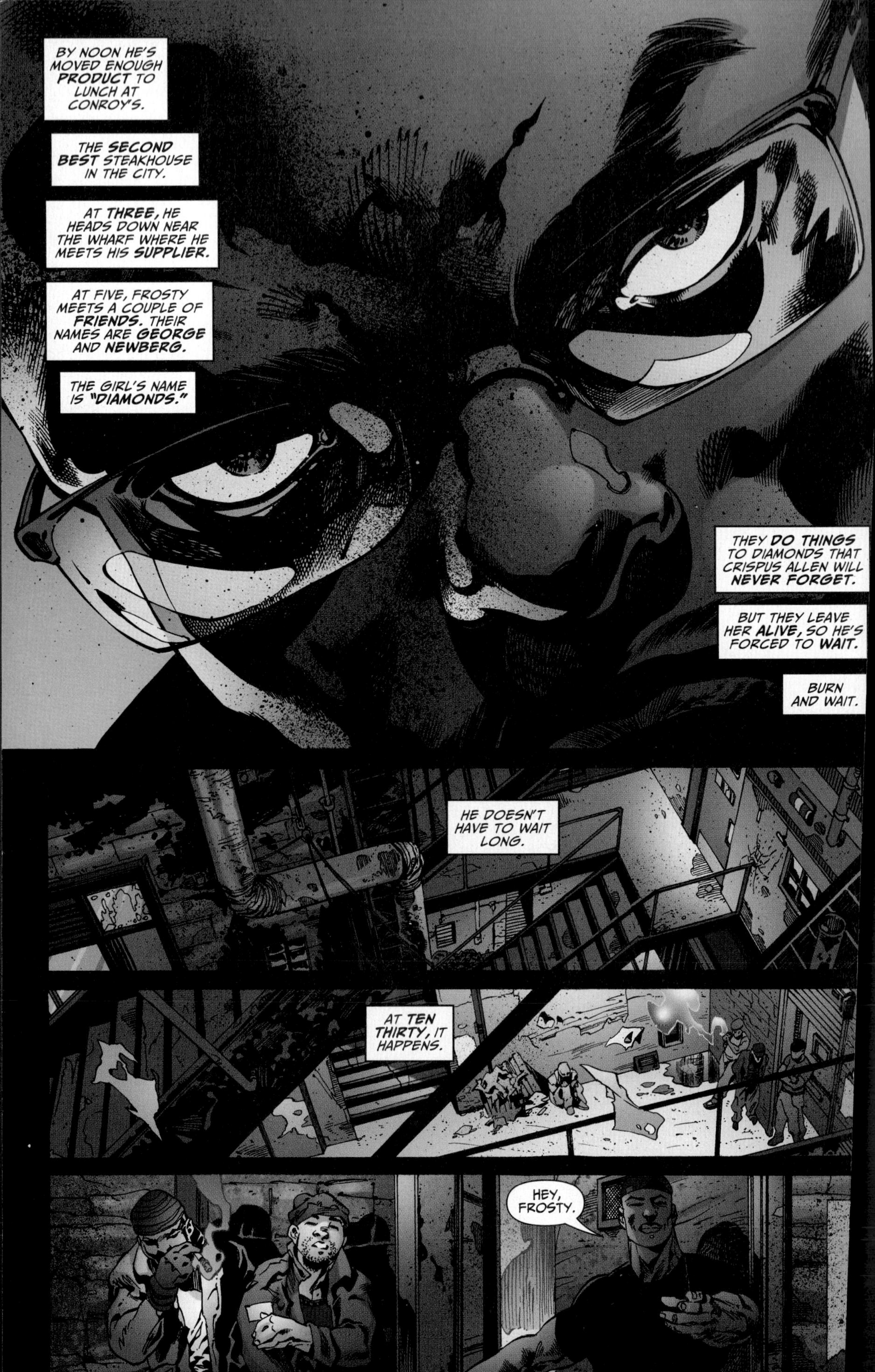
BY NOON HE'S MOVED ENOUGH PRODUCT TO LUNCH AT CONROY'S.
THE SECOND BEST STEAKHOUSE IN THE CITY.
AT THREE, HE HEADS DOWN NEAR THE WHARF WHERE HE MEETS HIS SUPPLIER.
AT FIVE, FROSTY MEETS A COUPLE OF FRIENDS. THEIR NAMES ARE GEORGE AND NEWBERG.
THE GIRL'S NAME IS "DIAMONDS."
THEY DO THINGS TO DIAMONDS THAT CRISPUS ALLEN WILL NEVER FORGET.
BUT THEY LEAVE HER ALIVE, SO HE'S FORCED TO WAIT.
BURN AND WAIT.
HE DOESN'T HAVE TO WAIT LONG.
AT TEN THIRTY, IT HAPPENS.
HEY, FROSTY.

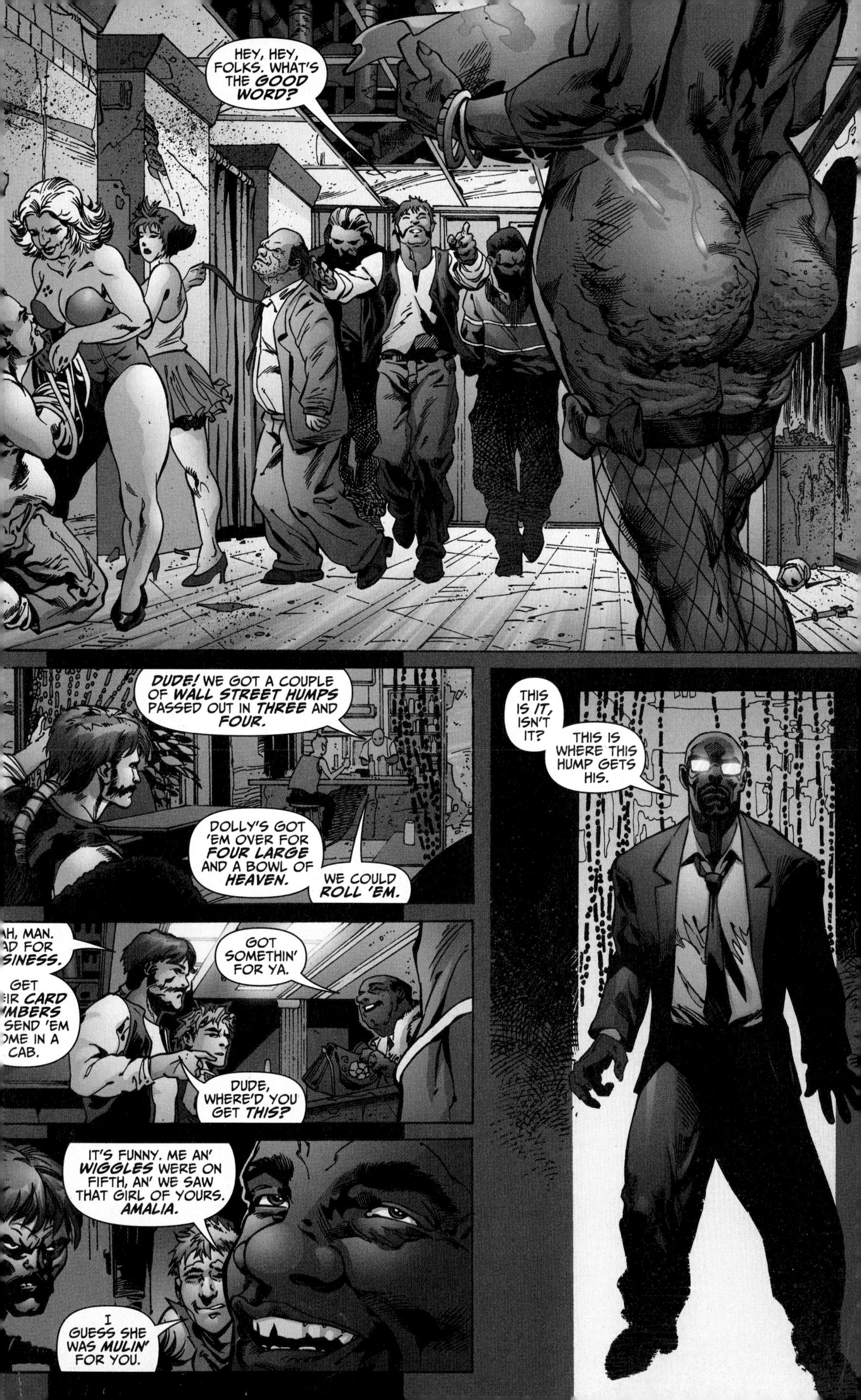

HEY, HEY, FOLKS. WHAT'S THE GOOD WORD?
DUDE! WE GOT A COUPLE OF WALL STREET HUMPS PASSED OUT IN THREE AND FOUR.
DOLLY'S GOT 'EM OVER FOR FOUR LARGE AND A BOWL OF HEAVEN.
WE COULD ROLL 'EM.
AH, MAN. AD FOR SINESS.
GET EIR CARD MBERS SEND 'EM OME IN A CAB.
GOT SOMETHIN' FOR YA.
DUDE, WHERE'D YOU GET THIS?
IT'S FUNNY. ME AN' WIGGLES WERE ON FIFTH, AN' WE SAW THAT GIRL OF YOURS. AMALIA.
I GUESS SHE WAS MULIN' FOR YOU.
THIS IS IT, ISN'T IT?
THIS IS WHERE THIS HUMP GETS HIS.

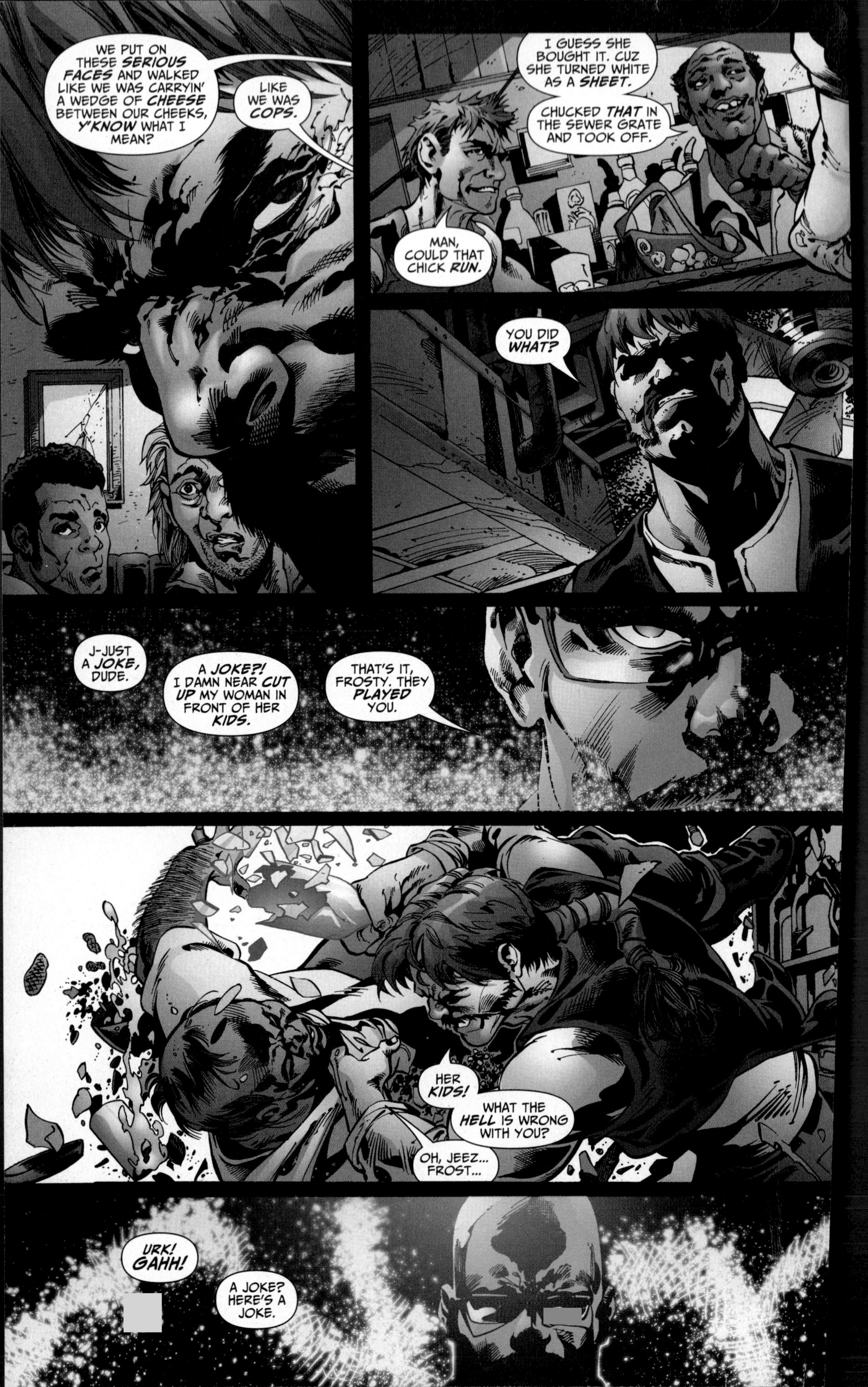

WE PUT ON THESE SERIOUS FACES AND WALKED LIKE WE WAS CARRYIN' A WEDGE OF CHEESE BETWEEN OUR CHEEKS, Y'KNOW WHAT I MEAN?
LIKE WE WAS COPS.
I GUESS SHE BOUGHT IT. CUZ SHE TURNED WHITE AS A SHEET.
CHUCKED THAT IN THE SEWER GRATE AND TOOK OFF.
MAN, COULD THAT CHICK RUN.
YOU DID WHAT?
J-JUST A JOKE, DUDE.
A JOKE?! I DAMN NEAR CUT UP MY WOMAN IN FRONT OF HER KIDS.
THAT'S IT, FROSTY. THEY PLAYED YOU.
HER KIDS!
WHAT THE HELL IS WRONG WITH YOU?
OH, JEEZ... FROST...
URK! GAHH!
A JOKE? HERE'S A JOKE.

GAHHHHHARRRRRRRR!

AH-AHHHHHHHH!

THAT'S A *DAMN* JOKE!

GOD.

HE'S DYIN', DUDE.

WHAT THE--

OKAY...

WELL, I GUESS LET'S *FINISH* THIS.

STOP! NAH...

EVERY-BODY KNOWS *YOU* CAN'T KEEP YOUR MOUTH SHUT.

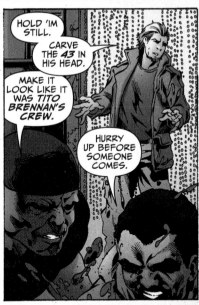

HOLD 'IM STILL.

CARVE THE *43* IN HIS HEAD.

MAKE IT LOOK LIKE IT WAS *TITO BRENNAN'S* CREW.

HURRY UP BEFORE SOMEONE COMES.

NAH... NAH...COME ON...

URK! GAHH!

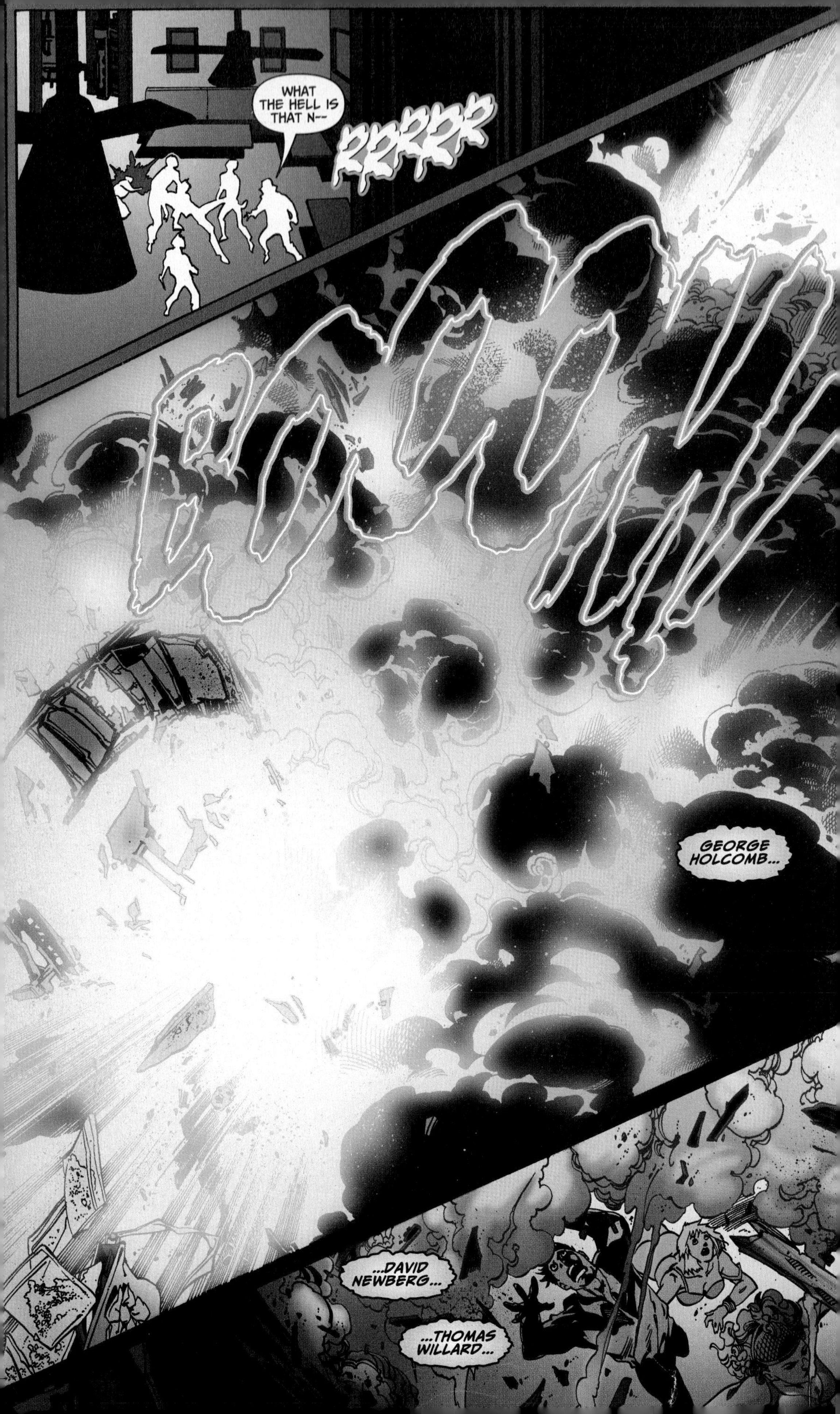
WHAT THE HELL IS THAT N--
RRRRR
BOOOOM
GEORGE HOLCOMB...
...DAVID NEWBERG...
...THOMAS WILLARD...

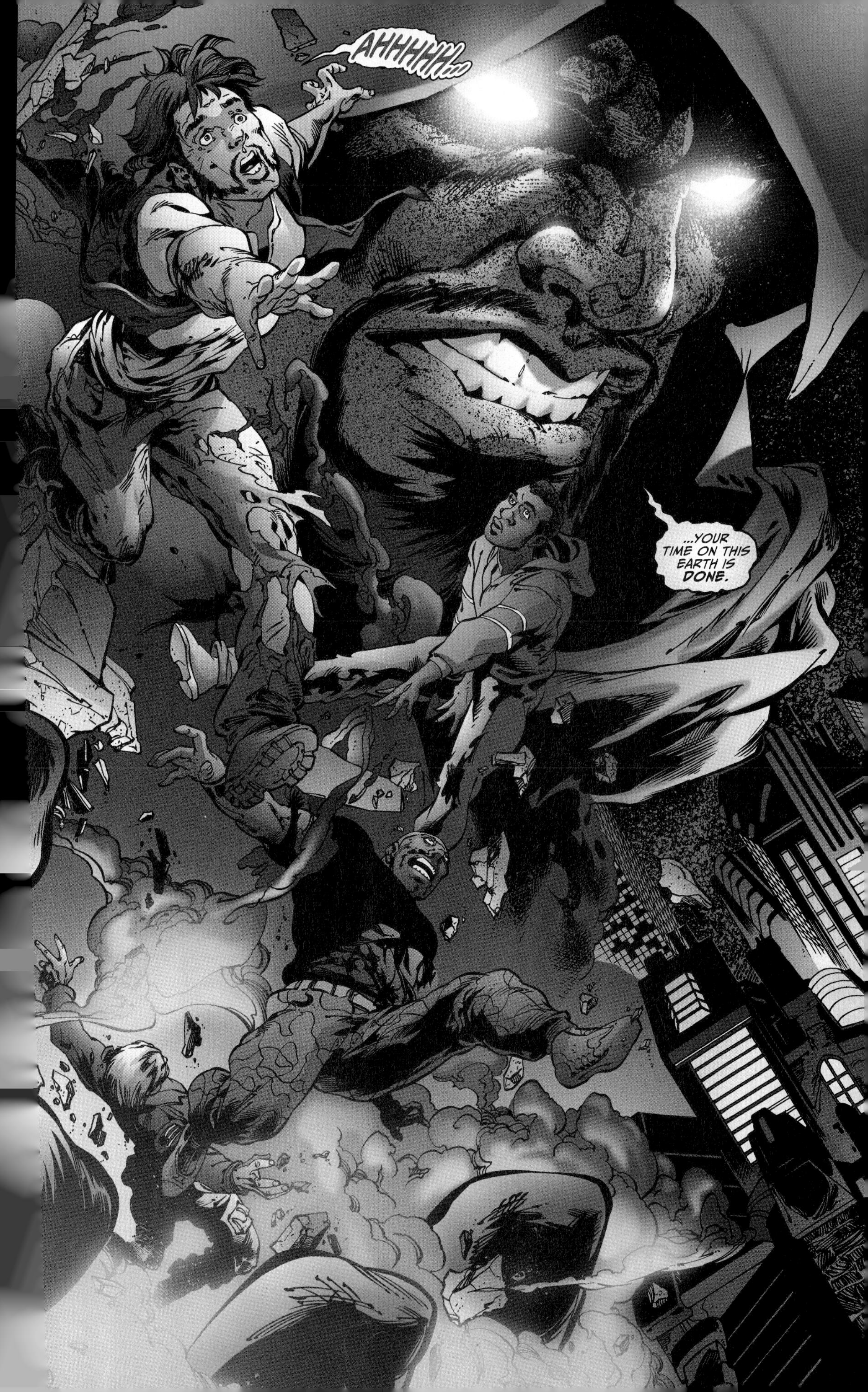
AHHHHH...
...YOUR TIME ON THIS EARTH IS DONE.

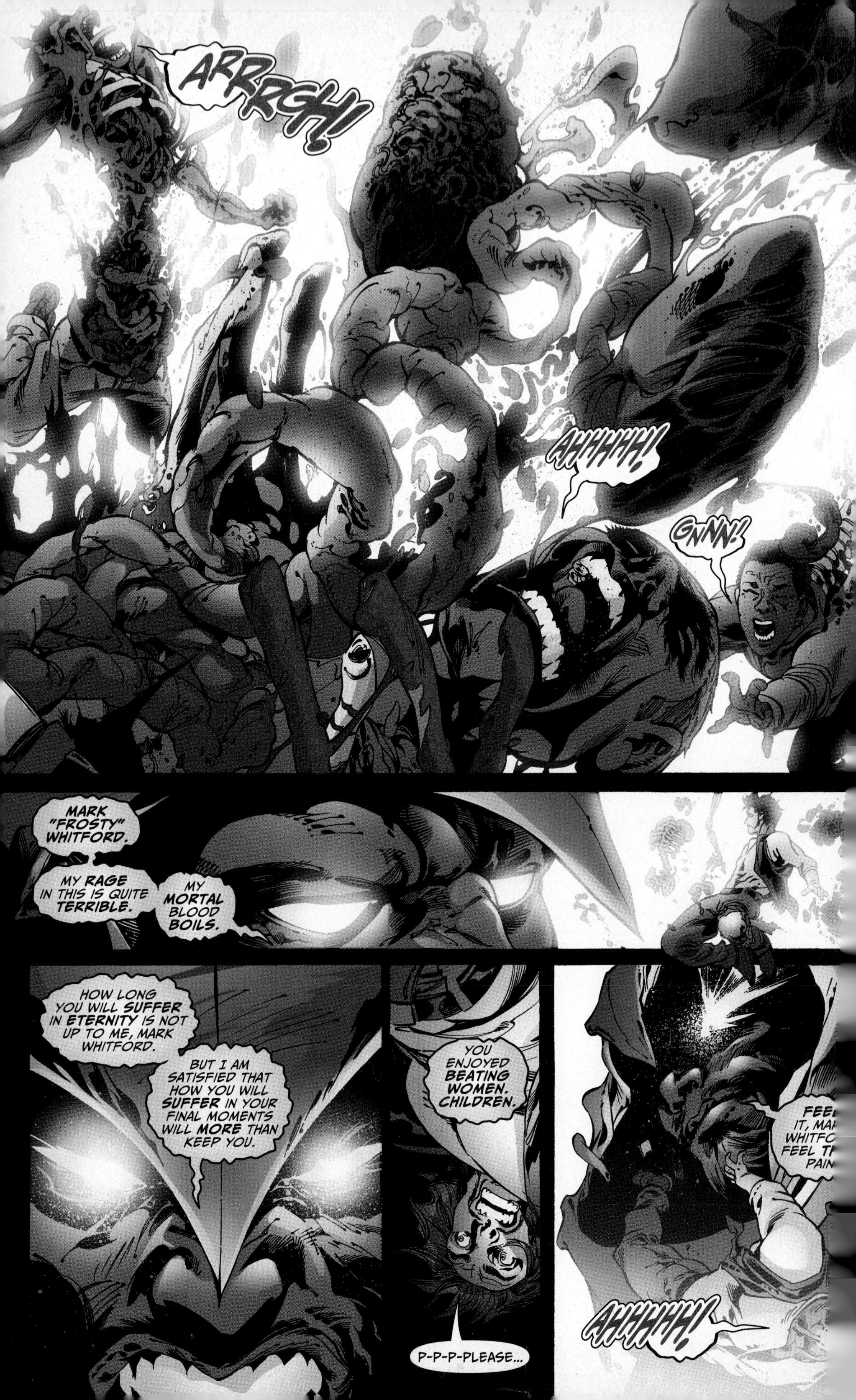
ARRRGH!
AHHHHH!
GNNN!
MARK "FROSTY" WHITFORD.
MY RAGE IN THIS IS QUITE TERRIBLE.
MY MORTAL BLOOD BOILS.
HOW LONG YOU WILL SUFFER IN ETERNITY IS NOT UP TO ME, MARK WHITFORD.
BUT I AM SATISFIED THAT HOW YOU WILL SUFFER IN YOUR FINAL MOMENTS WILL MORE THAN KEEP YOU.
YOU ENJOYED BEATING WOMEN. CHILDREN.
P-P-P-PLEASE...
AHHHHH!

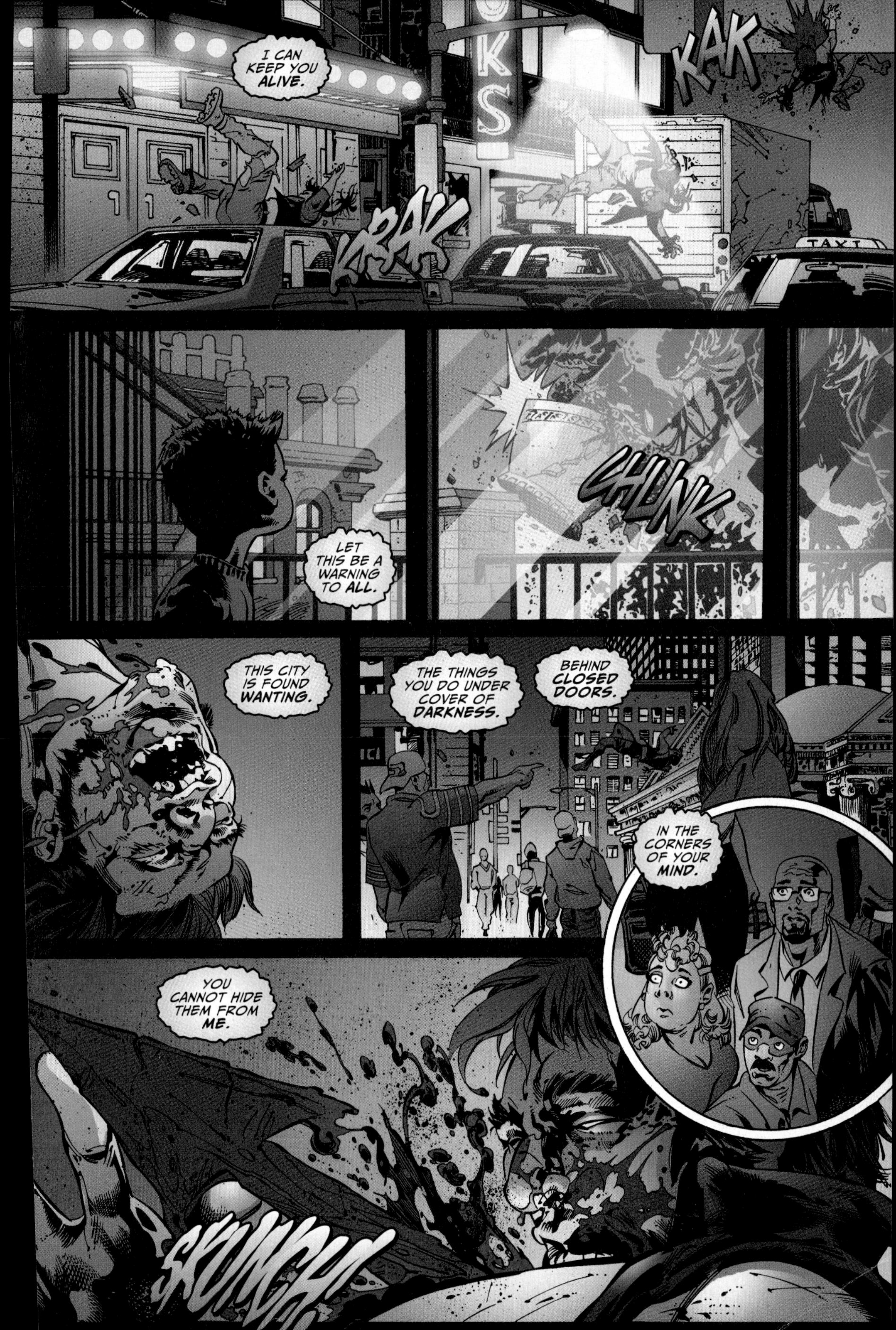
I CAN KEEP YOU ALIVE.
KAK
KRAK
TAXI
CHUNK
LET THIS BE A WARNING TO ALL.
THIS CITY IS FOUND WANTING.
THE THINGS YOU DO UNDER COVER OF DARKNESS.
BEHIND CLOSED DOORS.
IN THE CORNERS OF YOUR MIND.
YOU CANNOT HIDE THEM FROM ME.
SKUNCH!

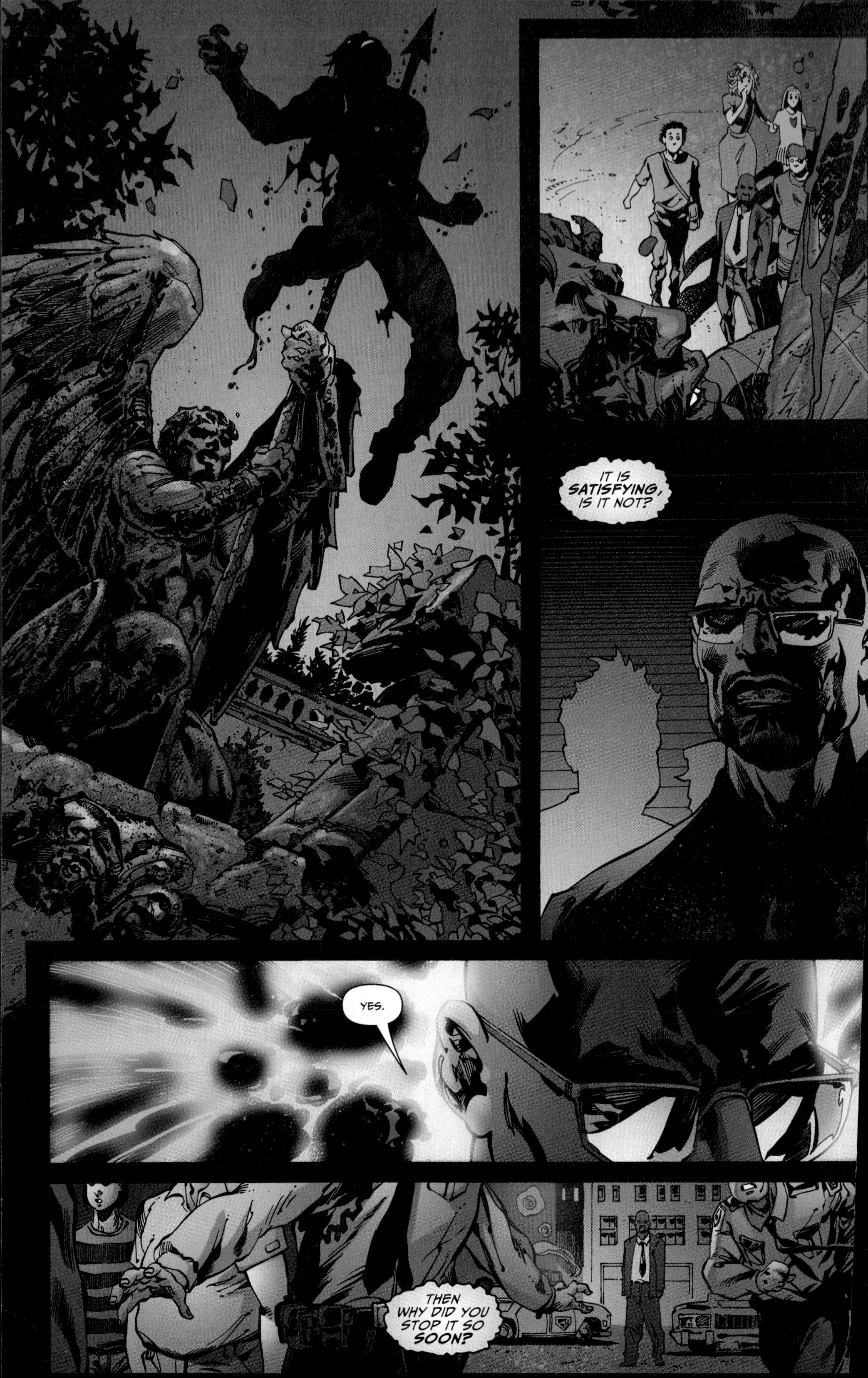
IT IS SATISFYING, IS IT NOT?
YES.
THEN WHY DID YOU STOP IT SO SOON?

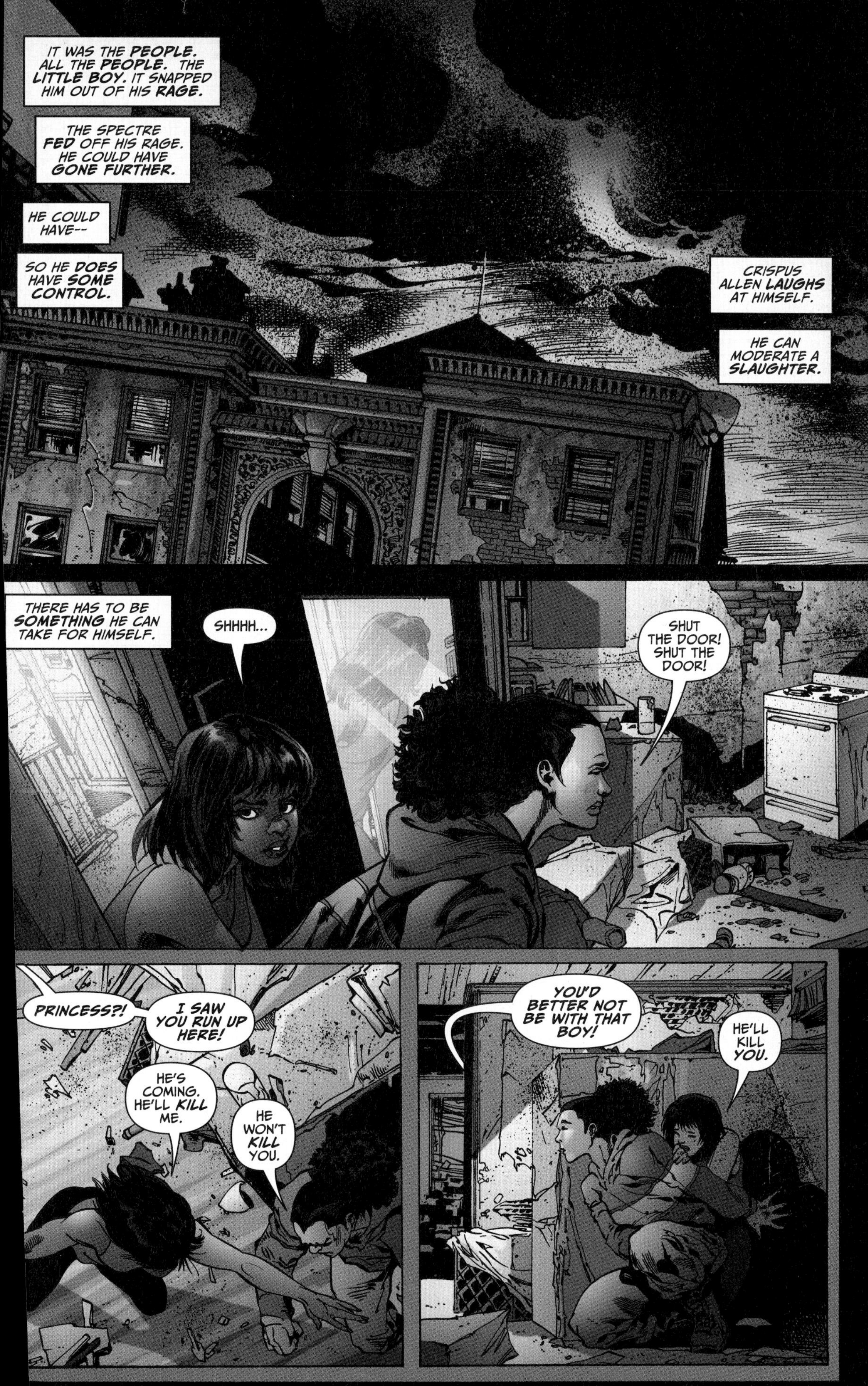

IT WAS THE PEOPLE. ALL THE PEOPLE. THE LITTLE BOY. IT SNAPPED HIM OUT OF HIS RAGE.
THE SPECTRE FED OFF HIS RAGE. HE COULD HAVE GONE FURTHER.
HE COULD HAVE--
SO HE DOES HAVE SOME CONTROL.
CRISPUS ALLEN LAUGHS AT HIMSELF.
HE CAN MODERATE A SLAUGHTER.
THERE HAS TO BE SOMETHING HE CAN TAKE FOR HIMSELF.
SHHHH...
SHUT THE DOOR! SHUT THE DOOR!
PRINCESS?!
I SAW YOU RUN UP HERE!
HE'S COMING. HE'LL KILL ME.
HE WON'T KILL YOU.
YOU'D BETTER NOT BE WITH THAT BOY!
HE'LL KILL YOU.

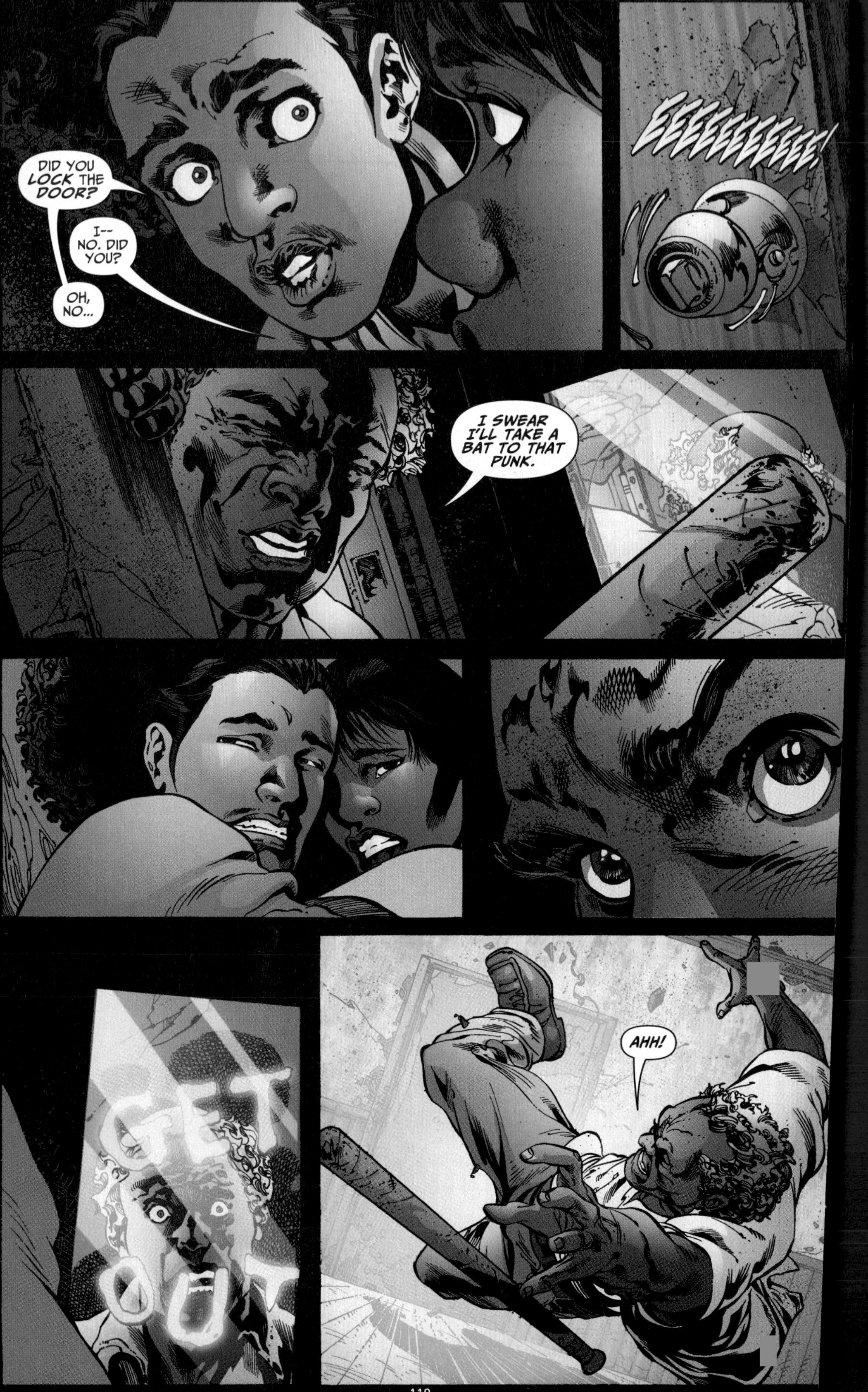
DID YOU LOCK THE DOOR?
I-- NO. DID YOU?
OH, NO...
EEEEEEEEEE!
I SWEAR I'LL TAKE A BAT TO THAT PUNK.
GET OUT
AHH!

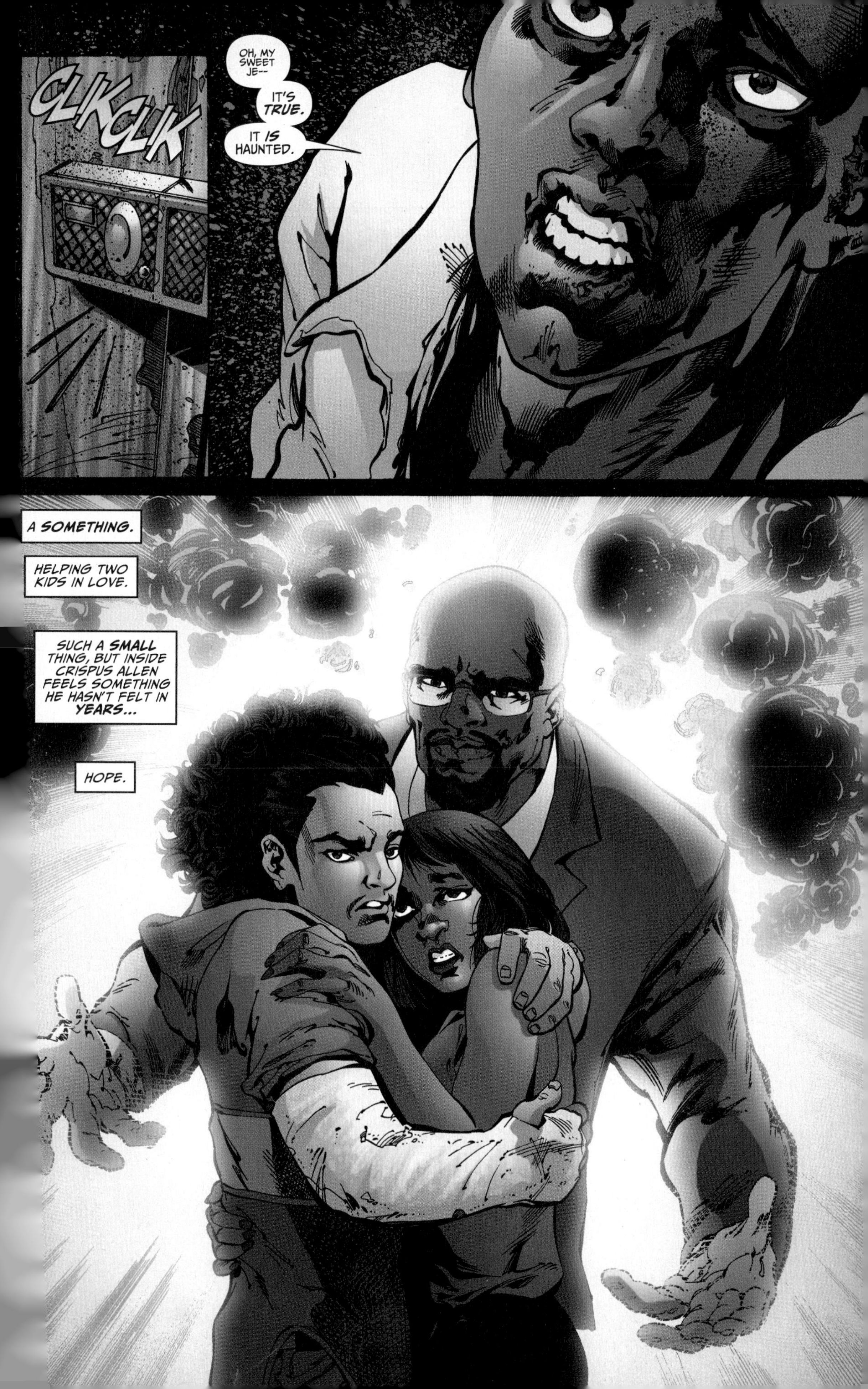
CLIKCLIK
OH, MY SWEET JE--
IT'S TRUE.
IT IS HAUNTED.
A SOMETHING.
HELPING TWO KIDS IN LOVE.
SUCH A SMALL THING, BUT INSIDE CRISPUS ALLEN FEELS SOMETHING HE HASN'T FELT IN YEARS...
HOPE.

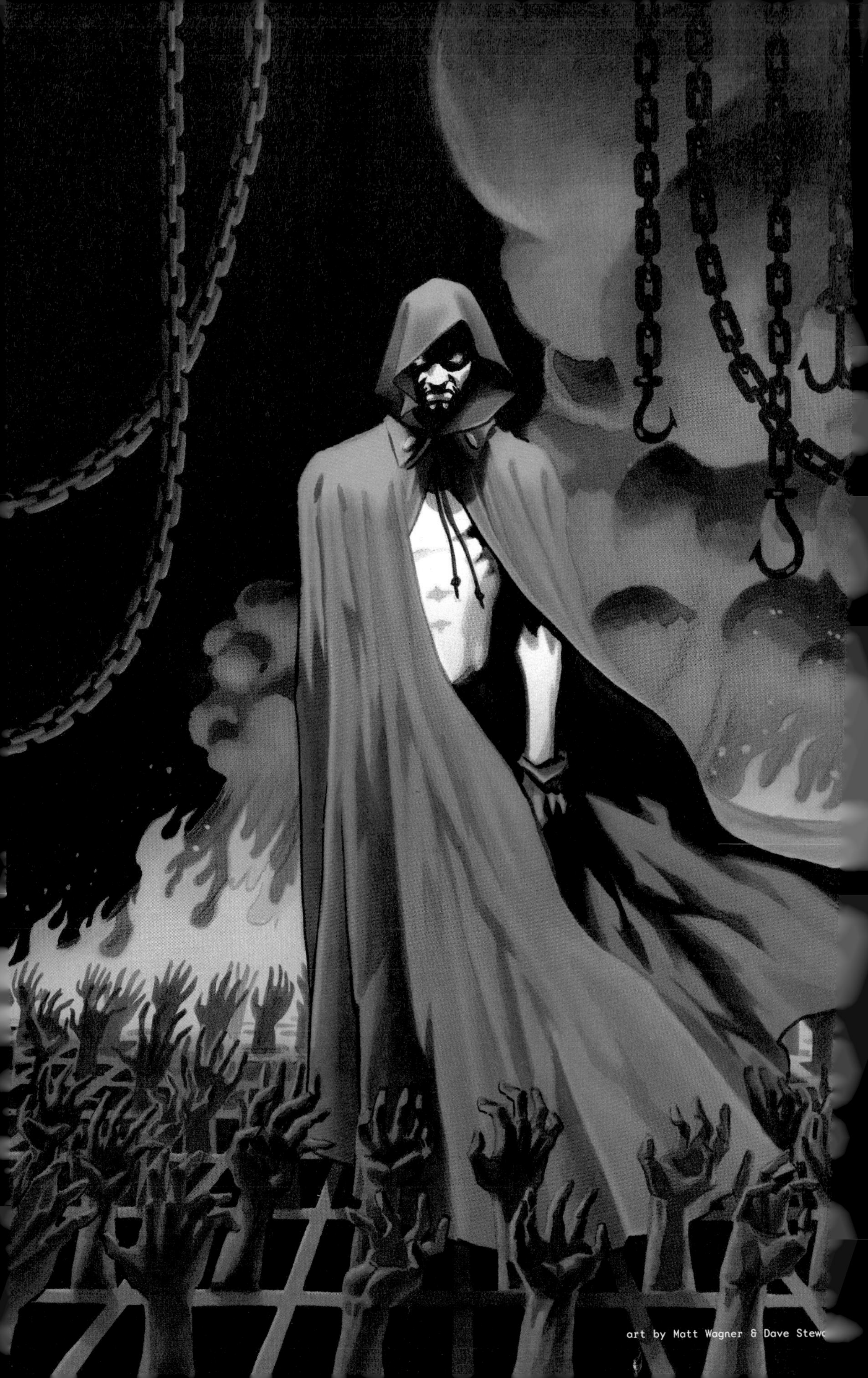
art by Matt Wagner & Dave Stewa

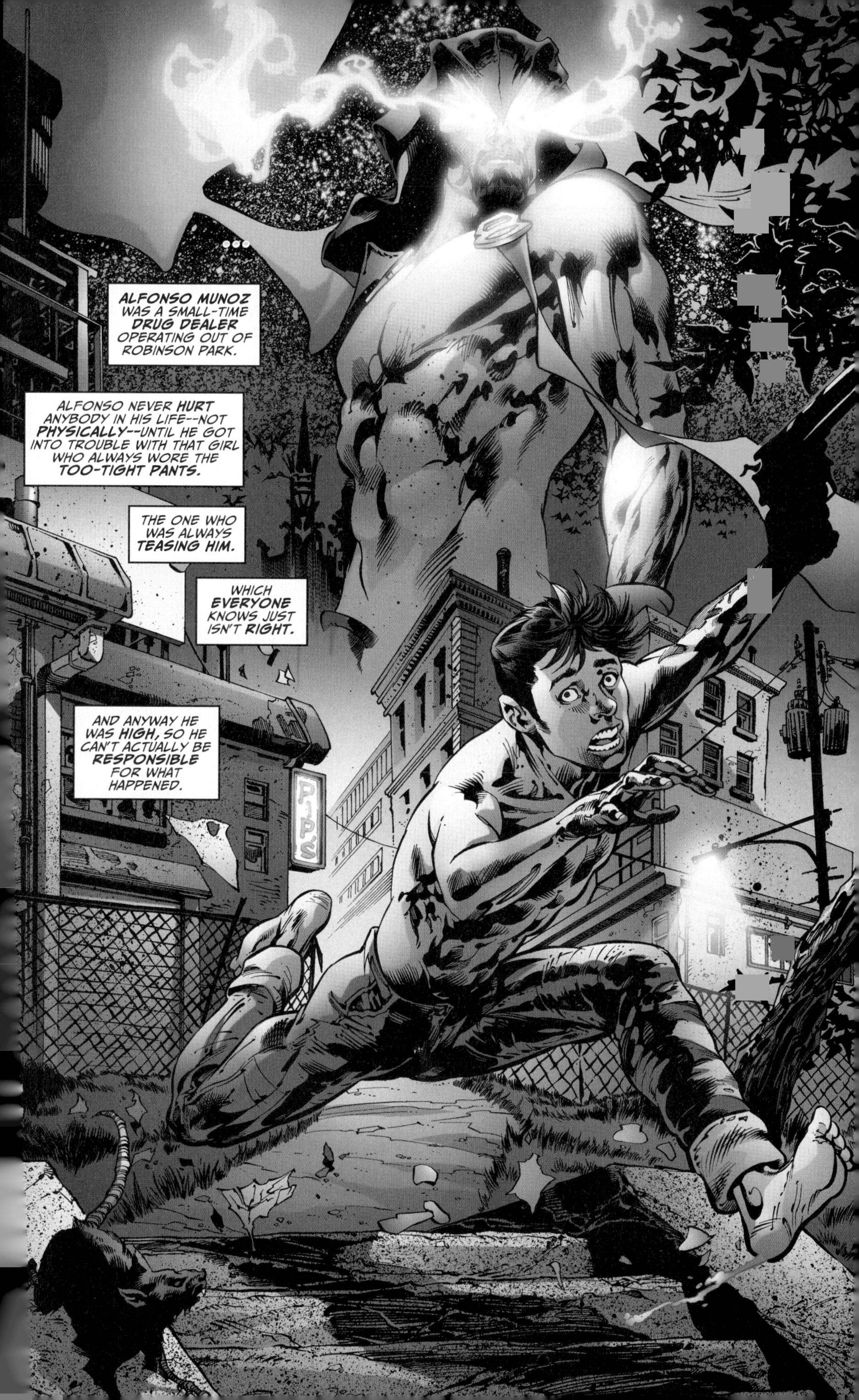
...
ALFONSO MUNOZ WAS A SMALL-TIME DRUG DEALER OPERATING OUT OF ROBINSON PARK.
ALFONSO NEVER HURT ANYBODY IN HIS LIFE--NOT PHYSICALLY--UNTIL HE GOT INTO TROUBLE WITH THAT GIRL WHO ALWAYS WORE THE TOO-TIGHT PANTS.
THE ONE WHO WAS ALWAYS TEASING HIM.
WHICH EVERYONE KNOWS JUST ISN'T RIGHT.
AND ANYWAY HE WAS HIGH, SO HE CAN'T ACTUALLY BE RESPONSIBLE FOR WHAT HAPPENED.
PIP'S

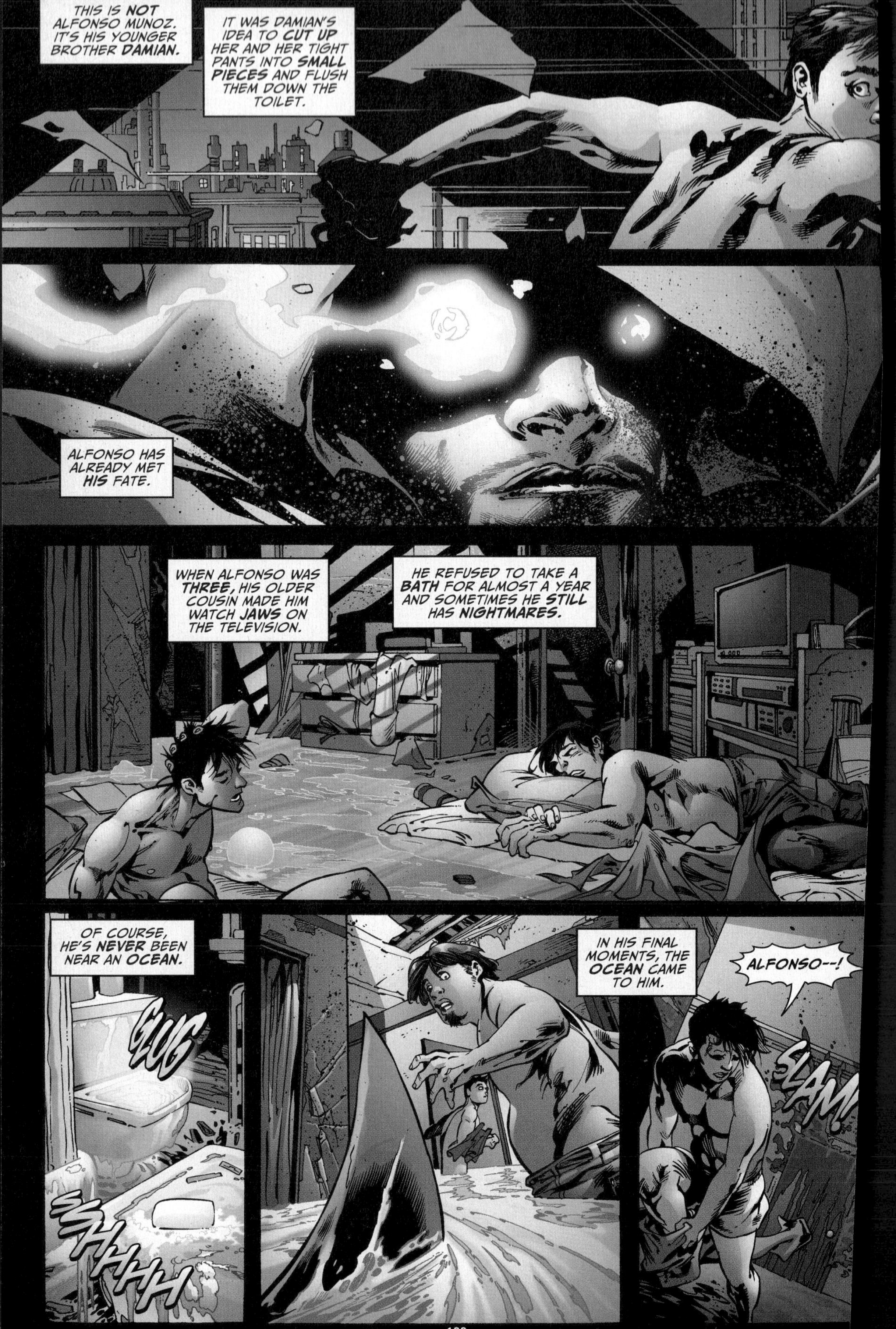
THIS IS NOT ALFONSO MUNOZ. IT'S HIS YOUNGER BROTHER DAMIAN.
IT WAS DAMIAN'S IDEA TO CUT UP HER AND HER TIGHT PANTS INTO SMALL PIECES AND FLUSH THEM DOWN THE TOILET.
ALFONSO HAS ALREADY MET HIS FATE.
WHEN ALFONSO WAS THREE, HIS OLDER COUSIN MADE HIM WATCH JAWS ON THE TELEVISION.
HE REFUSED TO TAKE A BATH FOR ALMOST A YEAR AND SOMETIMES HE STILL HAS NIGHTMARES.
OF COURSE, HE'S NEVER BEEN NEAR AN OCEAN.
GLUG
SHHHHH
IN HIS FINAL MOMENTS, THE OCEAN CAME TO HIM.
ALFONSO--!
SLAM!

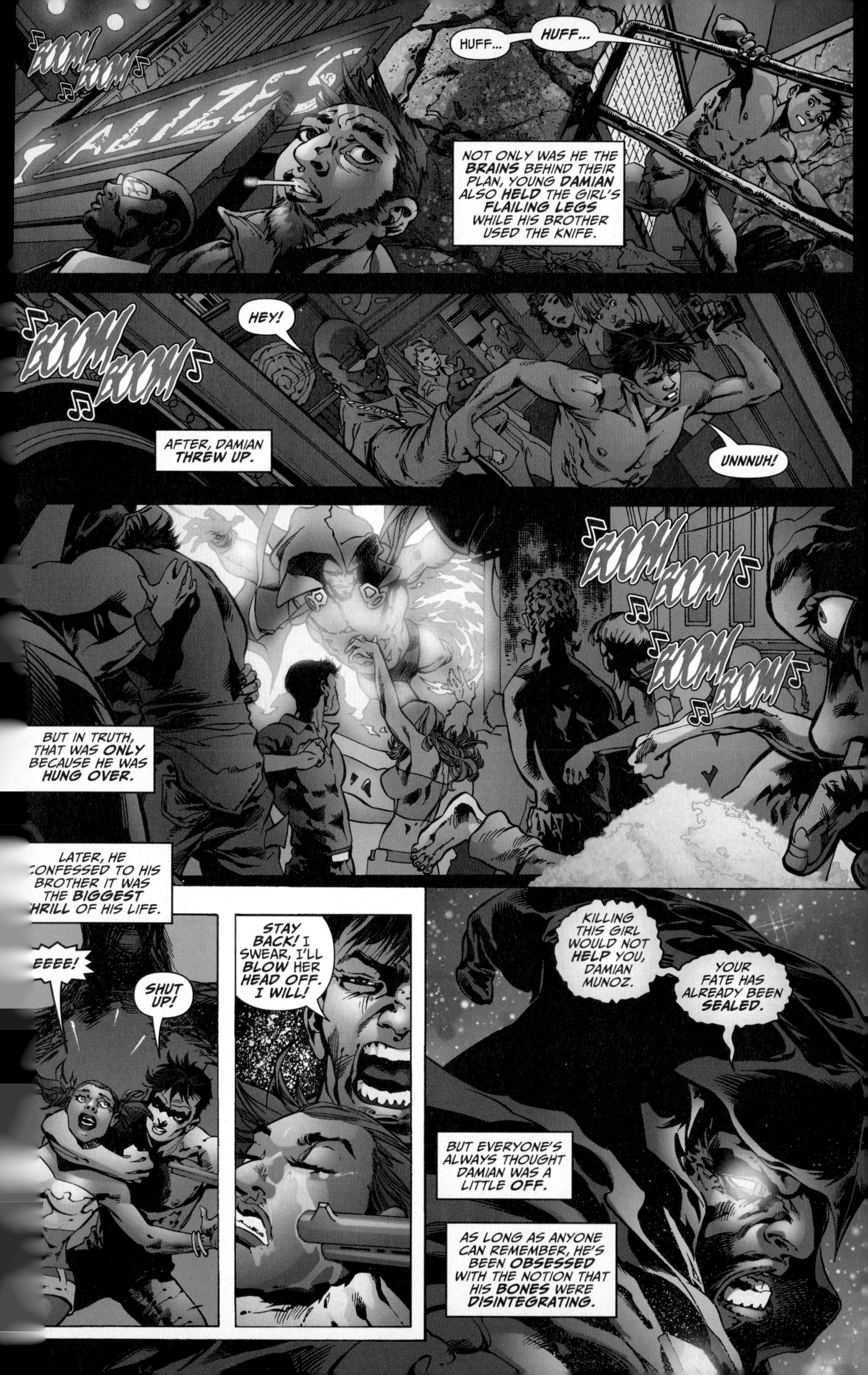
BOOM BOOM
HUFF... HUFF...
NOT ONLY WAS HE THE BRAINS BEHIND THEIR PLAN, YOUNG DAMIAN ALSO HELD THE GIRL'S FLAILING LEGS WHILE HIS BROTHER USED THE KNIFE.
BOOM BOOM
HEY!
AFTER, DAMIAN THREW UP.
UNNNUH!
BOOM BOOM
BOOM BOOM
BUT IN TRUTH, THAT WAS ONLY BECAUSE HE WAS HUNG OVER.
LATER, HE CONFESSED TO HIS BROTHER IT WAS THE BIGGEST THRILL OF HIS LIFE.
EEEE!
SHUT UP!
STAY BACK! I SWEAR, I'LL BLOW HER HEAD OFF. I WILL!
KILLING THIS GIRL WOULD NOT HELP YOU, DAMIAN MUNOZ.
YOUR FATE HAS ALREADY BEEN SEALED.
BUT EVERYONE'S ALWAYS THOUGHT DAMIAN WAS A LITTLE OFF.
AS LONG AS ANYONE CAN REMEMBER, HE'S BEEN OBSESSED WITH THE NOTION THAT HIS BONES WERE DISINTEGRATING.

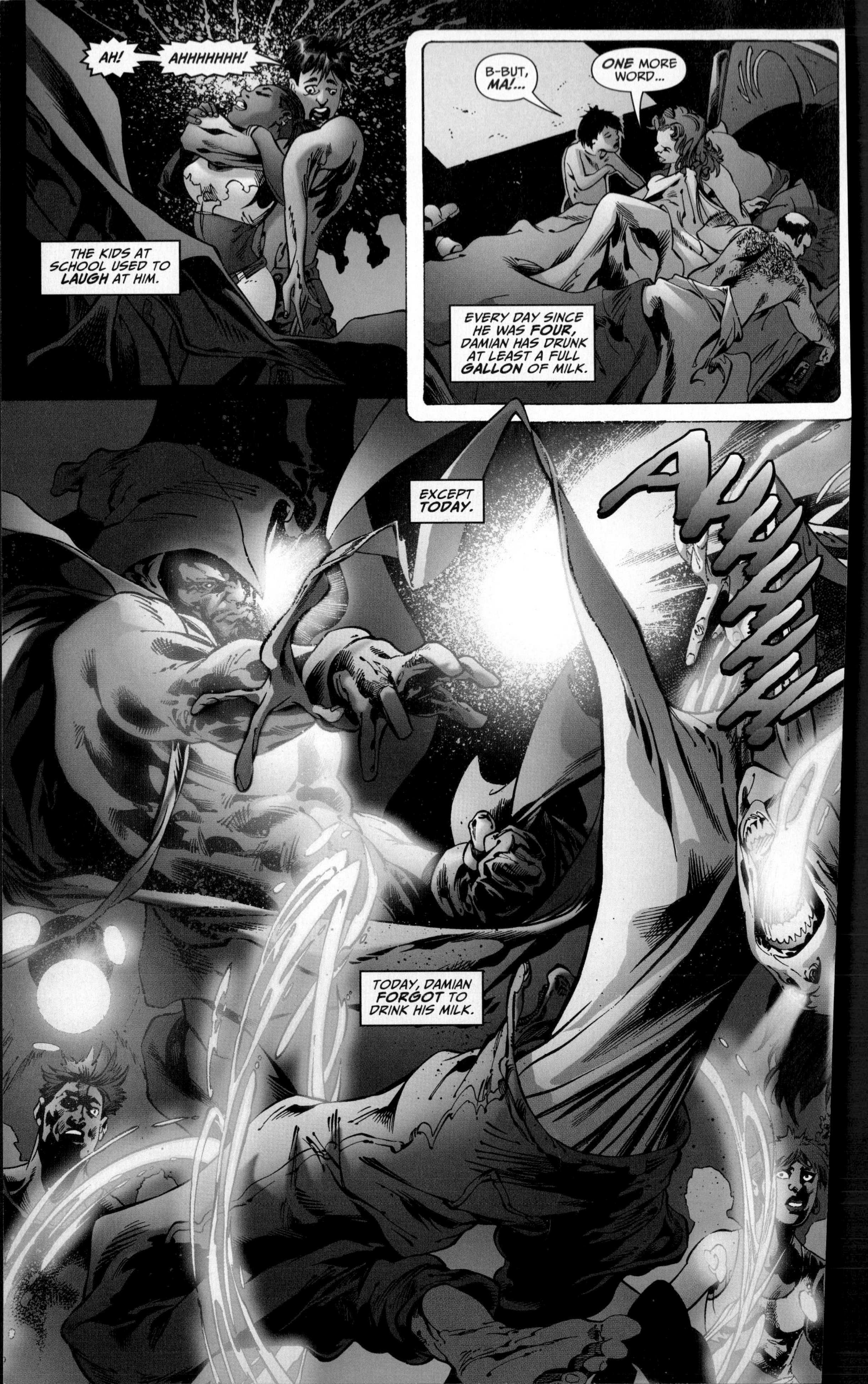
AH!
AHHHHHHH!
THE KIDS AT SCHOOL USED TO LAUGH AT HIM.
B-BUT, MA!...
ONE MORE WORD...
EVERY DAY SINCE HE WAS FOUR, DAMIAN HAS DRUNK AT LEAST A FULL GALLON OF MILK.
EXCEPT TODAY.
TODAY, DAMIAN FORGOT TO DRINK HIS MILK.

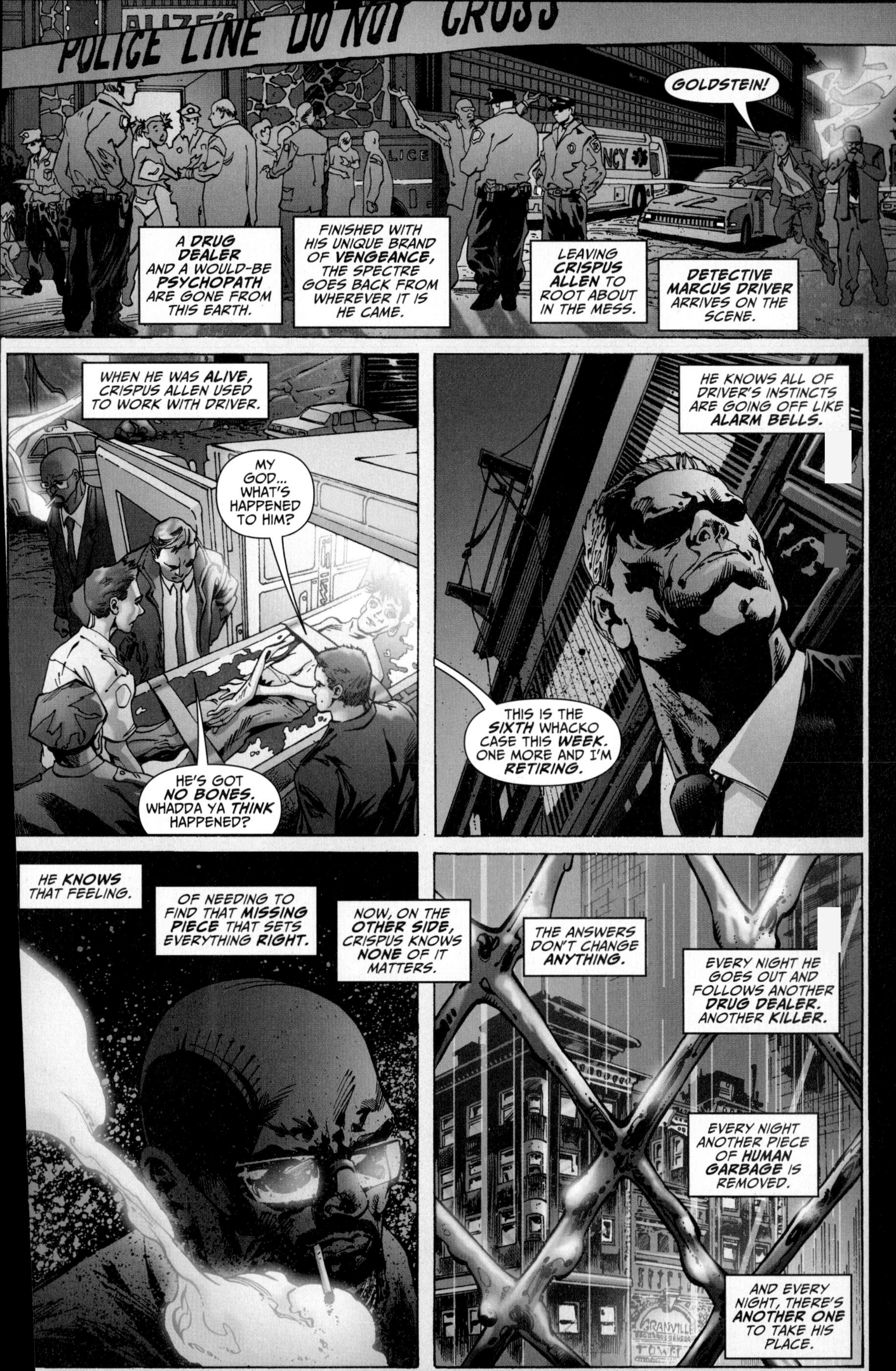
POLICE LINE DO NOT CROSS
GOLDSTEIN!
A DRUG DEALER AND A WOULD-BE PSYCHOPATH ARE GONE FROM THIS EARTH.
FINISHED WITH HIS UNIQUE BRAND OF VENGEANCE, THE SPECTRE GOES BACK FROM WHEREVER IT IS HE CAME.
LEAVING CRISPUS ALLEN TO ROOT ABOUT IN THE MESS.
DETECTIVE MARCUS DRIVER ARRIVES ON THE SCENE.
WHEN HE WAS ALIVE, CRISPUS ALLEN USED TO WORK WITH DRIVER.
MY GOD... WHAT'S HAPPENED TO HIM?
HE'S GOT NO BONES. WHADDA YA THINK HAPPENED?
HE KNOWS ALL OF DRIVER'S INSTINCTS ARE GOING OFF LIKE ALARM BELLS.
THIS IS THE SIXTH WHACKO CASE THIS WEEK. ONE MORE AND I'M RETIRING.
HE KNOWS THAT FEELING.
OF NEEDING TO FIND THAT MISSING PIECE THAT SETS EVERYTHING RIGHT.
NOW, ON THE OTHER SIDE, CRISPUS KNOWS NONE OF IT MATTERS.
THE ANSWERS DON'T CHANGE ANYTHING.
EVERY NIGHT HE GOES OUT AND FOLLOWS ANOTHER DRUG DEALER. ANOTHER KILLER.
EVERY NIGHT ANOTHER PIECE OF HUMAN GARBAGE IS REMOVED.
AND EVERY NIGHT, THERE'S ANOTHER ONE TO TAKE HIS PLACE.

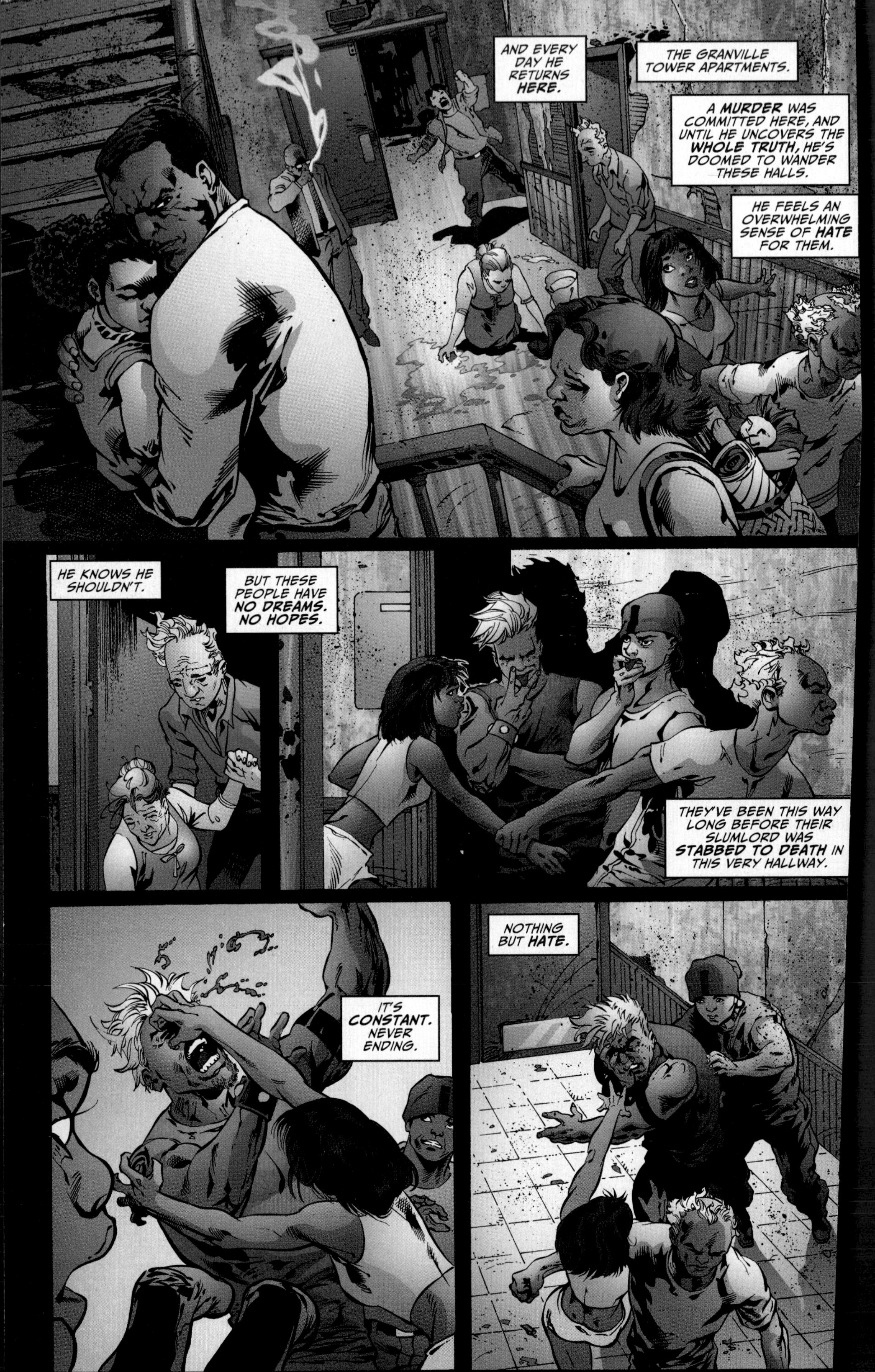
AND EVERY DAY HE RETURNS HERE.
THE GRANVILLE TOWER APARTMENTS.
A MURDER WAS COMMITTED HERE, AND UNTIL HE UNCOVERS THE WHOLE TRUTH, HE'S DOOMED TO WANDER THESE HALLS.
HE FEELS AN OVERWHELMING SENSE OF HATE FOR THEM.
HE KNOWS HE SHOULDN'T.
BUT THESE PEOPLE HAVE NO DREAMS. NO HOPES.
THEY'VE BEEN THIS WAY LONG BEFORE THEIR SLUMLORD WAS STABBED TO DEATH IN THIS VERY HALLWAY.
IT'S CONSTANT. NEVER ENDING.
NOTHING BUT HATE.

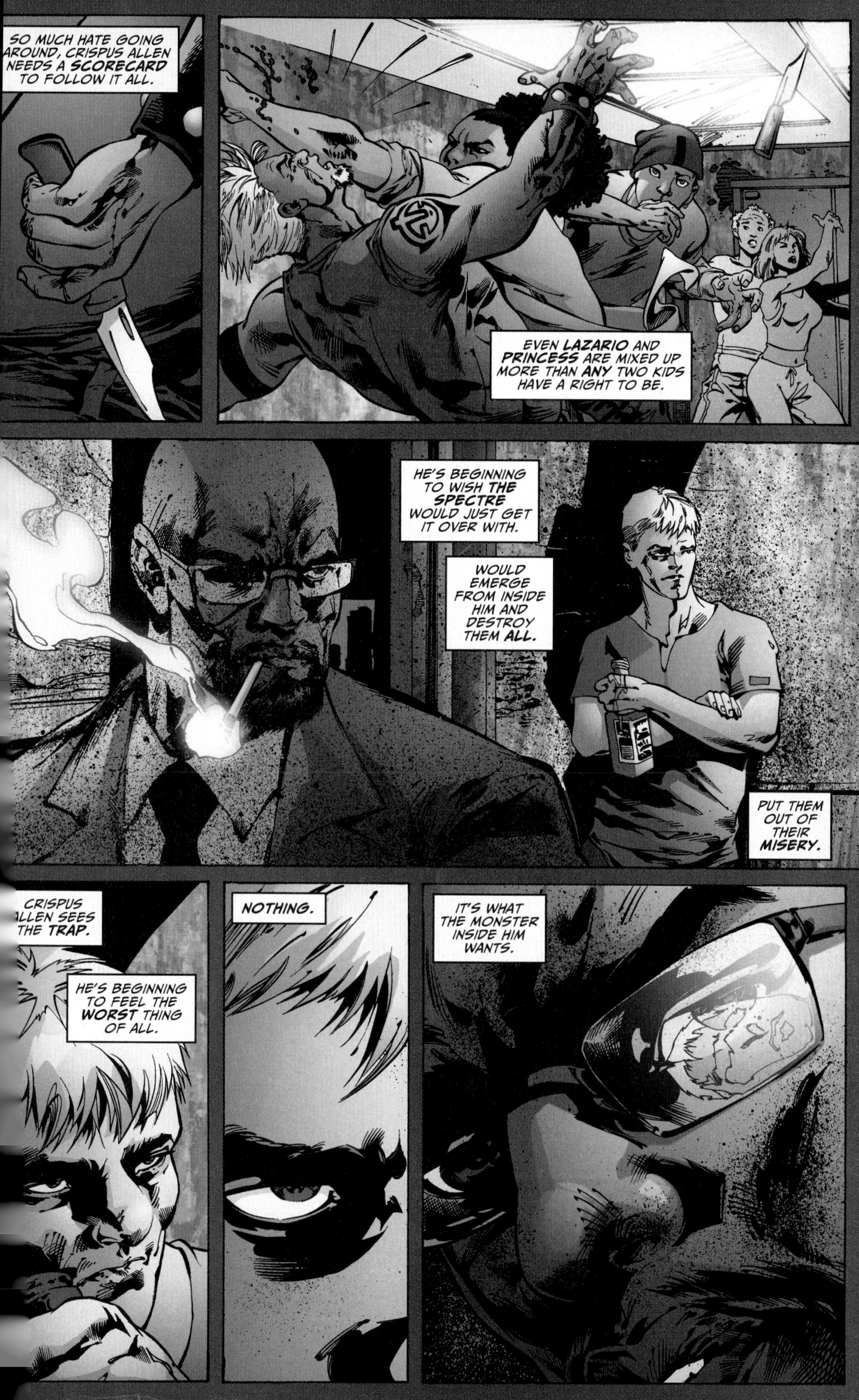
SO MUCH HATE GOING AROUND, CRISPUS ALLEN NEEDS A SCORECARD TO FOLLOW IT ALL.
EVEN LAZARIO AND PRINCESS ARE MIXED UP MORE THAN ANY TWO KIDS HAVE A RIGHT TO BE.
HE'S BEGINNING TO WISH THE SPECTRE WOULD JUST GET IT OVER WITH.
WOULD EMERGE FROM INSIDE HIM AND DESTROY THEM ALL.
PUT THEM OUT OF THEIR MISERY.
CRISPUS ALLEN SEES THE TRAP.
HE'S BEGINNING TO FEEL THE WORST THING OF ALL.
NOTHING.
IT'S WHAT THE MONSTER INSIDE HIM WANTS.

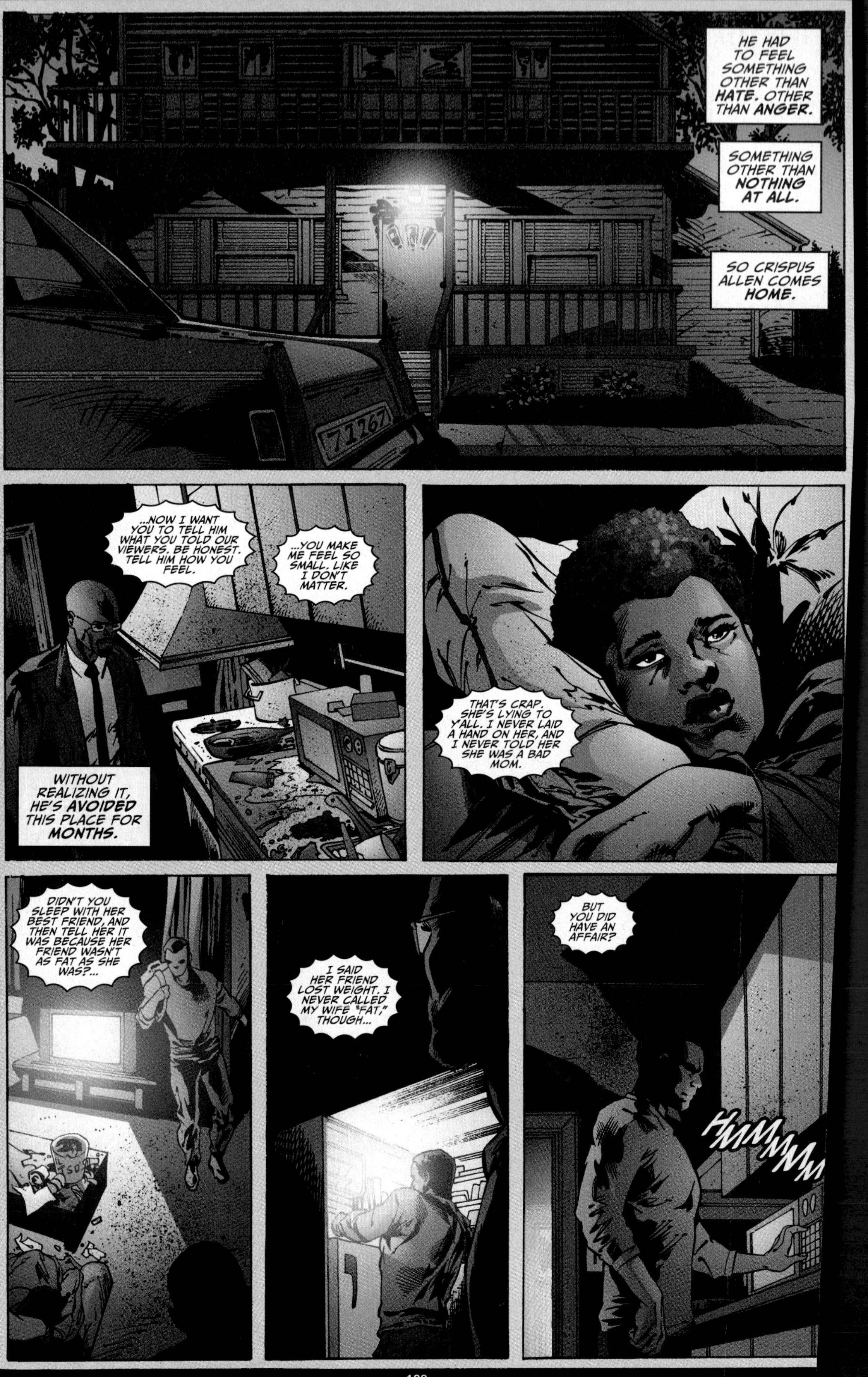

HE HAD TO FEEL SOMETHING OTHER THAN HATE. OTHER THAN ANGER.
SOMETHING OTHER THAN NOTHING AT ALL.
SO CRISPUS ALLEN COMES HOME.
71267
...NOW I WANT YOU TO TELL HIM WHAT YOU TOLD OUR VIEWERS. BE HONEST. TELL HIM HOW YOU FEEL.
...YOU MAKE ME FEEL SO SMALL. LIKE I DON'T MATTER.
WITHOUT REALIZING IT, HE'S AVOIDED THIS PLACE FOR MONTHS.
THAT'S CRAP. SHE'S LYING TO Y'ALL. I NEVER LAID A HAND ON HER, AND I NEVER TOLD HER SHE WAS A BAD MOM.
DIDN'T YOU SLEEP WITH HER BEST FRIEND, AND THEN TELL HER IT WAS BECAUSE HER FRIEND WASN'T AS FAT AS SHE WAS?...
I SAID HER FRIEND LOST WEIGHT. I NEVER CALLED MY WIFE "FAT," THOUGH...
BUT YOU DID HAVE AN AFFAIR?
KMMMMMM

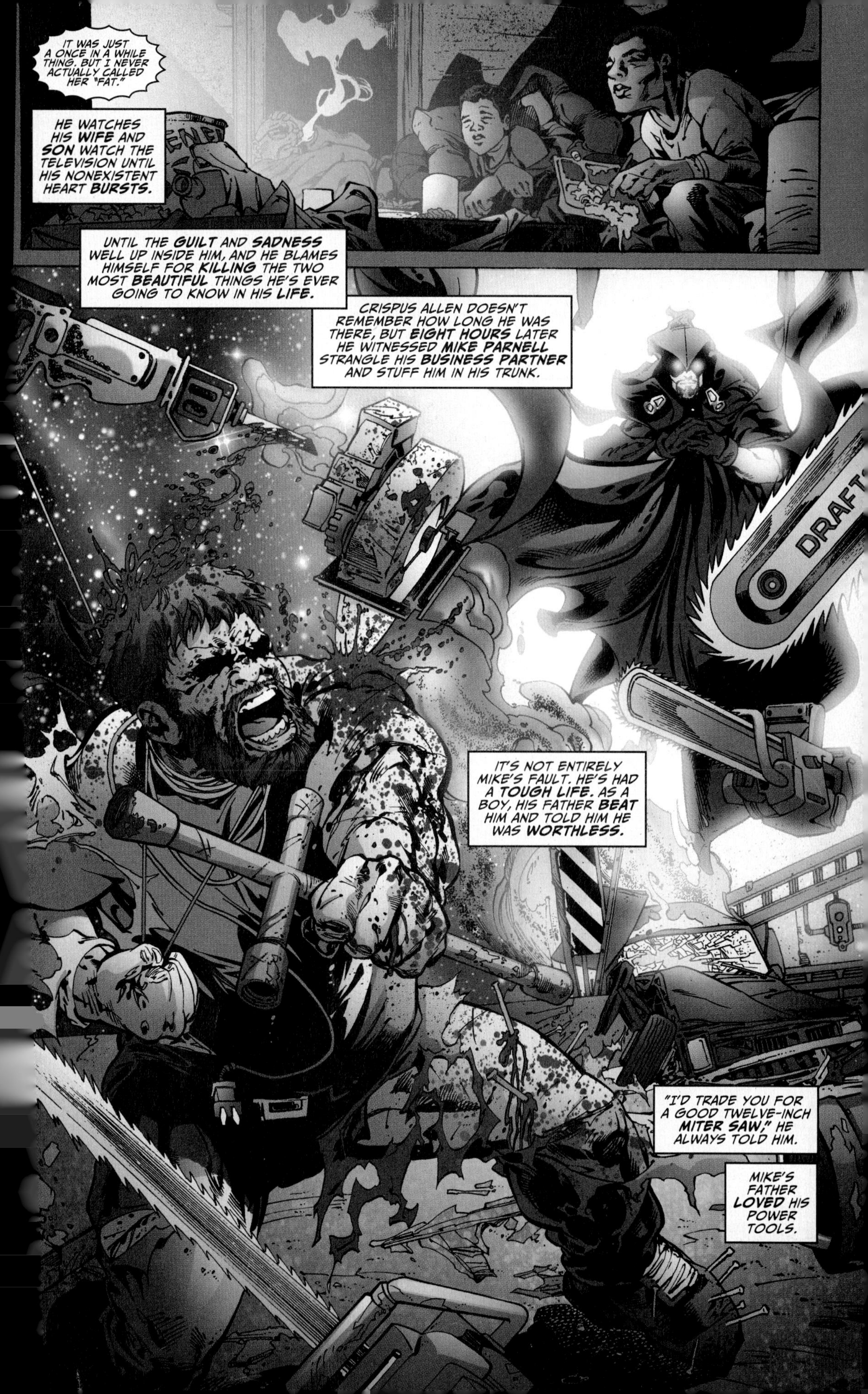
IT WAS JUST A ONCE IN A WHILE THING. BUT I NEVER ACTUALLY CALLED HER "FAT."
HE WATCHES HIS WIFE AND SON WATCH THE TELEVISION UNTIL HIS NONEXISTENT HEART BURSTS.
UNTIL THE GUILT AND SADNESS WELL UP INSIDE HIM, AND HE BLAMES HIMSELF FOR KILLING THE TWO MOST BEAUTIFUL THINGS HE'S EVER GOING TO KNOW IN HIS LIFE.
CRISPUS ALLEN DOESN'T REMEMBER HOW LONG HE WAS THERE, BUT EIGHT HOURS LATER HE WITNESSED MIKE PARNELL STRANGLE HIS BUSINESS PARTNER AND STUFF HIM IN HIS TRUNK.
DRAFT
IT'S NOT ENTIRELY MIKE'S FAULT. HE'S HAD A TOUGH LIFE. AS A BOY, HIS FATHER BEAT HIM AND TOLD HIM HE WAS WORTHLESS.
"I'D TRADE YOU FOR A GOOD TWELVE-INCH MITER SAW," HE ALWAYS TOLD HIM.
MIKE'S FATHER LOVED HIS POWER TOOLS.

HE DOESN'T EVEN **WAIT** FOR THE POLICE TO COME.

ABOUT NOW, HE IMAGINES, **MARCUS DRIVER** IS PICKING UP **CHUNKS** OF **JACK PARNELL** ALL THE WAY DOWN TO THE **RIVER**.

WHAT DOES IT MATTER?

WHAT DOES **ANYBODY** MATTER?

HIS **COP'S** INSTINCTS MAKE HIM STOP.

WEDDING BAND. **MARRIED.** LOOKS LIKE A **REGULAR JOE.**

WHAT'S HE DOING IN **GOTHAM** AT THIS HOUR?

-:SOB:-

NNNUUUHH... NNNN...

OH, GOD. OH, GOD...GOD, **PLEASE** TELL ME WHAT TO DO... UHNNN...BREATHE... BREATHE...

BEEP BEEP BEEP

HEY!...

JACK, IT'S **DOUG.** YOU'RE NEVER GONNA B--

...I'M NOT AVAILABLE TO TAKE YOUR CALL, BUT IT SURE IS **DANG** IMPORTANT TO ME, SO LEAVE A NICE MESSAGE AT THE TONE...

BEEEEEP!

DAMMIT, JACK PICK UP! I'M ST IN THE **DAMN** C THAT GIRL YOU L ME WITH...SHE T MY **WALLET!**

YOU SWOR THIS KIND C THING **NEVE** HAPPENS! W AM I SUPPO TO TELL CAR

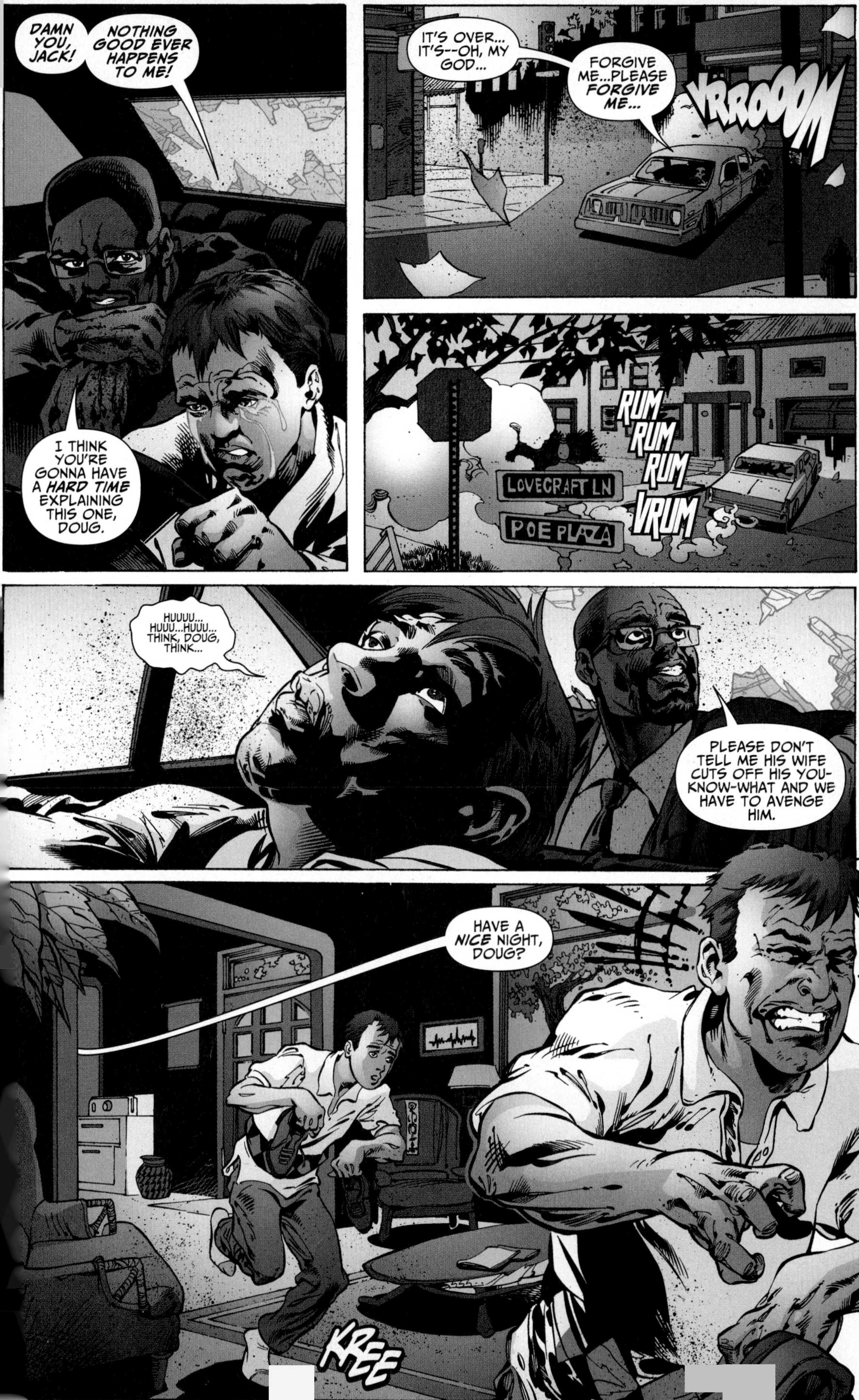
DAMN YOU, JACK!
NOTHING GOOD EVER HAPPENS TO ME!
I THINK YOU'RE GONNA HAVE A HARD TIME EXPLAINING THIS ONE, DOUG.
IT'S OVER... IT'S--OH, MY GOD...
FORGIVE ME...PLEASE FORGIVE ME...
VRROOOM
LOVECRAFT LN
POE PLAZA
RUM RUM RUM VRUM
HUUUU... HUUU...HUUU... THINK, DOUG, THINK...
PLEASE DON'T TELL ME HIS WIFE CUTS OFF HIS YOU-KNOW-WHAT AND WE HAVE TO AVENGE HIM.
HAVE A NICE NIGHT, DOUG?
KREE

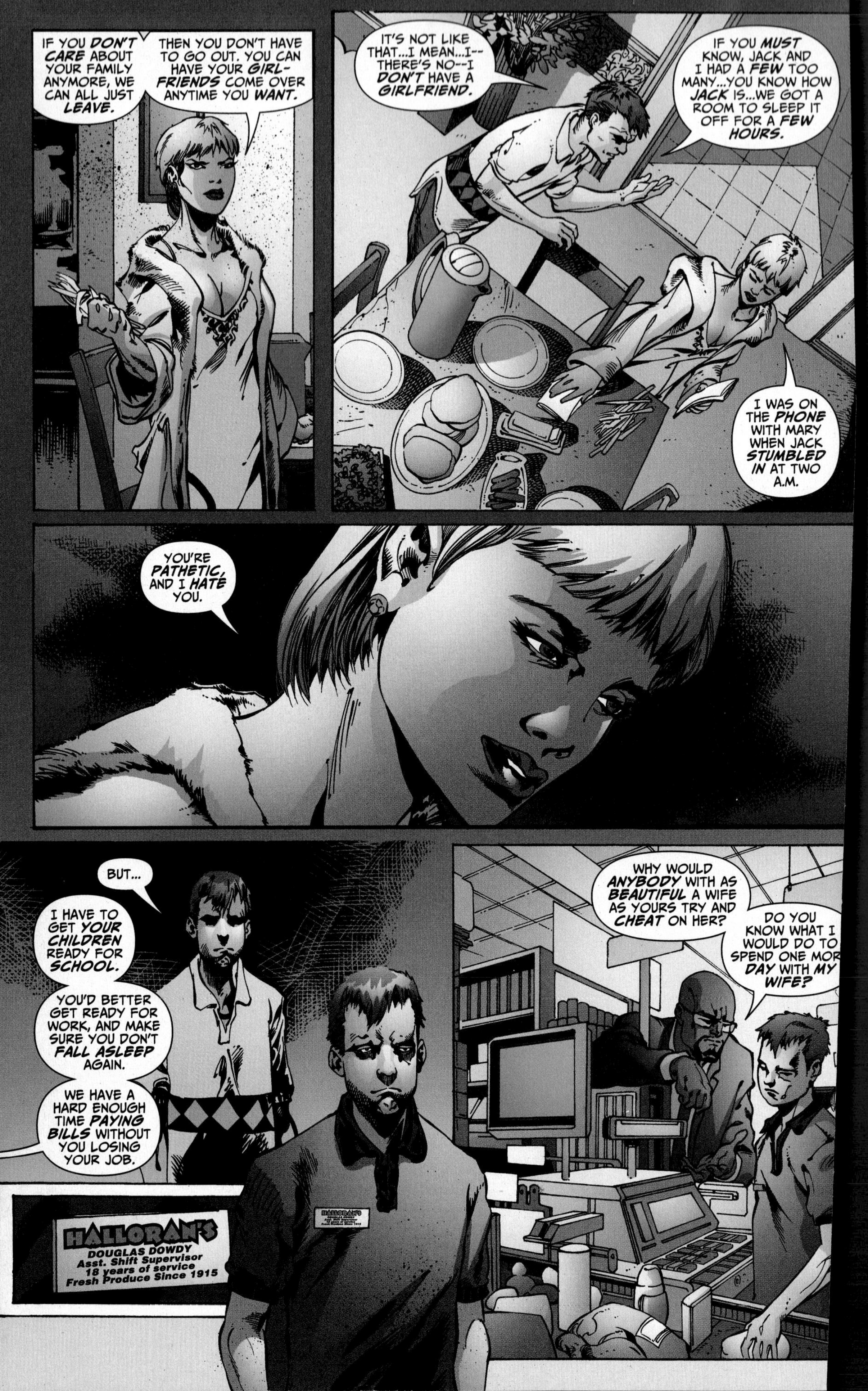
IF YOU DON'T CARE ABOUT YOUR FAMILY ANYMORE, WE CAN ALL JUST LEAVE.
THEN YOU DON'T HAVE TO GO OUT. YOU CAN HAVE YOUR GIRL-FRIENDS COME OVER ANYTIME YOU WANT.
IT'S NOT LIKE THAT...I MEAN...I--THERE'S NO--I DON'T HAVE A GIRLFRIEND.
IF YOU MUST KNOW, JACK AND I HAD A FEW TOO MANY...YOU KNOW HOW JACK IS...WE GOT A ROOM TO SLEEP IT OFF FOR A FEW HOURS.
I WAS ON THE PHONE WITH MARY WHEN JACK STUMBLED IN AT TWO A.M.
YOU'RE PATHETIC, AND I HATE YOU.
BUT...
I HAVE TO GET YOUR CHILDREN READY FOR SCHOOL.
YOU'D BETTER GET READY FOR WORK, AND MAKE SURE YOU DON'T FALL ASLEEP AGAIN.
WE HAVE A HARD ENOUGH TIME PAYING BILLS WITHOUT YOU LOSING YOUR JOB.
HALLORAN'S
DOUGLAS DOWDY
Asst. Shift Supervisor
18 years of service
Fresh Produce Since 1915
WHY WOULD ANYBODY WITH AS BEAUTIFUL A WIFE AS YOURS TRY AND CHEAT ON HER?
DO YOU KNOW WHAT I WOULD DO TO SPEND ONE MOR DAY WITH MY WIFE?

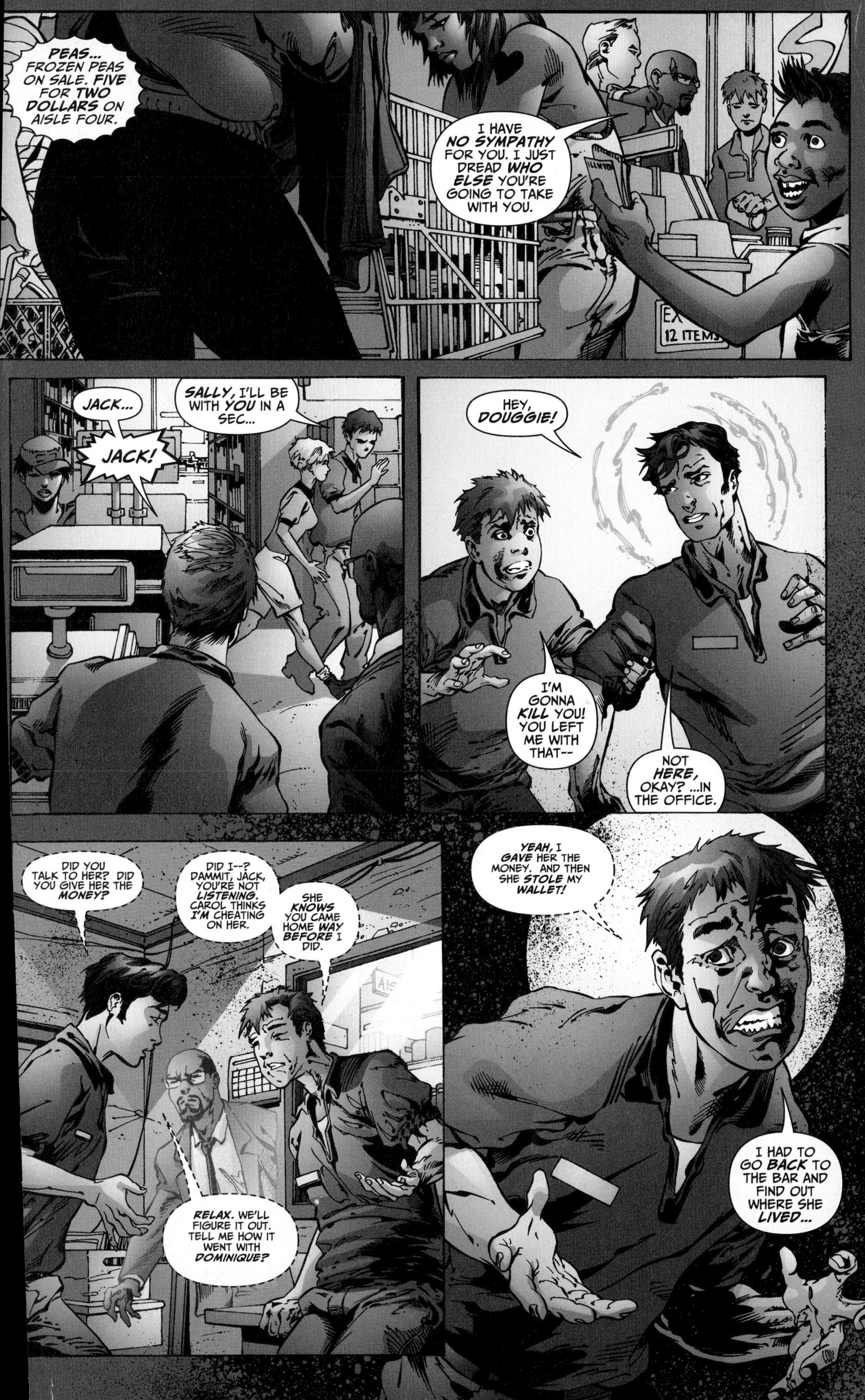
PEAS... FROZEN PEAS ON SALE. FIVE FOR TWO DOLLARS ON AISLE FOUR.
I HAVE NO SYMPATHY FOR YOU. I JUST DREAD WHO ELSE YOU'RE GOING TO TAKE WITH YOU.
EX 12 ITEMS
JACK...
SALLY, I'LL BE WITH YOU IN A SEC...
JACK!
HEY, DOUGGIE!
I'M GONNA KILL YOU! YOU LEFT ME WITH THAT--
NOT HERE, OKAY? ...IN THE OFFICE.
DID YOU TALK TO HER? DID YOU GIVE HER THE MONEY?
DID I--? DAMMIT, JACK, YOU'RE NOT LISTENING. CAROL THINKS I'M CHEATING ON HER.
SHE KNOWS YOU CAME HOME WAY BEFORE I DID.
RELAX. WE'LL FIGURE IT OUT. TELL ME HOW IT WENT WITH DOMINIQUE?
YEAH, I GAVE HER THE MONEY. AND THEN SHE STOLE MY WALLET!
I HAD TO GO BACK TO THE BAR AND FIND OUT WHERE SHE LIVED...

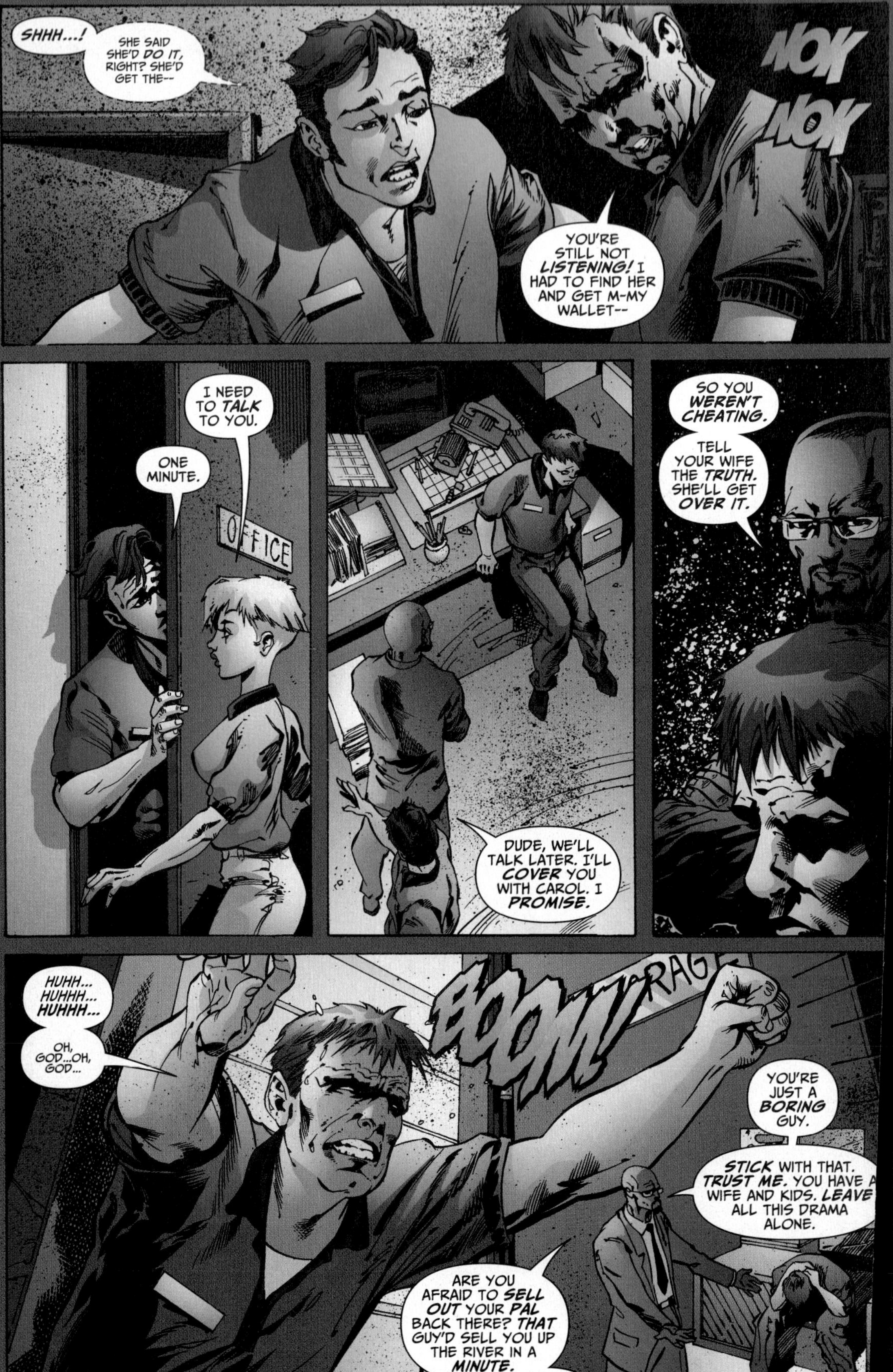
SHHH...!
SHE SAID SHE'D DO IT, RIGHT? SHE'D GET THE--
NOK NOK
YOU'RE STILL NOT LISTENING! I HAD TO FIND HER AND GET M-MY WALLET--
I NEED TO TALK TO YOU.
ONE MINUTE.
OFFICE
DUDE, WE'LL TALK LATER. I'LL COVER YOU WITH CAROL. I PROMISE.
SO YOU WEREN'T CHEATING.
TELL YOUR WIFE THE TRUTH. SHE'LL GET OVER IT.
HUHH... HUHHH... HUHHH...
OH, GOD...OH, GOD...
BOOM!
RAGE
YOU'RE JUST A BORING GUY.
STICK WITH THAT. TRUST ME. YOU HAVE A WIFE AND KIDS. LEAVE ALL THIS DRAMA ALONE.
ARE YOU AFRAID TO SELL OUT YOUR PAL BACK THERE? THAT GUY'D SELL YOU UP THE RIVER IN A MINUTE.
WAKE UP, MAN.

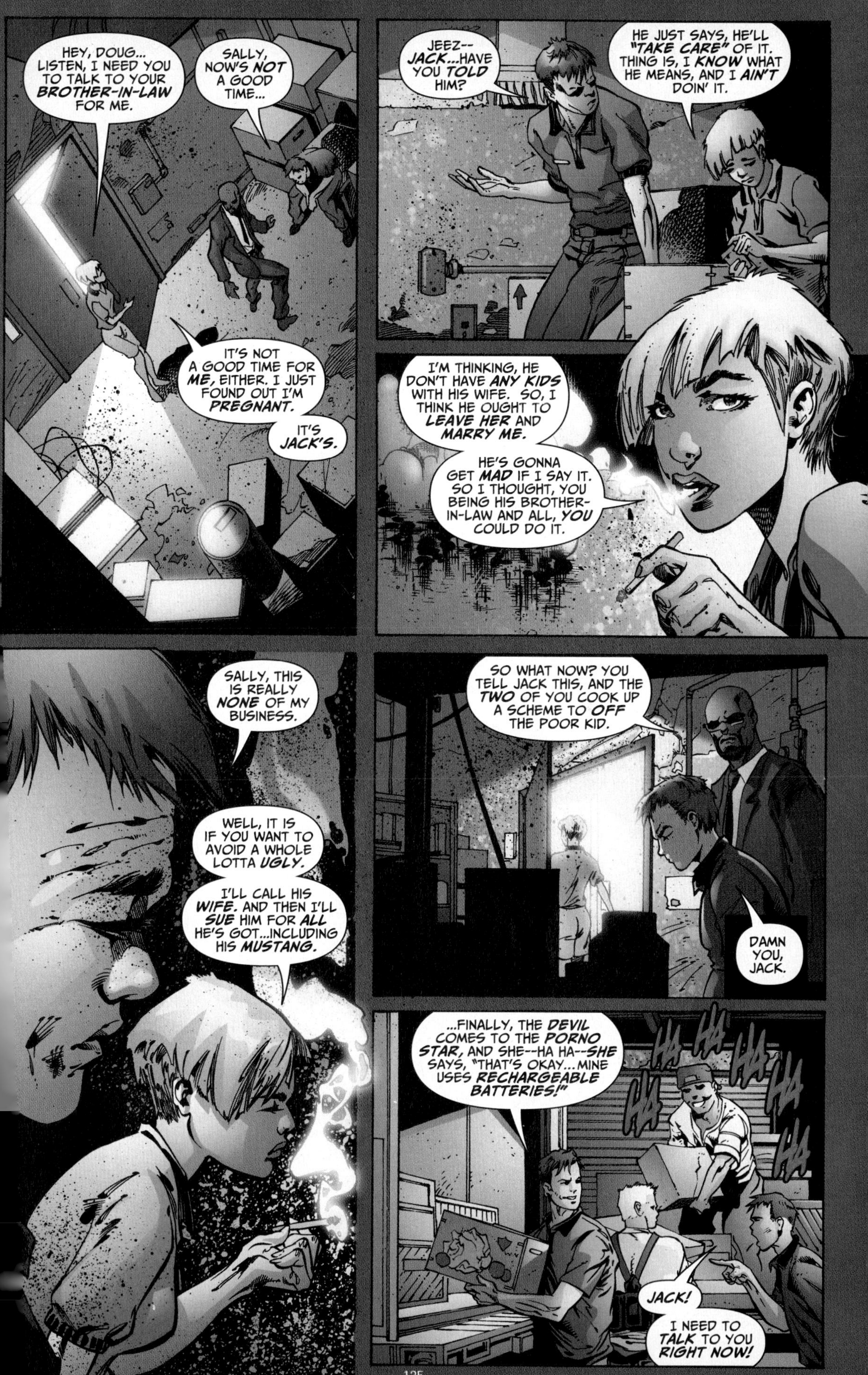
HEY, DOUG... LISTEN, I NEED YOU TO TALK TO YOUR BROTHER-IN-LAW FOR ME.
SALLY, NOW'S NOT A GOOD TIME...
IT'S NOT A GOOD TIME FOR ME, EITHER. I JUST FOUND OUT I'M PREGNANT.
IT'S JACK'S.
JEEZ-- JACK...HAVE YOU TOLD HIM?
HE JUST SAYS, HE'LL "TAKE CARE" OF IT. THING IS, I KNOW WHAT HE MEANS, AND I AIN'T DOIN' IT.
I'M THINKING, HE DON'T HAVE ANY KIDS WITH HIS WIFE. SO, I THINK HE OUGHT TO LEAVE HER AND MARRY ME.
HE'S GONNA GET MAD IF I SAY IT. SO I THOUGHT, YOU BEING HIS BROTHER-IN-LAW AND ALL, YOU COULD DO IT.
SALLY, THIS IS REALLY NONE OF MY BUSINESS.
WELL, IT IS IF YOU WANT TO AVOID A WHOLE LOTTA UGLY.
I'LL CALL HIS WIFE. AND THEN I'LL SUE HIM FOR ALL HE'S GOT...INCLUDING HIS MUSTANG.
SO WHAT NOW? YOU TELL JACK THIS, AND THE TWO OF YOU COOK UP A SCHEME TO OFF THE POOR KID.
DAMN YOU, JACK.
...FINALLY, THE DEVIL COMES TO THE PORNO STAR, AND SHE--HA HA--SHE SAYS, "THAT'S OKAY...MINE USES RECHARGEABLE BATTERIES!"
HA HA HA HA HA HA HA HA
JACK!
I NEED TO TALK TO YOU RIGHT NOW!

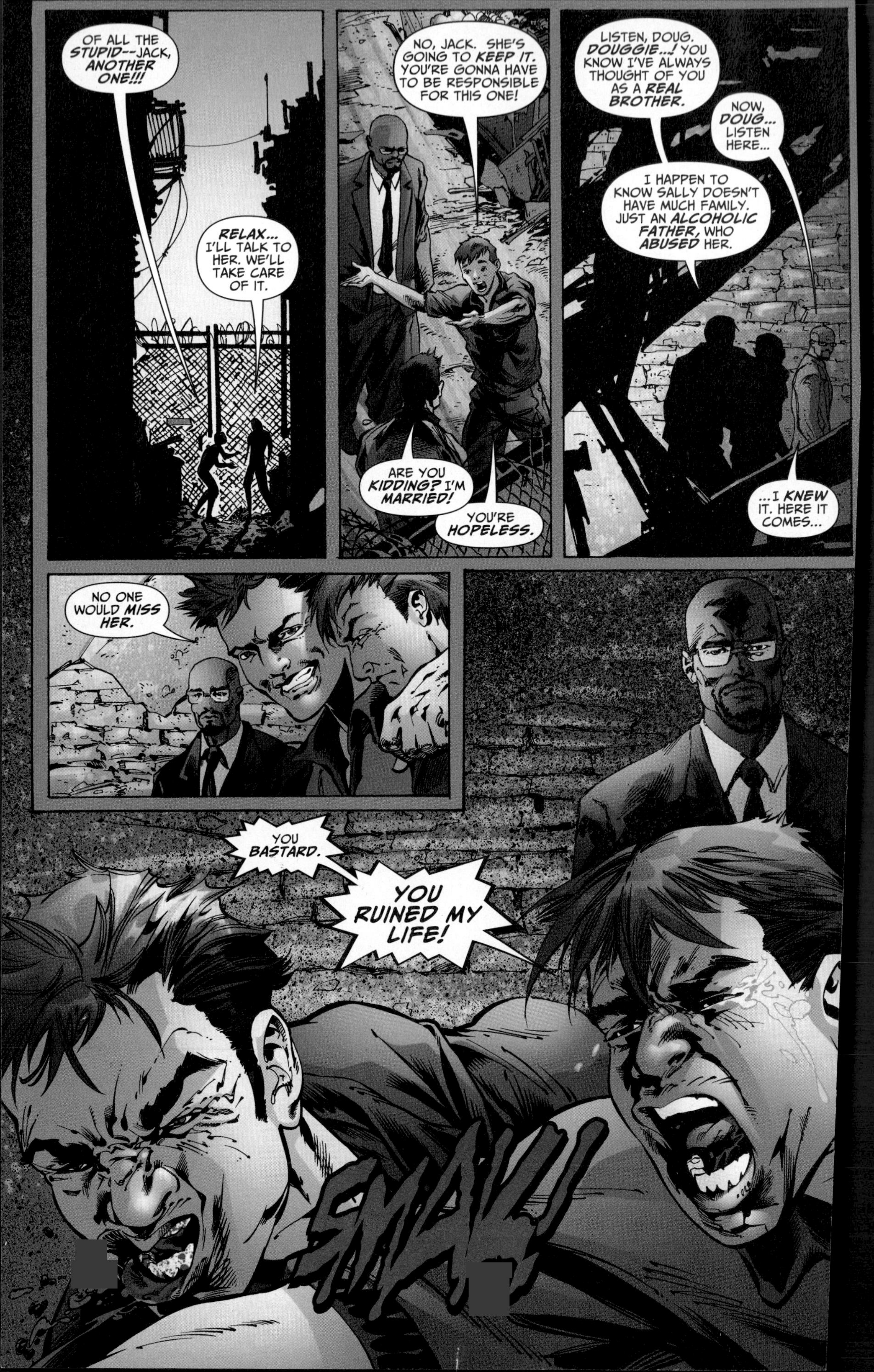
OF ALL THE STUPID--JACK, ANOTHER ONE!!!
RELAX... I'LL TALK TO HER. WE'LL TAKE CARE OF IT.
NO, JACK. SHE'S GOING TO KEEP IT. YOU'RE GONNA HAVE TO BE RESPONSIBLE FOR THIS ONE!
ARE YOU KIDDING? I'M MARRIED!
YOU'RE HOPELESS.
LISTEN, DOUG. DOUGGIE...! YOU KNOW I'VE ALWAYS THOUGHT OF YOU AS A REAL BROTHER.
NOW, DOUG... LISTEN HERE...
I HAPPEN TO KNOW SALLY DOESN'T HAVE MUCH FAMILY. JUST AN ALCOHOLIC FATHER, WHO ABUSED HER.
...I KNEW IT. HERE IT COMES...
NO ONE WOULD MISS HER.
YOU BASTARD.
YOU RUINED MY LIFE!

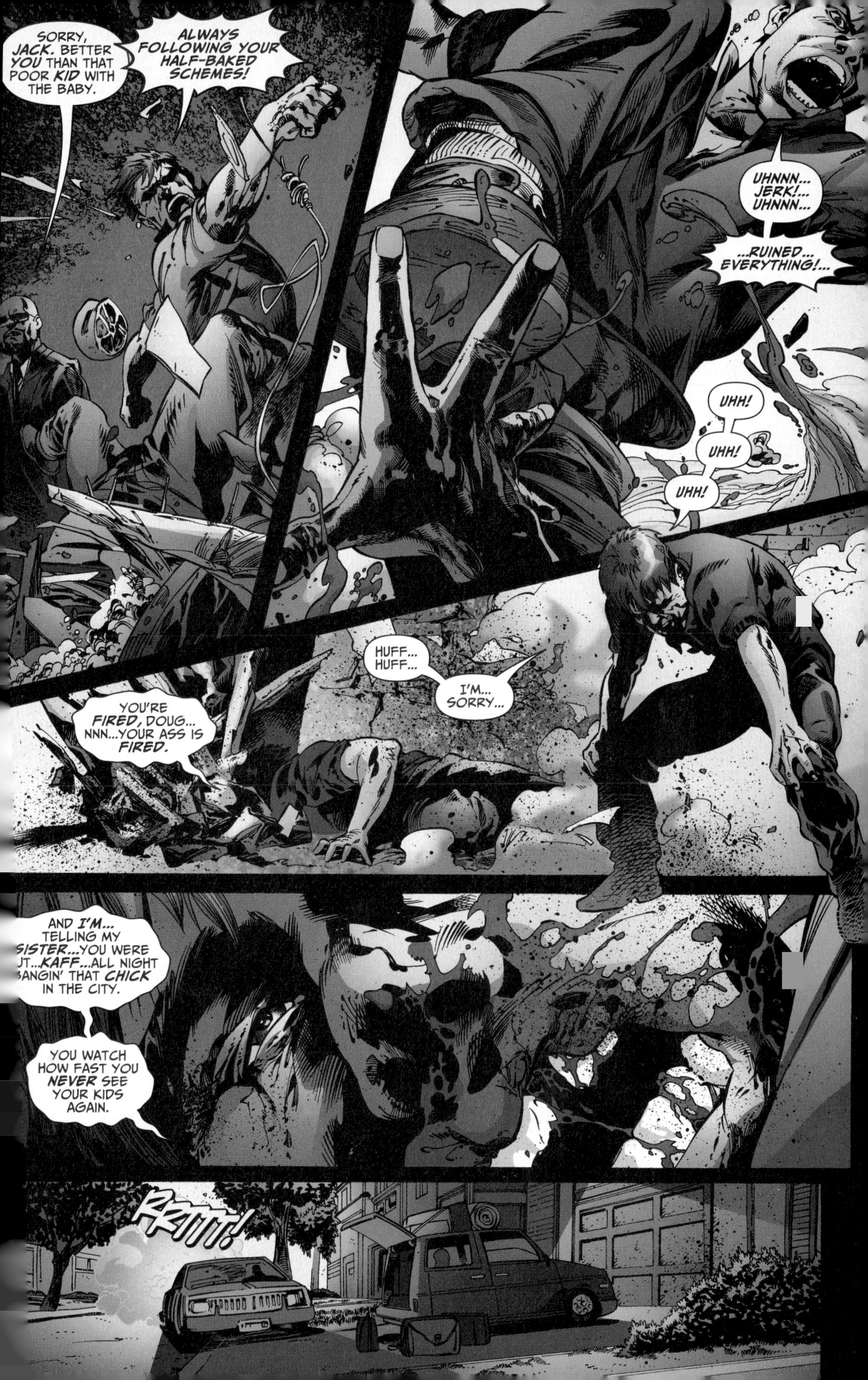

SORRY, JACK. BETTER YOU THAN THAT POOR KID WITH THE BABY.
ALWAYS FOLLOWING YOUR HALF-BAKED SCHEMES!
UHNNN... JERK!... UHNNN...
...RUINED... EVERYTHING!...
UHH!
UHH!
UHH!
HUFF... HUFF...
I'M... SORRY...
YOU'RE FIRED, DOUG... NNN...YOUR ASS IS FIRED.
AND I'M... TELLING MY SISTER...YOU WERE OUT...KAFF...ALL NIGHT BANGIN' THAT CHICK IN THE CITY.
YOU WATCH HOW FAST YOU NEVER SEE YOUR KIDS AGAIN.
RRTTT!

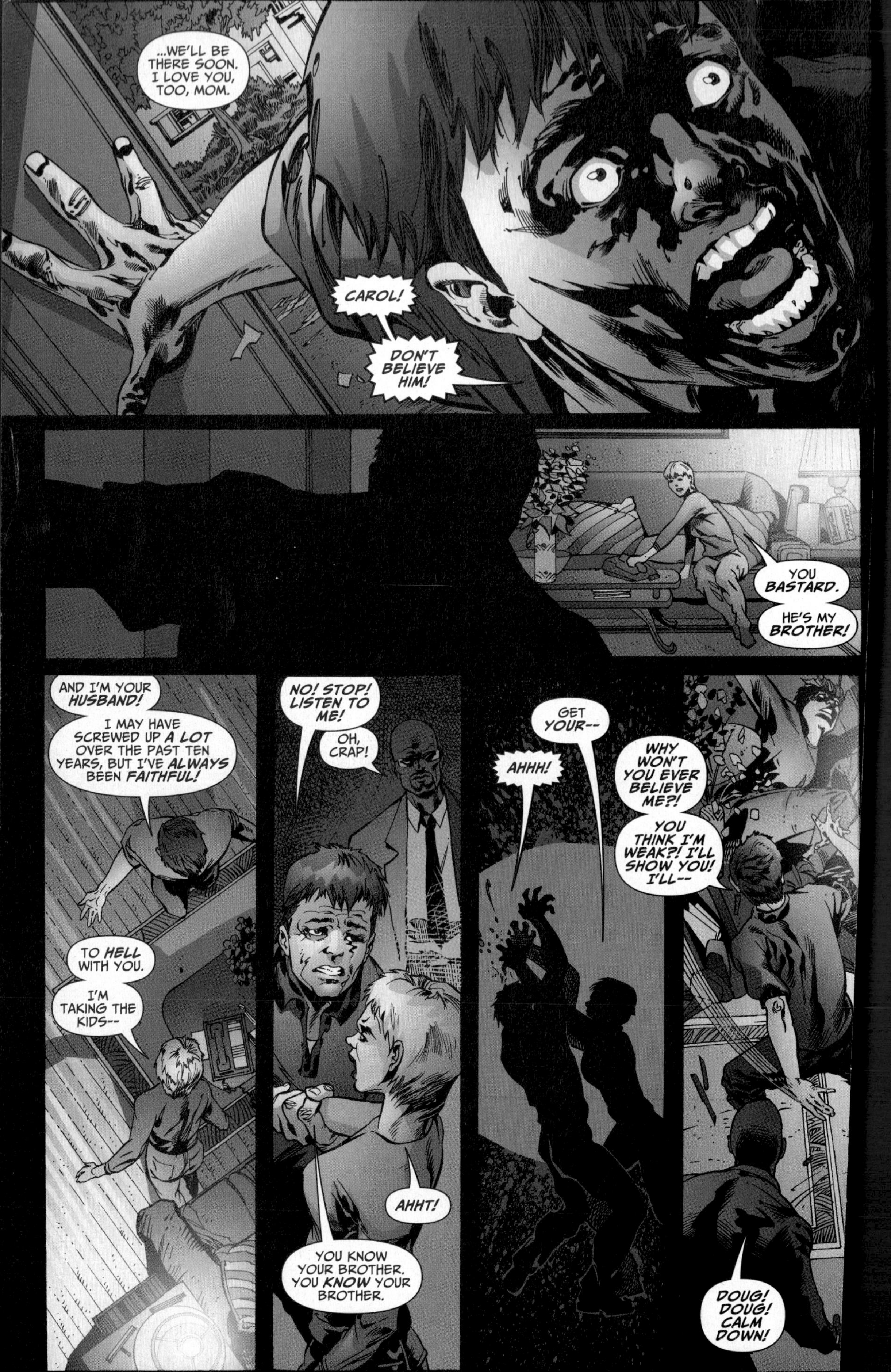
...WE'LL BE THERE SOON. I LOVE YOU, TOO, MOM.
CAROL!
DON'T BELIEVE HIM!
YOU BASTARD.
HE'S MY BROTHER!
AND I'M YOUR HUSBAND!
I MAY HAVE SCREWED UP A LOT OVER THE PAST TEN YEARS, BUT I'VE ALWAYS BEEN FAITHFUL!
TO HELL WITH YOU.
I'M TAKING THE KIDS--
NO! STOP! LISTEN TO ME!
OH, CRAP!
AHHT!
YOU KNOW YOUR BROTHER. YOU KNOW YOUR BROTHER.
GET YOUR--
AHHH!
WHY WON'T YOU EVER BELIEVE ME?!
YOU THINK I'M WEAK?! I'LL SHOW YOU! I'LL--
DOUG! DOUG! CALM DOWN!

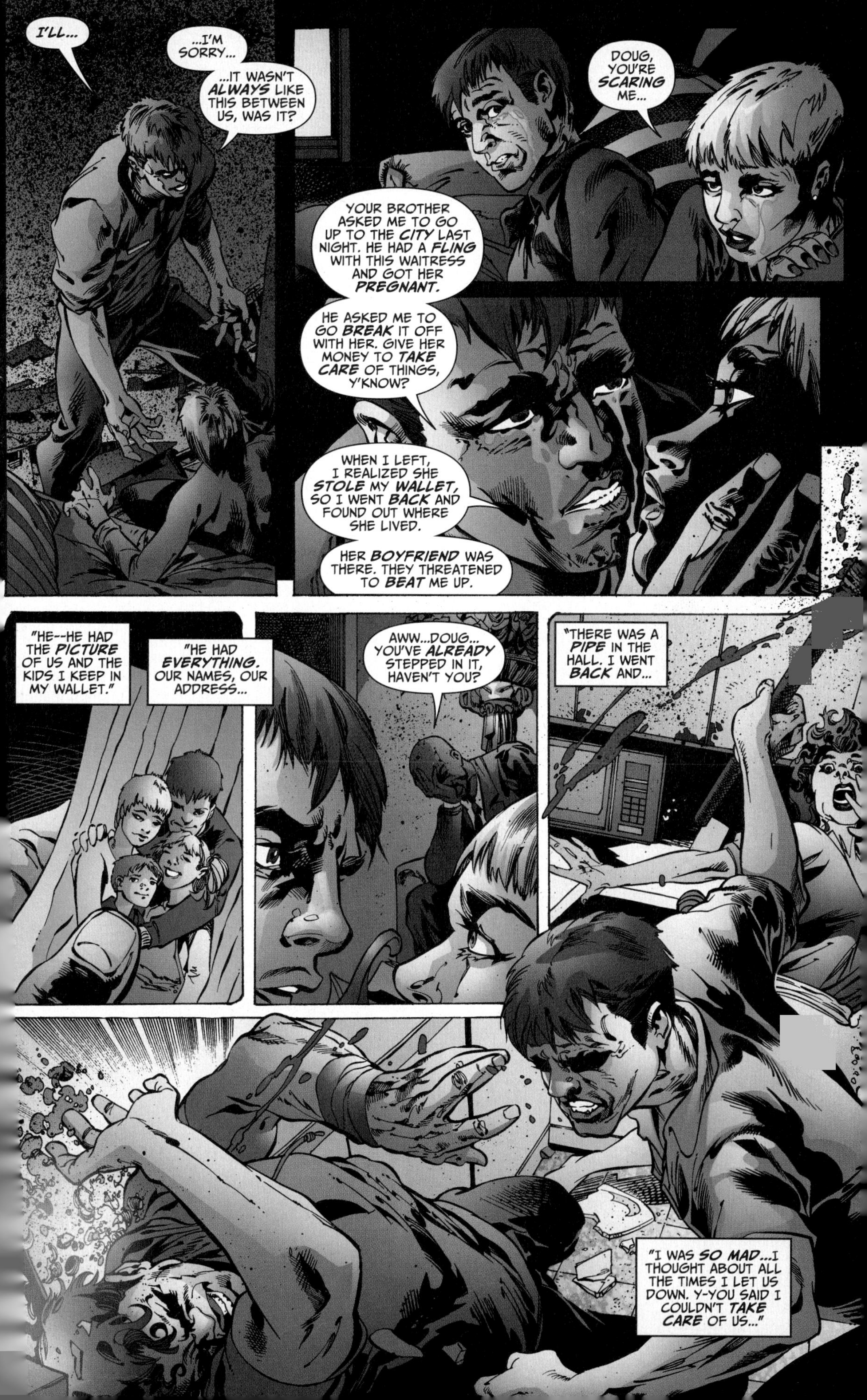

I'LL...
...I'M SORRY...
...IT WASN'T ALWAYS LIKE THIS BETWEEN US, WAS IT?
DOUG, YOU'RE SCARING ME...
YOUR BROTHER ASKED ME TO GO UP TO THE CITY LAST NIGHT. HE HAD A FLING WITH THIS WAITRESS AND GOT HER PREGNANT.
HE ASKED ME TO GO BREAK IT OFF WITH HER. GIVE HER MONEY TO TAKE CARE OF THINGS, Y'KNOW?
WHEN I LEFT, I REALIZED SHE STOLE MY WALLET, SO I WENT BACK AND FOUND OUT WHERE SHE LIVED.
HER BOYFRIEND WAS THERE. THEY THREATENED TO BEAT ME UP.
"HE--HE HAD THE PICTURE OF US AND THE KIDS I KEEP IN MY WALLET."
"HE HAD EVERYTHING. OUR NAMES, OUR ADDRESS...
AWW...DOUG... YOU'VE ALREADY STEPPED IN IT, HAVEN'T YOU?
"THERE WAS A PIPE IN THE HALL. I WENT BACK AND...
"I WAS SO MAD...I THOUGHT ABOUT ALL THE TIMES I LET US DOWN. Y-YOU SAID I COULDN'T TAKE CARE OF US..."

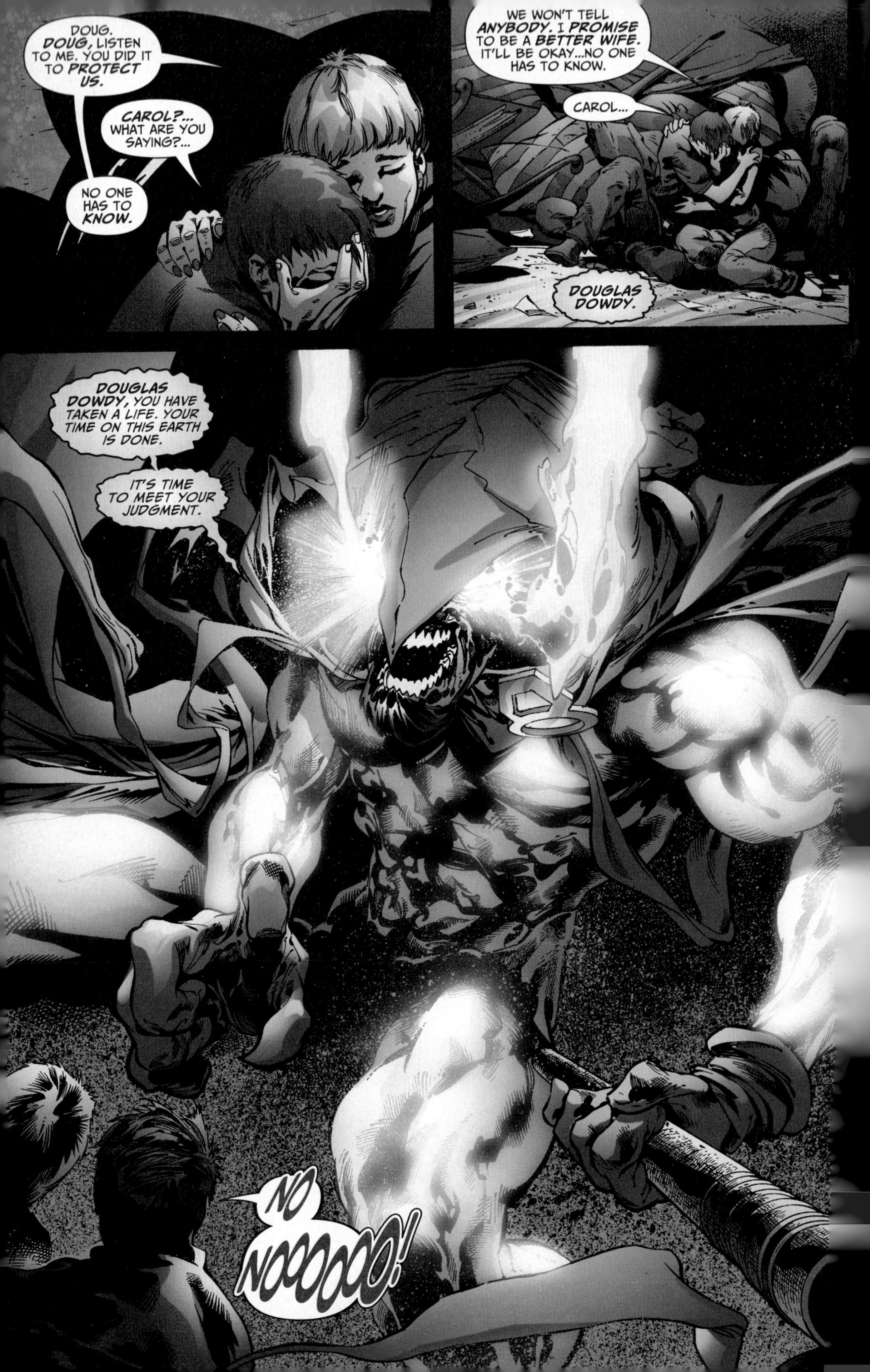
DOUG. DOUG, LISTEN TO ME. YOU DID IT TO PROTECT US.
CAROL?... WHAT ARE YOU SAYING?...
NO ONE HAS TO KNOW.
WE WON'T TELL ANYBODY. I PROMISE TO BE A BETTER WIFE. IT'LL BE OKAY...NO ONE HAS TO KNOW.
CAROL...
DOUGLAS DOWDY.
DOUGLAS DOWDY, YOU HAVE TAKEN A LIFE. YOUR TIME ON THIS EARTH IS DONE.
IT'S TIME TO MEET YOUR JUDGMENT.
NO NOOOOOO!

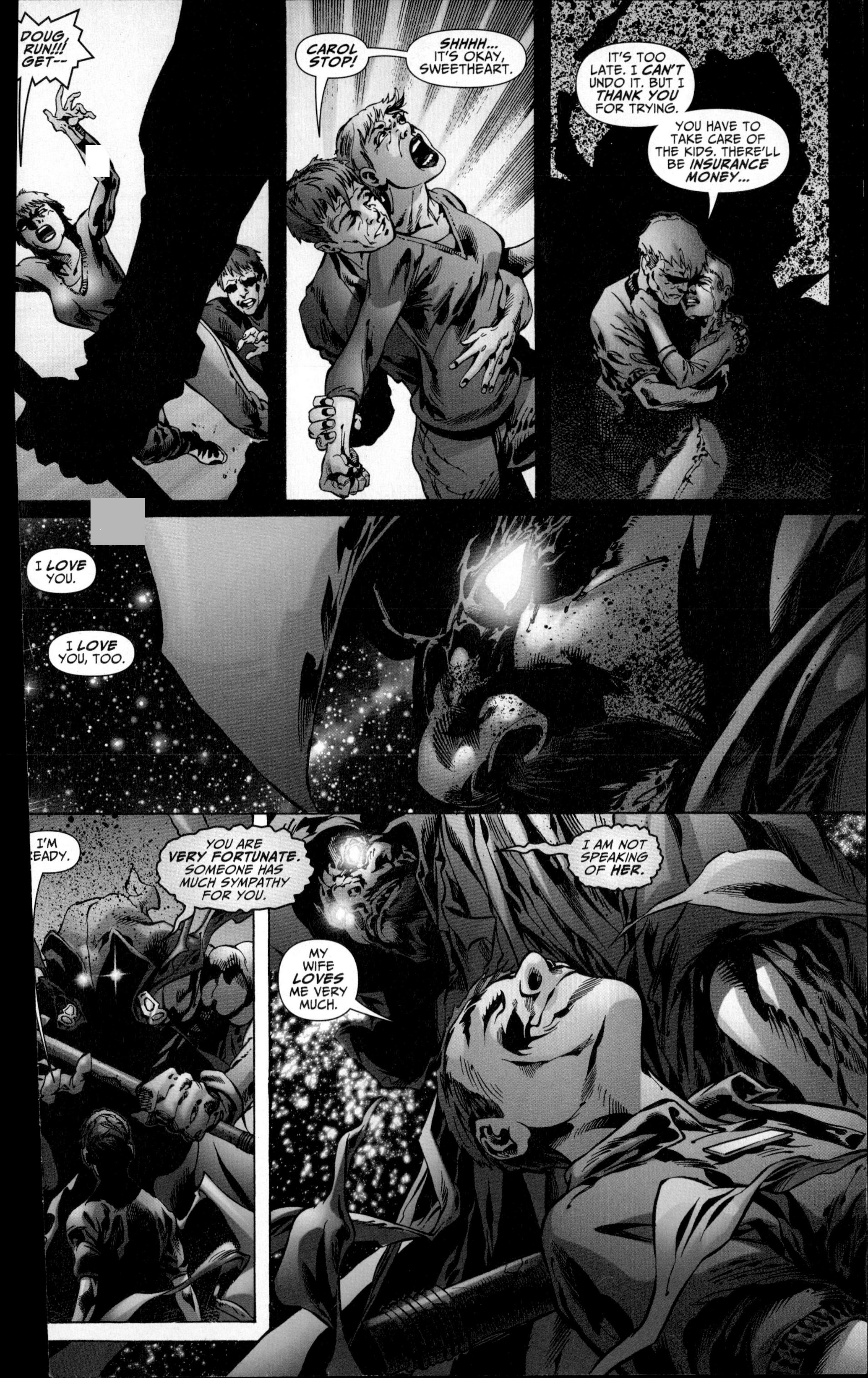
DOUG, RUN!!! GET--
CAROL STOP!
SHHHH... IT'S OKAY, SWEETHEART.
IT'S TOO LATE. I CAN'T UNDO IT. BUT I THANK YOU FOR TRYING.
YOU HAVE TO TAKE CARE OF THE KIDS. THERE'LL BE INSURANCE MONEY...
I LOVE YOU.
I LOVE YOU, TOO.
I'M READY.
YOU ARE VERY FORTUNATE. SOMEONE HAS MUCH SYMPATHY FOR YOU.
MY WIFE LOVES ME VERY MUCH.
I AM NOT SPEAKING OF HER.

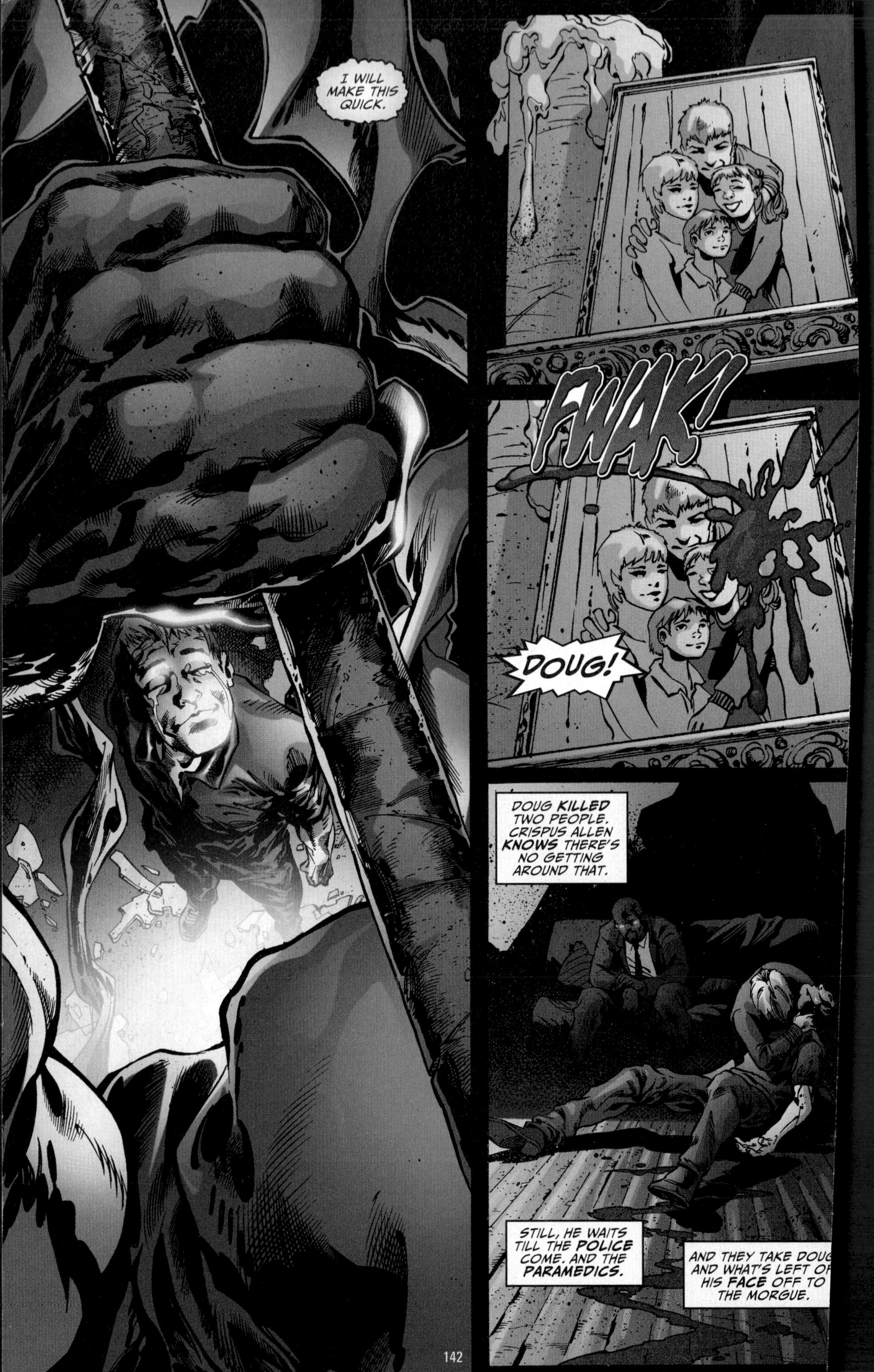
I WILL MAKE THIS QUICK.
FWAK!
DOUG!
DOUG KILLED TWO PEOPLE. CRISPUS ALLEN KNOWS THERE'S NO GETTING AROUND THAT.
STILL, HE WAITS TILL THE POLICE COME. AND THE PARAMEDICS.
AND THEY TAKE DOUG AND WHAT'S LEFT OF HIS FACE OFF TO THE MORGUE.

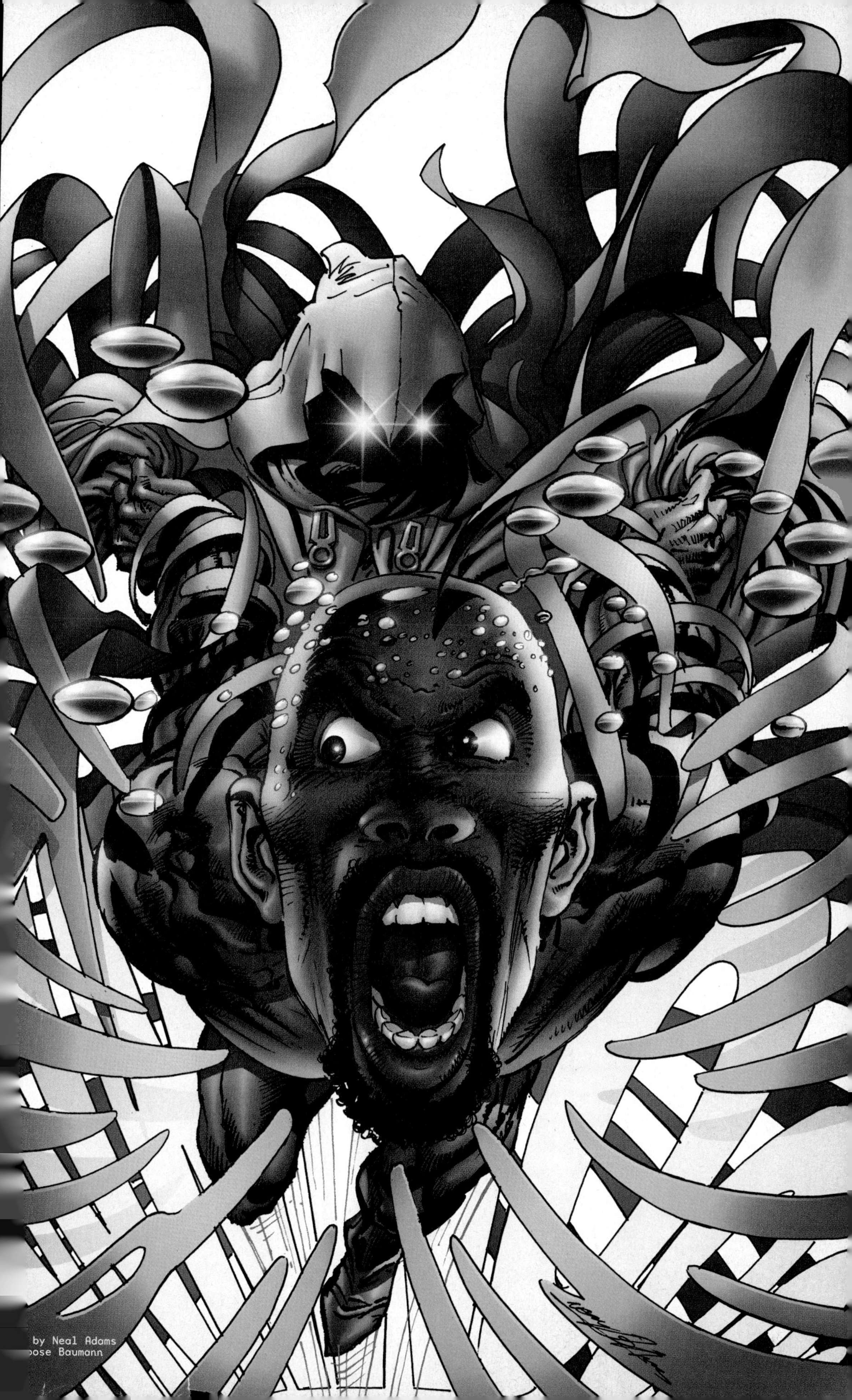

by Neal Adams
oose Baumann

READ MORE ADVENTURES OF YOUR FAVORITE HEROES IN THESE COLLECTIONS FROM DC COMICS:

KINGDOM COME

THE GREATEST SUPER HERO EPIC OF TOMORROW!
DC
ELSEWORLDS
KINGDOM COME
Mark WAID Alex ROSS

Mark Waid and **Alex Ross** deliver a grim tale of youth versus experience, tradition versus change and what defines a hero. KINGDOM COME is a riveting story pitting the old guard — Superman, Batman, Wonder Woman and their peers — against a new uncompromising generation.

WINNER OF FIVE EISNER AND HARVEY AWARDS, INCLUDING BEST LIMITED SERIES AND BEST ARTIST

IDENTITY CRISIS

NEW YORK TIMES BEST-SELLING AUTHOR OF THE ZERO GAME
BRAD MELTZER
RAGS MORALES MICHAEL BAIR
IDENTITY CRISIS
Introduction by JOSS WHEDON, creator of BUFFY THE VAMPIRE SLAYER and FIREFLY
"The IDENTITY CRISIS mystery involves the biggest DC heroes... and uses all of Mr. Meltzer's skills as a thriller novelist."
— The New York Times
DC

BRAD MELTZER
RAGS MORALES
MICHAEL BAIR

CRISIS ON INFINITE EARTHS

CRISIS
ON INFINITE EARTHS
MARV WOLFMAN
& GEORGE PÉREZ
DC

GEORGE PÉREZ

DC: THE NEW FRONTIER VOLUME 1

DC
DC: The New Frontier
VOLUME ONE
BY DARWYN COOKE WITH DAVE STEWART

DARWYN COOKE
DAVE STEWART

SEARCH THE GRAPHIC NOVELS SECTION OF

www.DCCOMICS.com

FOR ART AND INFORMATION ON ALL OF OUR BOO

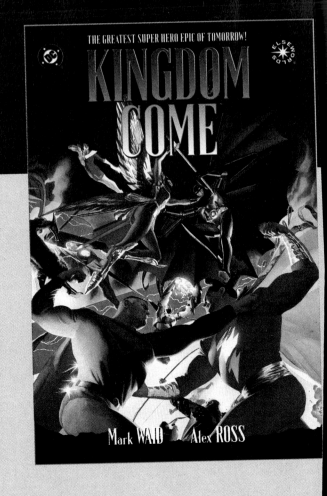

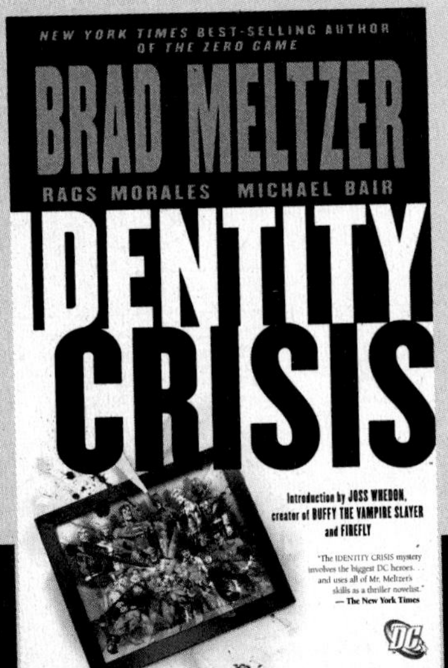